Zénaïde Alexeïevna Ragozin

Chaldea from the Earliest Times to the Rise of Assyria

Zénaïde Alexeïevna Ragozin

Chaldea from the Earliest Times to the Rise of Assyria

ISBN/EAN: 9783337236403

Printed in Europe, USA, Canada, Australia, Japan

Cover: Foto ©ninafisch / pixelio.de

More available books at **www.hansebooks.com**

CHALDEA

FROM THE EARLIEST TIMES TO THE RISE
OF ASSYRIA

(TREATED AS A GENERAL INTRODUCTION TO THE STUDY OF
ANCIENT HISTORY)

BY

ZÉNAÏDE A. RAGOZIN

MEMBER OF THE "SOCIÉTÉ ETHNOLOGIQUE" OF PARIS; OF THE "AMERICAN
ORIENTAL SOCIETY"; CORRESPONDING MEMBER OF THE "ATHÉNÉE
ORIENTAL" OF PARIS; AUTHOR OF "ASSYRIA," "MEDIA," ETC.

"He (Carlyle) says it is part of his creed that history is poetry, could we
tell it right."—EMERSON.
"Da mihi, Domine, scire quod sciendum est."—IMITATION OF CHRIST."
("Grant that the knowledge I get may be the knowledge worth having."—
Matthew Arnold's translation.)

THIRD EDITION

London
T. FISHER UNWIN
PATERNOSTER SQUARE
NEW YORK: G. P. PUTNAM'S SONS
MDCCCXCI

Entered at Stationers' Hall
By T. FISHER UNWIN.

Copyright by G. P. Putnam's Sons, 1886
(For the United States of America).

TO THE MEMBERS OF

THE CLASS,

IN LOVING REMEMBRANCE OF MANY HAPPY HOURS, THIS
VOLUME AND THE FOLLOWING ONES ARE AFFEC-
TIONATELY INSCRIBED BY THEIR FRIEND,

THE AUTHOR.

IDLEWILD PLANTATION,
SAN ANTONIO,

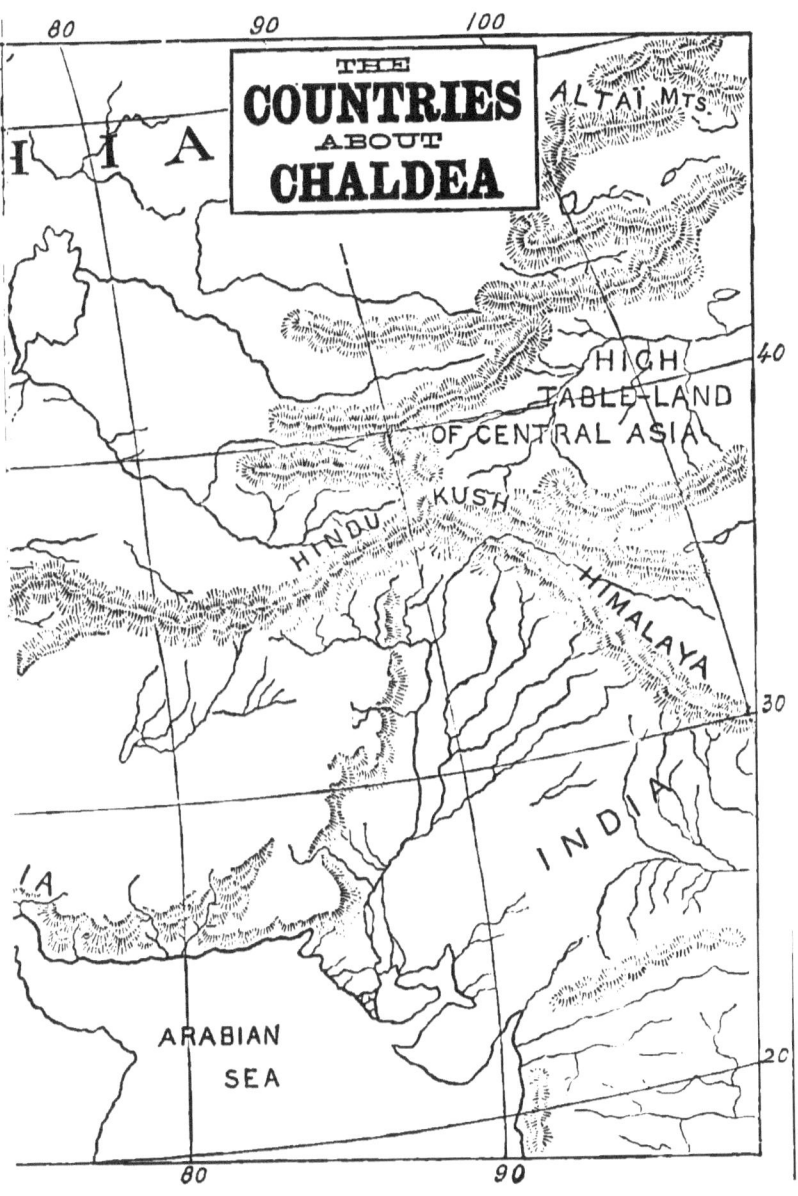

CLASSIFIED CONTENTS.

INTRODUCTION.

I.

MESOPOTAMIA.—THE MOUNDS.—THE FIRST SEARCHERS 1–18

§ 1. Complete destruction of Nineveh.—§§ 2–4. Xenophon and the "Retreat of the Ten Thousand." The Greeks pass the ruins of Calah and Nineveh, and know them not.—§ 5. Alexander's passage through Mesopotamia.—§ 6. The Arab invasion and rule.—§ 7. Turkish rule and mismanagement.—§ 8. Peculiar natural conditions of Mesopotamia.—§ 9. Actual desolate state of the country.—§ 10. The plains studded with Mounds. Their curious aspect.—§ 11. Fragments of works of art amidst the rubbish.—§ 12. Indifference and superstition of the Turks and Arabs.—§ 13. Exclusive absorption of European scholars in Classical Antiquity.—§ 14. Forbidding aspect of the Mounds, compared with other ruins.—§ 15. Rich, the first explorer.—§ 16. Botta's work and want of success.—§ 17. Botta's great discovery.—§ 18. Great sensation created by it.—§ 19. Layard's first expedition.

II.

LAYARD AND HIS WORK 19–35

§ 1. Layard's arrival at Nimrud. His excitement and dreams.—§ 2. Beginning of difficulties. The Ogre-like Pasha of Mossul.—§ 3. Opposition from the Pasha. His malice and cunning.—§ 4. Discovery of the gigantic head.

v

Fright of the Arabs, who declare it to be Nimrod.—§ 5.
Strange ideas of the Arabs about the sculptures.—§ 6. Layard's life in the desert.—§ 7. Terrible heat of summer.—§ 8.
Sand-storms and hot hurricanes.—§ 9. Layard's wretched
dwelling.—§ 10. Unsuccessful attempts at improvement.—
§ 11. In what the task of the explorer consists.—§ 12. Different modes of carrying on the work of excavation.

III.

THE RUINS 36–90

§ 1. Every country's culture and art determined by its geographical conditions.—§ 2. Chaldea's absolute deficiency in
wood and stone.—§ 3. Great abundance of mud fit for the
fabrication of bricks; hence the peculiar architecture of
Mesopotamia. Ancient ruins still used as quarries of bricks
for building. Trade of ancient bricks at Hillah.—§ 4. Various cements used.—§ 5. Construction of artificial platforms.
—§ 6. Ruins of Ziggurats; peculiar shape and uses of this
sort of buildings.—§ 7. Figures showing the immense amount
of labor used on these constructions.—§ 8. Chaldean architecture adopted unchanged by the Assyrians.—§ 9. Stone
used for ornament and casing of walls. Water transport in
old and modern times.—§ 10. Imposing aspect of the palaces.
—§ 11. Restoration of Sennacherib's palace by Fergusson.
—§ 12. Pavements of palace halls.—§ 13. Gateways and
sculptured slabs along the walls. Friezes in painted tiles.
—§ 14. Proportions of palace halls and roofing.—§ 15.
Lighting of halls.—§ 16. Causes of the kings' passion for
building.—§ 17. Drainage of palaces and platforms.—§ 18.
Modes of destruction.—§ 19. The Mounds a protection to
the ruins they contain. Refilling the excavations.—§ 20.
Absence of ancient tombs in Assyria.—§ 21. Abundance and
vastness of cemeteries in Chaldea.—§ 22. Warka (Erech)
the great Necropolis. Loftus' description.—§ 23. "Jar-coffins."—§ 24. "Dish-cover" coffins.—§ 25. Sepulchral vaults.
—§ 26. "Slipper-shaped" coffins.—§ 27. Drainage of sepulchral mounds.—§ 28. Decoration of walls in painted clay
cones.—§ 29. De Sarzec's discoveries at Tell-Loh.

IV.

THE BOOK OF THE PAST.—THE LIBRARY OF
  NINEVEH 92–115

§ 1. Object of making books.—§ 2. Books not always of paper.—§ 3. Universal craving for an immortal name.—§ 4. Insufficiency of records on various writing materials. Universal longing for knowledge of the remotest past.—§ 5. Monumental records.—§ 6. Ruins of palaces and temples, tombs and caves—the Book of the Past.—§§ 7–8. Discovery by Layard of the Royal Library at Nineveh.—§ 9. George Smith's work at the British Museum.—§ 10. His expeditions to Nineveh, his success and death.—§ 11. Value of the Library.—§§ 12–13. Contents of the Library.—§ 14. The Tablets.—§ 15. The cylinders and foundation-tablets.

CHALDEA.

I.

NOMADS AND SETTLERS.—THE FOUR STAGES OF
  CULTURE 116–126

§ 1. Nomads.—§ 2. First migrations.—§ 3. Pastoral life—the second stage.—§ 4. Agricultural life; beginnings of the State.—§ 5. City-building; royalty.—§ 6. Successive migrations and their causes.—§ 7. Formation of nations.

II.

THE GREAT RACES.—CHAPTER X. OF GENESIS   127–142

§ 1. Shinar.—§ 2. Berosus.—§ 3. Who were the settlers in Shinar?—§ 4. The Flood probably not universal.—§§ 5–6. The blessed race and the accursed, according to Genesis.—§ 7. Genealogical form of Chap. X. of Genesis.—§ 8. Eponyms.—§ 9. Omission of some white races from Chap. X.—§ 10. Omission of the Black Race.—§ 11. Omission of the Yellow Race. Characteristics of the Turanians.—§ 12.

The Chinese.—§ 13. Who were the Turanians? What became of the Cainites?—§ 14. Possible identity of both.—§ 15. The settlers in Shinar—Turanians.

III.

TURANIAN CHALDEA.—SHUMIR AND ACCAD.—
THE BEGINNINGS OF RELIGION . 146–181

§ 1. Shumir and Accad.—§ 2. Language and name.—§ 3. Turanian migrations and traditions.—§ 4. Collection of sacred texts.—§ 5. "Religiosity"—a distinctively human characteristic. Its first promptings and manifestations.—§ 6. The Magic Collection and the work of Fr. Lenormant.—§ 7. The Shumiro-Accads' theory of the world, and their elementary spirits.—§ 8. The incantation of the Seven Maskim.—§ 9. The evil spirits.—§ 10. The Arali.—§ 11. The sorcerers.—§ 12. Conjuring and conjurers.—§ 13. The beneficent Spirits. Êa.—§ 14. Meridug.—§ 15. A charm against an evil spell.—§ 16. Diseases considered as evil demons.—§ 17. Talismans. The *Kerubim*.—§ 18. More talismans.—§ 19. The demon of the South-West Wind.—§ 20. The first gods.—§ 21. *Ud*, the Sun.—§ 22. *Nin dar*, the nightly Sun.—§ 23. *Gibil*, Fire.—§ 24. Dawn of moral consciousness.—§ 25. Man's Conscience divinized.—§§ 26–28. Penitential Psalms.—§ 29. General character of Turanian religions.

APPENDIX TO CHAPTER III. 181–183

Professor L. Dyer's poetical version of the Incantation against the Seven Maskim.

IV.

CUSHITES AND SEMITES.—EARLY CHALDEAN
HISTORY 184–228

§ 1. Oannes.—§ 2. Were the second settlers Cushites or Semites?—§ 3. Cushite hypothesis. Earliest migrations.—§ 4. The Ethiopians and the Egyptians.—§ 5. The Canaanites.—§ 6. Possible Cushite station on the islets of the Persian Gulf.—§ 7. Colonization of Chaldea possibly by Cushites.—§ 8. Vagueness of very ancient chronology.—§ 9. Early dates.—§ 10. Exorbitant figures of Berosus.—§ 11. Early

Chaldea—a nursery of nations.—§ 12. Nomadic Semitic tribes.—§ 13. The tribe of Arphaxad.—§ 14. Ur of the Chaldees.—§ 15. Scholars divided between the Cushite and Semitic theories.—§ 16. History commences with Semitic culture.—§ 17. Priestly rule. The *patesis*.—§§ 18-19. Sharrukin I. (Sargon I.) of Agadê.—§§ 20-21. The second Sargon's literary labors.—§§ 22-23. Chaldean folk-lore, maxims and songs.—§ 24. Discovery of the elder Sargon's date—3800 B.C.—§ 25. Gudêa of Sirgulla and Ur-êa of Ur.—§ 26. Predominance of Shumir. Ur-êa and his son Dungi first kings of "Shumir and Accad."—§ 27. Their inscriptions and buildings. The Elamite invasion.—§ 28. Elam.—§§ 29-31. Khudur-Lagamar and Abraham.—§ 32. Hardness of the Elamite rule.—§ 33. Rise of Babylon.—§ 34. Hammurabi.—§ 35. Invasion of the Kasshi.

V.

BABYLONIAN RELIGION 229-257

§ 1. Babylonian calendar.—§ 2. Astronomy conducive to religious feeling.—§ 3. Sabeism.—§ 4. Priestcraft and astrology.—§ 5. Transformation of the old religion.—§ 6. Vague dawning of the monotheistic idea. Divine emanations.—§ 7. The Supreme Triad.—§ 8. The Second Triad.—§ 9. The five Planetary deities.—§§ 10-11. Duality of nature. Masculine and feminine principles. The goddesses.—§ 12. The twelve Great Gods and their Temples.—§ 13. The temple of Shamash at Sippar and Mr. Rassam's discovery.—§ 14. Survival of the old Turanian superstitions.—§ 15. Divination, a branch of Chaldean "Science."—§§ 16-17. Collection of one hundred tablets on divination. Specimens.—§ 18. The three classes of "wise men." "Chaldeans," in later times, a byword for "magician," and "astrologer."—§ 19. Our inheritance from the Chaldeans: the sun-dial, the week, the calendar, the Sabbath.

VI.

LEGENDS AND STORIES 258-293

§ 1. The Cosmogonies of different nations.—§ 2. The antiquity of the Sacred Books of Babylonia.—§ 3. The legend of Oannes, told by Berosus. Discovery, by Geo. Smith, of the

Creation Tablets and the Deluge Tablet.—§§ 4-5. Chaldean account of the Creation.—§ 6. The Cylinder with the human couple, tree and serpent.—§ 7. Berosus' account of the creation.—§ 8. The Sacred Tree. Sacredness of the Symbol.—§ 9. Signification of the Tree-Symbol. The Cosmic Tree.—§ 10. Connection of the Tree-Symbol and of Ziggurats with the legend of Paradise.—§ 11. The Ziggurat of Borsippa.—§ 12.—It is identified with the Tower of Babel.—§§ 13-14. Peculiar Orientation of the Ziggurats.—§ 15. Traces of legends about a sacred grove or garden.—§ 16. Mummu-Tiamat, the enemy of the gods. Battle of Bel and Tiamat.—§ 17. The Rebellion of the seven evil spirits, originally messengers of the gods.—§ 18. The great Tower and the Confusion of Tongues.

VII.

MYTHS.—HEROES AND THE MYTHICAL EPOS . 294-330

§ 1. Definition of the word Myth.—§ 2. The Heroes.—§ 3. The Heroic Ages and Heroic Myths. The National Epos.—§ 4. The oldest known Epic.—§ 5. Berosus' account of the Flood.—§ 6. Geo. Smith's discovery of the original Chaldean narrative.—§ 7. The Epic divided into books or Tablets.—§ 8. Izdubar the Hero of the Epic.—§ 9. Erech's humiliation under the Elamite Conquest. Izdubar's dream.—§ 10. Êabâni the Seer. Izdubar's invitation and promises to him.—§ 11. Message sent to Êabâni by Ishtar's handmaidens. His arrival at Erech.—§ 12. Izdubar and Êabâni's victory over the tyrant Khumbaba.—§ 13. Ishtar's love message. Her rejection and wrath. The two friends' victory over the Bull sent by her.—§ 14. Ishtar's vengeance. Izdubar's journey to the Mouth of the Rivers.—§ 15. Izdubar sails the Waters of Death and is healed by his immortal ancestor Hâsisadra.—§ 16. Izdubar's return to Erech and lament over Êabâni. The seer is translated among the gods.—§ 17. The Deluge narrative in the Eleventh Tablet of the Izdubar Epic.—§§ 18-21. Mythic and solar character of the Epic analyzed.—§ 22. Sun-Myth of the Beautiful Youth, his early death and resurrection.—§§ 23-24. Dumuzi-Tammuz, the husband of Ishtar. The festival of Dumuzi in June.—§ 25.

Ishtar's Descent to the Land of the Dead.—§ 26. Universality of the Solar and Chthonic Myths.

VIII.

RELIGION AND MYTHOLOGY.—IDOLATRY AND ANTHROPOMORPHISM.—THE CHALDEAN LEGENDS AND THE BOOK OF GENESIS.—RETROSPECT 331–336

§ 1. Definition of Mythology and Religion, as distinct from each other.—§§ 2–3. Instances of pure religious feeling in the poetry of Shumir and Accad.—§ 4. Religion often stifled by Mythology.—§§ 5–6. The conception of the immortality of the soul suggested by the sun's career.—§ 7. This expressed in the Solar and Chthonic Myths.—§ 8. Idolatry.—§ 9. The Hebrews, originally polytheists and idolators, reclaimed by their leaders to Monotheism.—§ 10. Their intercourse with the tribes of Canaan conducive to relapses.—§ 11. Intermarriage severely forbidden for this reason. Striking similarity between the Book of Genesis and the ancient Chaldean legends.—§ 13. Parallel between the two accounts of the creation.—§ 14. Anthropomorphism, different from polytheism and idolatry, but conducive to both.—§§ 15–17. Parallel continued.—§§ 18–19. Retrospect.

PRINCIPAL WORKS READ OR CONSULTED IN THE PREPARATION OF THIS VOLUME.

BAER, Wilhelm. DER VORGESCHICHTLICHE MENSCH. 1 vol., Leipzig: 1874.
BAUDISSIN, W. von. STUDIEN ZUR SEMITISCHEN RELIGIONSGESCHICHTE. 2 vols.
BUDGE, E. A. WALLIS. BABYLONIAN LIFE AND HISTORY. ("By-paths of Bible Knowledge" Series, V.) 1884. London: The Religious Tract Society. 1 vol.
——— HISTORY OF ESARHADDON. 1 vol.
BUNSEN, Chr. Carl Jos. GOTT IN DER GESCHICHTE, oder Der Fortschritt des Glaubens an eine sittliche Weltordnung. 3 vols. Leipzig: 1857.
CASTREN, ALEXANDER. KLEINERE SCHRIFTEN. St. Petersburg: 1862. 1 vol.
CORY. ANCIENT FRAGMENTS. London: 1876. 1 vol.
DELITZSCH, DR. FRIEDRICH. WO LAG DAS PARADIES? eine Biblisch-Assyriologische Studie. Leipzig: 1881. 1 vol.
——— DIE SPRACHE DER KOSSÄER. Leipzig: 1885 (or 1884?). 1 vol.
DUNCKER, MAX. GESCHICHTE DES ALTERTHUMS. Leipzig: 1878. Vol. 1st.
FERGUSSON, James. PALACES OF NINEVEH AND PERSEPOLIS RESTORED. 1 vol.
HAPPEL, Julius. DIE ALTCHINESISCHE REICHSRELIGION, vom Standpunkte der Vergleichenden Religionsgeschichte. 46 pages, Leipzig: 1882.
HAUPT, Paul. DER KEILINSCHRIFTLICHE SINTFLUTBERICHT, eine Episode des Babylonischen Nimrodepos. 36 pages. Göttingen: 1881

HOMMEL, DR. FRITZ. GESCHICHTE BABYLONIENS UND ASSYRIENS (first instalment, 160 pp., 1885 ; and second instalment, 160 pp., 1886). (Allgemeine Geschichte in einzelnen Darstellungen, Abtheilung 95 und 117.)

—— DIE VORSEMITISCHEN KULTUREN IN ÆGYPTEN UND BABYLONIEN. Leipzig : 1882 and 1883.

LAYARD, AUSTEN H. DISCOVERIES AMONG THE RUINS OF NINEVEH AND BABYLON. (American Edition.) New York : 1853. 1 vol.

—— NINEVEH AND ITS REMAINS. London : 1849. 2 vols.

LENORMANT, FRANÇOIS. LES PREMIÈRES CIVILISATIONS. Études d'Histoire et d'Archéologie. 1874. Paris : Maisonneuve et Cie. 2 vols.

—— LES ORIGINES DE L'HISTOIRE, d'après la Bible et les Traditions des Peuples Orientaux. Paris : Maisonneuve et Cie. 3 vol. 1er vol. 1880 ; 2e vol. 1882 ; 3e vol. 1884.

—— LA GENÈSE. Traduction d'après l'Hébreu. Paris : 1883. 1 vol.

—— DIE MAGIE UND WAHRSAGEKUNST DER CHALDÄER. Jena, 1878. 1 vol.

—— IL MITO DI ADONE-TAMMUZ nei Documenti cuneiformi. 32 pages. Firenze : 1879.

—— SUR LE NOM DE TAMMOUZ. (Extrait des Mémoires du Congrès international des Orientalistes.) 17 pages. Paris : 1873.

—— A MANUAL OF THE ANCIENT HISTORY OF THE EAST. Translated by E. Chevallier. American Edition. Philadelphia : 1871. 2 vols.

LOFTUS. CHALDEA AND SUSIANA. 1 vol. London : 1857.

LOTZ, GUILELMUS. QUÆSTIONES DE HISTORIA SABBATI. Lipsiae : 1883.

MAURY, ALFRED L. F. LA MAGIE ET L'ASTROLOGIE dans l'antiquité et en Moyen Age. Paris : 1877. 1 vol. Quatrième édition.

MASPERO, G. HISTOIRE ANCIENNE DES PEUPLES DE L'ORIENT. 3e édition, 1878. Paris : Hachette & Cie. 1 vol.

MÉNANT, Joachim. LA BIBLIOTHÈQUE DU PALAIS DE NINIVE. 1 vol. (Bibliothèque Orientale Elzévirienne.) Paris : 1880.

MEYER, EDUARD. GESCHICHTE DES ALTERTHUMS. Stuttgart : 1884. Vol. 1st.

MÜLLER, Max. LECTURES ON THE SCIENCE OF LANGUAGE. 2 vols. American edition. New York : 1875.

MÜRDTER, F. KURZGEFASSTE GESCHICHTE BABYLONIENS UND ASSYRIENS, mit besonderer Berücksichtigung des Alten Testaments. Mit Vorwort und Beigaben von Friedrich Delitzsch. Stuttgart: 1882. 1 vol.

OPPERT, Jules. L'IMMORTALITÉ DE L'AME CHEZ LES CHALDÉENS. 28 pages. (Extrait des Annales de Philosophie Chrétienne, 1874.) Perrot et Chipiez.

QUATREFAGES, A. de. L'ESPÈCE HUMAINE. Sixième edition. 1 vol. Paris: 1880.

RAWLINSON, George. THE FIVE GREAT MONARCHIES OF THE ANCIENT EASTERN WORLD. London: 1865. 1st and 2d vols.

RECORDS OF THE PAST. Published under the sanction of the Society of Biblical Archæology. Volumes I. III. V. VII. IX. XI.

SAYCE, A. H. FRESH LIGHT FROM ANCIENT MONUMENTS. ("By-Paths of Bible Knowledge" Series, II.) 3d edition, 1885. London: 1 vol.

——— THE ANCIENT EMPIRES OF THE EAST. 1 vol. London, 1884.

——— BABYLONIAN LITERATURE. 1 vol. London, 1884.

SCHRADER, Eberhard. KEILINSCHRIFTEN und Geschichtsforschung. Giessen: 1878. 1 vol.

——— DIE KEILINSCHRIFTEN und das Alte Testament. Giessen: 1883. 1 vol.

——— ISTAR'S HÖLLENFAHRT. 1 vol. Giessen: 1874.

——— ZUR FRAGE NACH DEM URSPRUNG DER ALTBABYLONISCHEN KULTUR. Berlin: 1884.

SMITH, George. ASSYRIA from the Earliest Times to the Fall of Nineveh. ("Ancient History from the Monuments" Series.) London: 1 vol.

TYLOR, Edward B. PRIMITIVE CULTURE. Second American Edition. 2 vols. New York: 1877.

ZIMMERN, Heinrich. BABYLONISCHE BUSSPSALMEN, umschrieben, übersetzt und erklärt. 17 pages, 4to. Leipzig: 1885.

Numerous Essays by Sir Henry Rawlinson, Friedr. Delitzsch, E. Schrader and others, in Mr. Geo. Rawlinson's translation of Herodotus, in the Calwer Bibellexikon, and in various periodicals, such as "Proceedings" and "Transactions" of the "Society of Biblical Archæology," "Jahrbücher für Protestantische Theologie," "Zeitschrift für Keilschriftforschung," "Gazette Archéologique," and others.

LIST OF ILLUSTRATIONS.

		PAGE
SHAMASH THE SUN-GOD. *From a tablet in the British Museum.*		*Frontispiece.*
1. CUNEIFORM CHARACTERS.	*Menant.*	10
2. TEMPLE OF ÊA AT ERIDHU	*Hommel.*	23
3. VIEW OF EUPHRATES NEAR BABYLON	*Babelon.*	31
4. MOUND OF BABIL	*Oppert.*	33
5. BRONZE DISH	*Perrot and Chipiez.*	35
6. BRONZE DISH (RUG PATTERN)	*Perrot and Chipiez.*	37
7. SECTION OF BRONZE DISH	*Perrot and Chipiez.*	39
8. VIEW OF NEBBI-YUNUS	*Babelon.*	41
9. BUILDING IN BAKED BRICK	*Perrot and Chipiez.*	43
10. MOUND OF NINEVEH	*Hommel.*	45
11. MOUND OF MUGHEIR (ANCIENT UR)	*Taylor.*	47
12. TERRACE WALL AT KHORSABAD	*Perrot and Chipiez.*	49
13. RAFT BUOYED BY INFLATED SKINS (ANCIENT)	*Kaulen.*	51
14. RAFT BUOYED BY INFLATED SKINS (MODERN)	*Kaulen.*	51
15. EXCAVATIONS AT MUGHEIR (UR)	*Hommel.*	53

			PAGE
16.	WARRIORS SWIMMING ON INFLATED SKINS . .	. *Babelon.*	55
17.	VIEW OF KOYUNJIK . . .	*Hommel.*	57
18.	STONE LION AT ENTRANCE OF A TEMPLE	*Perrot and Chipiez.*	59
19.	COURT OF HAREM AT KHORSABAD. RESTORED . .	*Perrot and Chipiez.*	61
20.	CIRCULAR PILLAR BASE . .	*Perrot and Chipiez.*	63
21.	INTERIOR VIEW OF HAREM CHAMBER.	*Perrot and Chipiez.*	65
22, 23.	COLORED FRIEZE IN ENAMELLED TILES .	*Perrot and Chipiez.*	67
24.	PAVEMENT SLAB	*Perrot and Chipiez.*	69
25.	SECTION OF ORNAMENTAL DOORWAY, KHORSABAD .	*Perrot and Chipiez.*	71
26.	WINGED LION WITH HUMAN HEAD	*Perrot and Chipiez.*	73
27.	WINGED BULL . .	*Perrot and Chipiez.*	75
28.	MAN-LION	*Perrot and Chipiez.*	77
29.	FRAGMENT OF ENAMELLED BRICK	*Perrot and Chipiez.*	79
30.	RAM'S HEAD IN ALABASTER,	*British Museum.*	81
31.	EBONY COMB	*Perrot and Chipiez.*	81
32.	BRONZE FORK AND SPOON	*Perrot and Chipiez.*	81
33.	ARMENIAN LOUVRE . . .	*Botta.*	83
34, 35.	VAULTED DRAINS . . .	*Perrot and Chipiez.*	84
36.	CHALDEAN JAR-COFFIN . .	*Taylor.*	85
37.	"DISH-COVER" TOMB AT MUGHEIR	*Taylor.*	87
38.	"DISH-COVER" TOMB . .	*Taylor.*	87
39.	SEPULCHRAL VAULT AT MUGHEIR	*Taylor.*	89
40.	STONE JARS FROM GRAVES .	*Hommel.*	89

			PAGE
41.	DRAIN IN MOUND	*Perrot and Chipiez.*	90
42.	WALL WITH DESIGNS IN TERRA-COTTA	*Loftus.*	91
43.	TERRA-COTTA CONE	*Loftus.*	91
44.	HEAD OF ANCIENT CHALDEAN	*Perrot and Chipiez.*	101
45.	SAME, PROFILE VIEW	*Perrot and Chipiez.*	101
46.	CUNEIFORM INSCRIPTION	*Perrot and Chipiez.*	107
47.	INSCRIBED CLAY TABLET	*Smith's Chald. Gen.*	109
48.	CLAY TABLET IN ITS CASE	*Hommel.*	111
49.	ANTIQUE BRONZE SETTING OF CYLINDER	*Perrot and Chipiez.*	112
50.	CHALDEAN CYLINDER AND IMPRESSION	*Perrot and Chipiez.*	113
51.	ASSYRIAN CYLINDER		113
52.	PRISM OF SENNACHERIB	*British Museum.*	115
53.	INSCRIBED CYLINDER FROM BORSIP	*Ménant.*	117
54.	DEMONS FIGHTING	*British Museum.*	165
55.	DEMON OF THE SOUTH-WEST WIND	*Perrot and Chipiez.*	169
56.	HEAD OF DEMON	*British Museum.*	170
57.	OANNES	*Smith's Chald. Gen.*	187
58.	CYLINDER OF SARGON FROM AGADÊ	*Hommel.*	207
59.	STATUE OF GUDÊA	*Hommel.*	217
60.	BUST INSCRIBED WITH NAME OF NEBO	*British Museum.*	243
61.	BACK OF TABLET WITH ACCOUNT OF FLOOD	*Smith's Chald. Gen.*	262
62.	BABYLONIAN CYLINDER	*Smith's Chald. Gen.*	266
63.	FEMALE WINGED FIGURES AND SACRED TREES	*British Museum.*	269

			PAGE
64.	WINGED SPIRITS BEFORE SACRED TREE	*Smith's Chald. Gen.*	270
65.	SARGON OF ASSYRIA BEFORE SACRED TREE	*Perrot and Chipiez.*	271
66.	EAGLE-HEADED FIGURE BEFORE SACRED TREE	*Perrot and Chipiez.*	273
67.	FOUR-WINGED HUMAN FIGURE BEFORE SACRED TREE	*Perrot and Chipiez.*	275
68.	TEMPLE AND HANGING GARDENS AT KOYUNJIK	*British Museum.*	277
69.	PLAN OF A ZIGGURAT	*Perrot and Chipiez.*	278
70.	"ZIGGURAT" RESTORED	*Perrot and Chipiez.*	279
71.	BIRS-NIMRUD	*Perrot and Chipiez.*	281
72, 73.	BEL FIGHTS DRAGON	*Perrot and Chipiez.*	289
74.	BATTLE BETWEEN BEL AND DRAGON	*Smith's Chald. Gen.*	291
75.	IZDUBAR AND LION	*Smith's Chald. Gen.*	306
76.	IZDUBAR AND LION	*British Museum.*	307
77.	IZDUBAR AND ÊABÂNI	*Smith's Chald. Gen.*	309
78.	IZDUBAR AND LION	*Perrot and Chipiez.*	310
79.	SCORPION-MAN	*Smith's Chald. Gen.*	311
80.	STONE OBJECT FOUND AT ABU-HABBA		312

INTRODUCTION.

I.

MESOPOTAMIA.—THE MOUNDS.—THE FIRST SEARCHERS.

1. In or about the year before Christ 606, Nineveh, the great city, was destroyed. For many hundred years had she stood in arrogant splendor, her palaces towering above the Tigris and mirrored in its swift waters; army after army had gone forth from her gates and returned laden with the spoils of conquered countries; her monarchs had ridden to the high place of sacrifice in chariots drawn by captive kings. But her time came at last. The nations assembled and encompassed her around. Popular tradition tells how over two years lasted the siege; how the very river rose and battered her walls; till one day a vast flame rose up to heaven; how the last of a mighty line of kings, too proud to surrender, thus saved himself, his treasures and his capital from the shame of bondage. Never was city to rise again where Nineveh had been.

2. Two hundred years went by. Great changes

had passed over the land. The Persian kings now held the rule of Asia. But their greatness also was leaning towards its decline and family discords undermined their power. A young prince had rebelled against his elder brother and resolved to tear the crown from him by main force. To accomplish this, he had raised an army and called 'n the help of Grecian hirelings. They came, 13,000 in number, led by brave and renowned generals, and did their duty by him; but their valor could not save him from defeat and death. Their own leader fell into an ambush, and they commenced their retreat under the most disastrous circumstances and with little hope of escape.

3. Yet they accomplished it. Surrounded by open enemies and false friends, tracked and pursued, through sandy wastes and pathless mountains, now parched with heat, now numbed with cold, they at last reached the sunny and friendly Hellespont. It was a long and weary march from Babylon on the Euphrates, near which city the great battle had been fought. They might not have succeeded had they not chosen a great and brave commander, Xenophon, a noble Athenian, whose fame as scholar and writer equals his renown as soldier and general. Few books are more interesting than the lively relation he has left of his and his companions' toils and sufferings in this expedition, known in history as "The Retreat of the Ten Thousand"—for to that number had the original 13,000 been reduced by battles, privations and disease. So cultivated a man could not fail, even in the midst of

danger and weighed down by care, to observe whatever was noteworthy in the strange lands which he traversed. So he tells us how one day his little army, after a forced march in the early morning hours and an engagement with some light troops of pursuers, having repelled the attack and thereby secured a short interval of safety, travelled on till they came to the banks of the Tigris. On that spot, he goes on, there was a vast desert city. Its wall was twenty-five feet wide, one hundred feet high and nearly seven miles in circuit. It was built of brick with a basement, twenty feet high, of stone. Close by the city there stood a stone pyramid, one hundred feet in width, and two hundred in height. Xenophon adds that this city's name was Larissa and that it had anciently been inhabited by Medes; that the king of Persia, when he took the sovereignty away from the Medes, besieged it, but could not in any way get possession of it, until, a cloud having obscured the sun, the inhabitants forsook the city and thus it was taken.

4. Some eighteen miles further on (a day's march) the Greeks came to another great deserted city, which Xenophon calls Mespila. It had a similar but still higher wall. This city, he tells us, had also been inhabited by Medes, and taken by the king of Persia. Now these curious ruins were all that was left of Kalah and Nineveh, the two Assyrian capitals. In the short space of two hundred years, men had surely not yet lost the memory of Nineveh's existence and rule, yet they trod the very site where it had stood and knew it not, and called its ruins by a

meaningless Greek name, handing down concerning it a tradition absurdly made up of true and fictitious details, jumbled into inextricable confusion. For Nineveh had been the capital of the Assyrian Empire, while the Medes were one of the nations who attacked and destroyed it. And though an eclipse of the sun—(the obscuring cloud could mean nothing else)—did occur, created great confusion and produced important results, it was at a later period and on an entirely different occasion. As to "the king of Persia," no such personage had anything whatever to do with the catastrophe of Nineveh, since the Persians had not yet been heard of at that time as a powerful people, and their country was only a small and insignificant principality, tributary to Media. So effectually had the haughty city been swept from the face of the earth!

5. Another hundred years brought on other and even greater changes. The Persian monarchy had followed in the wake of the empires that had gone before it and fallen before Alexander, the youthful hero of Macedon. As the conqueror's fleet of light-built Grecian ships descended the Euphrates towards Babylon, they were often hindered in their progress by huge dams of stone built across the river. The Greeks, with great labor, removed several, to make navigation more easy. They did the same on several other rivers,—nor knew that they were destroying the last remaining vestige of a great people's civilization,—for these dams had been used to save the water and distribute it into the numerous canals, which covered the arid coun-

try with their fertilizing network. They may have been told what travellers are told in our own days by the Arabs—that these dams had been constructed once upon a time by Nimrod, the Hunter-King. For some of them remain even still, showing their huge, square stones, strongly united by iron cramps, above the water before the river is swollen with the winter rains.

6. More than one-and-twenty centuries have rolled since then over the immense valley so well named Mesopotamia—"the Land between the Rivers,"—and each brought to it more changes, more wars, more disasters, with rare intervals of rest and prosperity. Its position between the East and the West, on the very high-road of marching armies and wandering tribes, has always made it one of the great battle grounds of the world. About one thousand years after Alexander's rapid invasion and short-lived conquest, the Arabs overran the country, and settled there, bringing with them a new civilization and the new religion given them by their prophet Mohammed, which they thought it their mission to carry, by force of word or sword, to the bounds of the earth. They even founded there one of the principal seats of their sovereignty, and Baghdad yielded not greatly in magnificence and power to Babylon of old.

7. Order, laws, and learning now flourished for a few hundred years, when new hordes of barbarous people came pouring in from the East, and one of them, the Turks, at last established itself in the land and stayed. They rule there now. The valley of

the Tigris and Euphrates is a province of the Ottoman or Turkish Empire, which has its capital in Constantinople; it is governed by pashas, officials sent by the Turkish government, or the "Sublime Porte," as it is usually called, and the ignorant, oppressive, grinding treatment to which it has now been subjected for several hundred years has reduced it to the lowest depth of desolation. Its wealth is exhausted, its industry destroyed, its prosperous cities have disappeared or dwindled into insignificance. Even Mossul, built by the Arabs on the right bank of the Tigris, opposite the spot where Nineveh once stood, one of their finest cities, famous for the manufacturing of the delicate cotton tissue to which it gave its name—(*muslin, mousseline*)—would have lost all importance, had it not the honor to be the chief town of a Turkish district and to harbor a pasha. And Baghdad, although still the capital of the whole province, is scarcely more than the shadow of her former glorious self; and her looms no longer supply the markets of the world with wonderful shawls and carpets, and gold and silver tissues of marvellous designs.

8. Mesopotamia is a region which must suffer under neglect and misgovernment even more than others; for, though richly endowed by nature, it is of a peculiar formation, requiring constant care and intelligent management to yield all the return of which it is capable. That care must chiefly consist in distributing the waters of the two great rivers and their affluents over all the land by means of an intricate system of canals, regulated by a complete and

well-kept set of dams and sluices, with other simpler arrangements for the remoter and smaller branches. The yearly inundations caused by the Tigris and Euphrates, which overflow their banks in spring, are not sufficient; only a narrow strip of land on each side is benefited by them. In the lowlands towards the Persian Gulf there is another inconvenience: the country there being perfectly flat, the waters accumulate and stagnate, forming vast pestilential swamps where rich pastures and wheat-fields should be—and have been in ancient times. In short, if left to itself, Upper Mesopotamia, (ancient Assyria), is unproductive from the barrenness of its soil, and Lower Mesopotamia, (ancient Chaldea and Babylonia), runs to waste, notwithstanding its extraordinary fertility, from want of drainage.

9. Such is actually the condition of the once populous and flourishing valley, owing to the principles on which the Turkish rulers carry on their government. They look on their remoter provinces as mere sources of revenue for the state and its officials. But even admitting this as their avowed and chief object, they pursue it in an altogether wrong-headed and short-sighted way. The people are simply and openly plundered, and no portion of what is taken from them is applied to any uses of local public utility, as roads, irrigation, encouragement of commerce and industry and the like : what is not sent home to the Sultan goes into the private pouches of the pasha and his many subaltern officials. This is like taking the milk and omitting to feed the cow. The consequence is, the people lose their interest in

work of any kind, leave off striving for an increase of property which they will not be permitted to enjoy, and resign themselves to utter destitution with a stolid apathy most painful to witness. The land has been brought to such a degree of impoverishment that it is actually no longer capable of producing crops sufficient for a settled population. It is cultivated only in patches along the rivers, where the soil is rendered so fertile by the yearly inundations as to yield moderate returns almost unasked, and that mostly by wandering tribes of Arabs or of Kurds from the mountains to the north, who raise their tents and leave the spot the moment they have gathered in their little harvest—if it has not been appropriated first by some of the pasha's tax-collectors or by roving parties of Bedouins—robber-tribes from the adjoining Syrian and Arabian deserts, who, mounted on their own matchless horses, are carried across the open border with as much facility as the drifts of desert sand so much dreaded by travellers. The rest of the country is left to nature's own devices and, wherever it is not cut up by mountains or rocky ranges, offers the well-known twofold character of steppe-land: luxuriant grassy vegetation during one-third of the year and a parched, arid waste the rest of the time, except during the winter rains and spring floods.

10. A wild and desolate scene! Imposing too in its sorrowful grandeur, and well suited to a land which may be called a graveyard of empires and nations. The monotony of the landscape would be unbroken, but for certain elevations and hillocks of

strange and varied shapes, which spring up, as it were, from the plain in every direction ; some are high and conical or pyramidal in form, others are quite extensive and rather flat on the summit, others again long and low, and all curiously unconnected with each other or any ridge of hills or mountains. This is doubly striking in Lower Mesopotamia or Babylonia, proverbial for its excessive flatness. The few permanent villages, composed of mud-huts or plaited reed-cabins, are generally built on these eminences, others are used as burying-grounds, and a mosque, the Mohammedan house of prayer, sometimes rises on one or the other. They are pleasing objects in the beautiful spring season, when corn-fields wave on their summits, and their slopes, as well as all the surrounding plains, are clothed with the densest and greenest of herbage, enlivened with countless flowers of every hue, till the surface of the earth looks, from a distance or from a height, as gorgeous as the richest Persian carpet. But, on approaching nearer to these hillocks or mounds, an unprepared traveller would be struck by some peculiar features. Their substance being rather soft and yielding, and the winter rains pouring down with exceeding violence, their sides are furrowed in many places with ravines, dug by the rushing streams of rain-water. These streams of course wash down much of the substance itself and carry it far into the plain, where it lies scattered on the surface quite distinct from the soil. These washings are found to consist not of earth or sand, but of rubbish, something like that which lies in heaps wherever a house is being built or demolished, and to contain innumerable fragments of bricks, pottery, stone evidently worked by the hand and chisel; many of these fragments moreover bearing inscriptions in complicated characters composed of one curious figure shaped like the head of an arrow, and used in every possible position and combination,—like this:

A 𒀭𒀭 𒀭𒀭𒀭 𒀭𒀭𒀭 𒀭𒀭𒀭𒀭

1.—CUNEIFORM CHARACTERS.

11. In the crevices or ravines themselves, the waters having cleared away masses of this loose rubbish, have laid bare whole sides of walls of solid brick-work, sometimes even a piece of a human head or limb, or a corner of sculptured stone-slab, always of colossal size and bold, striking execution. All this tells its own tale and the conclusion is self-apparent: that these elevations are not natural hillocks or knolls, but artificial mounds, heaps of earth and building materials which have been at some time placed there by men, then, collapsing and crumbling to rubbish from neglect, have concealed within their ample sides all that remains of those ancient structures and works of art, clothed themselves in verdure, and deceitfully assumed all the outward signs of natural hills.

12. The Arabs never thought of exploring these curious heaps. Mohammedan nations, as a rule, take little interest in relics of antiquity; moreover they are very superstitious, and, as their religious law strictly forbids them to represent the human

form either in painting or sculpture lest such reproduction might lead ignorant and misguided people back to the abominations of idolatry, so they look on relics of ancient statuary with suspicion amounting to fear and connect them with magic and witchcraft. It is, therefore, with awe not devoid of horror that they tell travellers that the mounds contain underground passages which are haunted not only by wild beasts, but by evil spirits—for have not sometimes strange figures carved in stone been dimly perceived in the crevices? Better instructed foreigners have long ago assumed that within these mounds must be entombed whatever ruins may be preserved of the great cities of yore. Their number formed no objection, for it was well known how populous the valley had been in the days of its splendor, and that, besides several famous cities, it could boast no end of smaller ones, often separated from each other by a distance of only a few miles. The long low mounds were rightly supposed to represent the ancient walls, and the higher and vaster ones to have been the site of the palaces and temples. The Arabs, though utterly ignorant of history of any kind, have preserved in their religion some traditions from the Bible, and so it happens that out of these wrecks of ages some biblical names still survive. Almost everything of which they do not know the origin, they ascribe to Nimrod; and the smaller of the two mounds opposite Mosul, which mark the spot where Nineveh itself once stood, they call "Jonah's Mound," and stoutly believe the mosque which crowns it, surrounded by a comparatively prosperous village, to contain the tomb of Jonah himself, the prophet who was sent to rebuke and warn the wicked city. As the Mohammedans honor the Hebrew prophets, the whole mound is sacred in their eyes in consequence.

13. If travellers had for some time been aware of these general facts concerning the Mounds, it was many years before their curiosity and interest were so far aroused as to make them go to the trouble and expense of digging into them, in order to find out what they really contained. Until within the last hundred years or so, not only the general public, but even highly cultivated men and distinguished scholars, under the words "study of antiquity," understood no more than the study of so-called "*Classical* Antiquity," i.e., of the language, history and literature of the Greeks and Romans, together with the ruins, works of art, and remains of all sorts left by these two nations. Their knowledge of other empires and people they took from the Greek and Roman historians and writers, without doubting or questioning their statements, or—as we say now—without subjecting their statements to any criticism. Moreover, European students in their absorption in and devotion to classical studies, were too apt to follow the example of their favorite authors and to class the entire rest of the world, as far as it was known in ancient times, under the sweeping and somewhat contemptuous by-name of "Barbarians," thus allowing them but a secondary importance and an inferior claim to attention.

14. Things began greatly to change towards the

end of the last century. Yet the mounds of Assyria and Babylonia were still suffered to keep their secret unrevealed. This want of interest may be in part explained by their peculiar nature. They are so different from other ruins. A row of massive pillars or of stately columns cut out on the clear blue sky, with the desert around or the sea at their feet,—a broken arch or battered tombstone clothed with ivy and hanging creepers, with the blue and purple mountains for a background, are striking objects which first take the eye by their beauty, then invite inspection by the easy approach they offer. But these huge, shapeless heaps! What labor to remove even a small portion of them! And when that is done, who knows whether their contents will at all repay the effort and expense?

15. The first European whose love of learning was strong enough to make him disregard all such doubts and difficulties, was Mr. Rich, an Englishman. He was not particularly successful, nor were his researches very extensive, being carried on entirely with his private means; yet his name will always be honorably remembered, for he was *the first* who went to work with pickaxe and shovel, who hired men to dig, who measured and described some of the principal mounds on the Euphrates, thus laying down the groundwork of all later and more fruitful explorations in that region. It was in 1820 and Mr. Rich was then political resident or representative of the East India Company at Baghdad. He also tried the larger of the two mounds opposite Mosul, encouraged by the report that, a

short time before he arrived there, a sculpture representing men and animals had been disclosed to view. Unfortunately he could not procure even a fragment of this treasure, for the people of Mosul, influenced by their *ulema*--(doctor of the law) —who had declared these sculptures to be "idols of the infidels," had walked across the river from the city in a body and piously shattered them to atoms. Mr. Rich had not the good luck to come across any such find himself, and after some further efforts, left the place rather disheartened. He carried home to England the few relics he had been able to obtain. In the absence of more important ones, they were very interesting, consisting in fragments of inscriptions, of pottery, in engraved stone, bricks and pieces of bricks. After his death all these articles were placed in the British Museum, where they formed the foundation of the present noble Chaldea-Assyrian collection of that great institution. Nothing more was undertaken for years, so that it could be said with literal truth that, up to 1842, "a case three feet square inclosed all that remained, not only of the great city Nineveh, but of Babylon itself!" *

16. The next in the field was Mr. Botta, appointed French Consul at Mosul in 1842. He began to dig at the end of the same year, and naturally attached himself specially to the larger of the two mounds opposite Mosul, named KOYUNJIK, after a small village at its base. This mound is the Mespila of

---

* Layard's "Discoveries at Nineveh," Introduction.

Xenophon. He began enthusiastically, and worked on for over three months, but repeated disappointments were beginning to produce discouragement, when one day a peasant from a distant village happened to be looking on at the small party of workmen. He was much amused on observing that every—to him utterly worthless—fragment of alabaster, brick or pottery, was carefully picked out of the rubbish, most tenderly handled and laid aside, and laughingly remarked that they might be better repaid for their trouble, if they would try the mound on which his village was built, for that lots of such rubbish had kept continually turning up, when they were digging the foundations of their houses.

17. Mr. Botta had by this time fallen into a rather hopeless mood; yet he did not dare to neglect the hint, and sent a few men to the mound which had been pointed out to him, and which, as well as the village on the top of it, bore the name of KHORSABAD. His agent began operations from the top. A well was sunk into the mound, and very soon brought the workmen to the top of a wall, which, on further digging, was found to be lined along its base with sculptured slabs of some soft substance much like gypsum or limestone. This discovery quickly brought Mr. Botta to the spot, in a fever of excitement. He now took the direction of the works himself, had a trench dug from the outside straight into the mound, wide and deep, towards the place already laid open from above. What was his astonishment on finding that he had entered a hall entirely lined all round, except where interruptions

indicated the place of doorways leading into other rooms, with sculptured slabs similar to the one first discovered, and representing scenes of battles, sieges and the like. He walked as in a dream. It was a new and wonderful world suddenly opened. For these sculptures evidently recorded the deeds of the builder, some powerful conqueror and king. And those long and close lines engraved in the stone, all along the slabs, in the same peculiar character as the short inscriptions on the bricks that lay scattered on the plain—they must surely contain the text to these sculptured illustrations. But who is to read them? They are not like any known writing in the world and may remain a sealed book forever. Who, then, was the builder? To what age belong these structures? Which of the wars we read about are here portrayed? None of these questions, which must have strangely agitated him, could Mr. Botta have answered at the time. But not the less to him remains the glory of having, first of living men, entered the palace of an Assyrian king.

18. Mr. Botta henceforth devoted himself exclusively to the mound of Khorsabad. His discovery created an immense sensation in Europe. Scholarly indifference was not proof against so unlooked-for a shock; the revulsion was complete and the spirit of research and enterprise was effectually aroused, not to slumber again. The French consul was supplied by his government with ample means to carry on excavations on a large scale. If the first success may be considered as merely a great piece of good fortune, the following ones were certainly due to

intelligent, untiring labor and ingenuous scholarship. We see the results in Botta's voluminous work "Monuments de Ninive" * and in the fine Assyrian collection of the Louvre, in the first room of which is placed, as is but just, the portrait of the man to whose efforts and devotion it is due.

19. The great English investigator Layard, then a young and enthusiastic scholar on his Eastern travels, passing through Mosul in 1842, found Mr. Botta engaged on his first and unpromising attempts at Koyunjik, and subsequently wrote to him from Constantinople exhorting him to persist and not give up his hopes of success. He was one of the first to hear of the astounding news from Khorsabad, and immediately determined to carry out a long-cherished project of his own, that of exploring a large mound known among the Arabs under the name of NIMRUD, and situated somewhat lower on the Tigris, near that river's junction with one of its chief tributaries, the Zab. The difficulty lay in procuring the necessary funds. Neither the trustees of the British Museum nor the English Government were at first willing to incur such considerable expense on what was still looked upon as very uncertain chances. It was a private gentleman, Sir Stratford Canning, then English minister at Constantinople, who generously came forward, and announced himself willing to meet the outlay within certain limits, while authorities at home were to

---

* In five huge folio volumes, one of text, two of inscriptions, and two of illustrations. The title shows that Botta erroneously imagined the ruins he had discovered to be those of Nineveh itself.

be solicited and worked upon. So Mr. Layard was enabled to begin operations on the mound which he had specially selected for himself in the autumn of 1845, the year after that in which the building of Khorsabad was finally laid open by Botta. The results of his expedition were so startlingly vast and important, and the particulars of his work on the Assyrian plains are so interesting and picturesque, that they will furnish ample materials for a separate chapter.

II.

LAYARD AND HIS WORK.

1. IN the first part of November, 1845, we find the enthusiastic and enterprising young scholar on the scene of his future exertions and triumphs. His first night in the wilderness, in a ruinous Arab village amidst the smaller mounds of Nimrud, is vividly described by him:—"I slept little during the night. The hovel in which we had taken shelter, and its inmates, did not invite slumber; but such scenes and companions were not new to me; they could have been forgotten, had my brain been less excited. Hopes, long-cherished, were now to be realized, or were to end in disappointment. Visions of palaces underground, of gigantic monsters, of sculptured figures, and endless inscriptions floated before me. After forming plan after plan for removing the earth, and extricating these treasures, I fancied myself wandering in a maze of chambers from which I could find no outlet. Then again, all was reburied, and I was standing on the grass-covered mound."

2. Although not doomed to disappointment in the end, these hopes were yet to be thwarted in many ways before the visions of that night became

reality. For many and various were the difficulties which Layard had to contend with during the following months as well as during his second expedition in 1848. The material hardships of perpetual camping out in an uncongenial climate, without any of the simplest conveniences of life, and the fevers and sickness repeatedly brought on by exposure to winter rains and summer heat, should perhaps be counted among the least of them, for they had their compensations. Not so the ignorant and ill-natured opposition, open or covert, of the Turkish authorities. That was an evil to which no amount of philosophy could ever fully reconcile him. His experiences in that line form an amusing collection. Luckily, the first was also the worst. The pasha whom he found installed at Mosul was, in appearance and temper, more like an ogre than a man. He was the terror of the country. His cruelty and rapacity knew no bounds. When he sent his tax-collectors on their dreaded round, he used to dismiss them with this short and pithy instruction: " Go, destroy, eat ! " (i.e. " plunder "), and for his own profit had revived several kinds of contributions which had been suffered to fall into disuse, especially one called " tooth-money,"—" a compensation in money, levied upon all villages in which a man of such rank is entertained, for the wear and tear of his teeth in masticating the food he condescends to receive from the inhabitants."

3. The letters with which Layard was provided secured him a gracious reception from this amiable personage, who allowed him to begin operations

on the great mound of Nimrud with the party of Arab workmen whom he had hired for the purpose. Some time after, it came to the Pasha's knowledge that a few fragments of gold leaf had been found in the rubbish and he even procured a small particle as sample. He immediately concluded, as the Arab chief had done, that the English traveller was digging for hidden treasure—an object far more intelligible to them than that of disinterring and carrying home a quantity of old broken stones. This incident, by arousing the great man's rapacity, might have caused him to put a stop to all further search, had not Layard, who well knew that treasure of this kind was not likely to be plentiful in the ruins, immediately proposed that his Excellency should keep an agent at the mound, to take charge of all the precious metals which might be discovered there in the course of the excavations. The Pasha raised no objections at the moment, but a few days later announced to Layard that, to his great regret, he felt it his duty to forbid the continuation of the work, since he had just learned that the diggers were disturbing a Mussulman burying-ground. As the tombs of true believers are held very sacred and inviolable by Mohammedans, this would have been a fatal obstacle, had not one of the Pasha's own officers confidentially disclosed to Layard that the tombs were *sham ones*, that he and his men had been secretly employed to fabricate them, and for two nights had been bringing stones for the purpose from the surrounding villages. "We have destroyed more

tombs of true believers," said the Aga,—(officer)—
" in making sham ones, than ever you could have
defiled. We have killed our horses and ourselves
in carrying those accursed stones." Fortunately
the Pasha, whose misdeeds could not be tolerated
even by a Turkish government, was recalled about
Christmas, and succeeded by an official of an entirely different stamp, a man whose reputation for
justice and mildness had preceded him, and whose
arrival was accordingly greeted with public rejoic-
ings. Operations at the mound now proceeded for
some time rapidly and successfully. But this very
success at one time raised new difficulties for our
explorers.

4. One day, as Layard was returning to the
mound from an excursion, he was met on the way
by two Arabs who had ridden out to meet him at
full speed, and from a distance shouted to him in
the wildest excitement : " Hasten, O Bey! hasten
to the diggers! for they have found Nimrod himself. It is wonderful, but it is true! we have seen
him with our eyes. There is no God but God!"
Greatly puzzled, he hurried on and, descending into
the trench, found that the workmen had uncovered
a gigantic head, the body to which was still imbedded in earth and rubbish. This head, beautifully sculptured in the alabaster furnished by the
neighboring hills, surpassed in height the tallest
man present. The great shapely features, in their
majestic repose, seemed to guard some mighty
secret and to defy the bustling curiosity of those
who gazed on them in wonder and fear. " One of

the workmen, on catching the first glimpse of the monster, had thrown down his basket and run off toward Mossul as fast as his legs could carry him."

5. The Arabs came in crowds from the sur-

2.—TEMPLE OF EA AT ERIDHU (ABU-SHAHREIN). BACK-STAIRS.
(Hommel.)

rounding encampments; they could scarcely be persuaded that the image was of stone, and contended that it was not the work of men's hands, but of infidel giants of olden times. The commotion soon spread to Mosul, where the terrified workman, "entering breathless into the bazars, announced to every one he met that Nimrod had appeared." The authorities of the town were alarmed, put their heads together and decided that such idolatrous proceedings were an outrage to religion. The consequence was that Layard was requested by his friend Ismail-Pasha to suspend operations for awhile, until the excitement should have subsided, a request with which he thought it wisest to comply without remonstrance, lest the people of Mosul might come out in force and deal with his precious find as they had done with the sculptured figure at Koyunjik in Rich's time. The alarm, however, did not last long. Both Arabs and Turks soon became familiar with the strange creations which kept emerging out of the earth, and learned to discuss them with great calm and gravity. The colossal bulls and lions with wings and human heads, of which several pairs were discovered, some of them in a state of perfect preservation, were especially the objects of wonder and conjectures, which generally ended in a curse " on all infidels and their works," the conclusion arrived at being that " the idols " were to be sent to England, to form gateways to the palace of the Queen. And when some of these giants, now in the British Museum, were actually removed, with infinite pains and labor, to be dragged down to the Tigris, and floated down the river on rafts, there was no end to the astonishment of Layard's simple friends. On one such occasion an Arab Sheikh, or chieftain, whose tribe had engaged to assist in moving one of the winged bulls, opened his heart to him. " In the name of the Most High," said he, "tell me, O Bey, what you are going to do with these stones. So many thousands of purses spent on such things! Can it be, as you say, that your people learn wisdom from them? or is it as his reverence the Cadi declares, that they are to go to the palace of your Queen, who, with the rest of the unbelievers, worships these idols? As for wisdom, these figures will not teach you to make any better knives, or scissors, or chintzes, and it is in the making of these things that the English show their wisdom."

6. Such was the view very generally taken of Layard's work by both Turks and Arabs, from the Pasha down to the humblest digger in his band of laborers, and he seldom felt called upon to play the missionary of science, knowing as he did that all such efforts would be but wasted breath. This want of intellectual sympathy did not prevent the best understanding from existing between himself and these rangers of the desert. The primitive life which he led amongst them for so many months, the kindly hospitality which he invariably experienced at their hands during the excursions made and the visits he paid to different Bedouin tribes in the intervals of recreation which he was compelled to allow himself from time to time—these are among the most pleasurable memories of those wonderful, dreamlike years. He lingers on them lovingly and retraces them through many a page of both his books*—pages which, for their picturesque vivid-

---
* "Nineveh and its Remains," and "Discoveries in Nineveh and Babylon."

ness, must be perused with delight even by such as are but slightly interested in the discovery of buried palaces and winged bulls. One longs to have been with him through some of those peerless evenings when, after a long day's work, he sat before his cabin in the cool starlight, watching the dances with which those indefatigable Arabs, men and women, solaced themselves deep into the night, while the encampment was lively with the hum of voices, and the fires lit to prepare the simple meal. One longs to have shared in some of those brisk rides across plains so thickly enamelled with flowers, that it seemed a patchwork of many colors, and "the dogs, as they returned from hunting, issued from the long grass dyed red, yellow, or blue, according to the flowers through which they had last forced their way,"—the joy of the Arab's soul, which made the chief, Layard's friend, continually exclaim, "rioting in the luxuriant herbage and scented air, as his mare waded through the flowers:—'What delight has God given us equal to this? It is the only thing worth living for. What do the dwellers in cities know of true happiness? They never have seen grass or flowers! May God have pity on them!'" How glorious to watch the face of the desert changing its colors almost from day to day, white succeeding to pale straw color, red to white, blue to red, lilac to blue, and bright gold to that, according to the flowers with which it decked itself! Out of sight stretches the gorgeous carpet, dotted with the black camel's-hair tents ot the Arabs, enlivened with flocks of sheep and camels, and whole studs of horses of noble breed which are brought out from Mosul and left to graze at liberty, in the days of healthy breezes and fragrant pastures.

7. So much for spring. A beautiful, a perfect season, but unfortunately as brief as it is lovely, and too soon succeeded by the terrible heat and long drought of summer, which sometimes set in so suddenly as hardly to give the few villagers time to gather in their crops. Chaldea or Lower Mesopotamia is in this respect even worse off than the higher plains of Assyria. A temperature of 120° in the shade is no unusual occurrence in Baghdad; true, it can be reduced to 100° in the cellars of the houses by carefully excluding the faintest ray of light, and it is there that the inhabitants mostly spend their days in summer. The oppression is such that Europeans are entirely unmanned and unfitted for any kind of activity. "Camels sicken, and birds are so distressed by the high temperature, that they sit in the date-trees about Baghdad, with their mouths open, panting for fresh air."*

8. But the most frightful feature of a Mesopotamian summer is the frequent and violent sand-storms, during which travellers, in addition to all the dangers offered by snow-storms—being buried alive and losing their way—are exposed to that of suffocation not only from the furnace-like heat of the desert-wind, but from the impalpable sand, which is whirled and driven before it, and fills the eyes, mouth

---

* Rawlinson's "Five Great Monarchies of the Ancient World," Vol. I., Chap. II.

and nostrils of horse and rider. The three miles' ride from Layard's encampment to the mound of Nimrud must have been something more than pleasant morning exercise in such a season, and though the deep trenches and wells afforded a comparatively cool and delightful retreat, he soon found that fever was the price to be paid for the indulgence, and was repeatedly laid up with it. "The verdure of the plain," he says in one place, "had perished almost in a day. Hot winds, coming from the desert, had burnt up and carried away the shrubs; flights of locusts, darkening the air, had destroyed the few patches of cultivation, and had completed the havoc commenced by the heat of the sun. . . . Violent whirlwinds occasionally swept over the face of the country. They could be seen as they advanced from the desert, carrying along with them clouds of dust and sand. Almost utter darkness prevailed during their passage, which lasted generally about an hour, and nothing could resist their fury. On returning home one afternoon after a tempest of the kind, I found no traces of my dwellings; they had been completely carried away. Ponderous wooden frame-works had been borne over the bank and hurled some hundred yards distant; the tents had disappeared, and my furniture was scattered over the plain."

9. Fortunately it would not require much labor to restore the wooden frames to their proper place and reconstruct the reed-plaited, mud-plastered walls as well as the roof composed of reeds and boughs— such being the sumptuous residences of which Lay-

ard shared the largest with various domestic animals, from whose immediate companionship he was saved by a thin partition, the other hovels being devoted to the wives, children and poultry of his host, to his own servants and different household uses. But the time came when not even this accommodation, poor as it was, could be enjoyed with any degree of comfort. When the summer heat set in in earnest, the huts became uninhabitable from their closeness and the vermin with which they swarmed, while a canvas tent, though far preferable in the way of airiness and cleanliness, did not afford sufficient shelter.

10. "In this dilemma," says Layard, "I ordered a recess to be cut into the bank of the river where it rose perpendicularly from the water's edge. By screening the front with reeds and boughs of trees, and covering the whole with similar materials, a small room was formed. I was much troubled, however, with scorpions and other reptiles, which issued from the earth forming the walls of my apartment; and later in the summer by the gnats and sandflies which hovered on a calm night over the river." It is difficult to decide between the respective merits of this novel summer retreat and of the winter dwelling, ambitiously constructed of mud bricks dried in the sun, and roofed with solid wooden beams. This imposing residence, in which Layard spent the last months of his first winter in Assyria, would have been sufficient protection against wind and weather, after it had been duly coated with mud. Unfortunately a heavy shower fell before it was quite completed, and so saturated the bricks

that they did not dry again before the following spring. "The consequence was," he pleasantly remarks, "that the only verdure on which my eyes were permitted to feast before my return to Europe, was furnished by my own property—the walls in the interior of the rooms being continually clothed with a crop of grass."

11. These few indications are sufficient to give a tolerably clear idea of what might be called "Pleasures and hardships of an explorer's life in the desert." As for the work itself, it is simple enough in the telling, although it must have been extremely wearisome and laborious in the performance. The simplest way to get at the contents of a mound, would be to remove all the earth and rubbish by carting it away,—a piece of work which our searchers might no doubt have accomplished with great facility, had they had at their disposal a few scores of thousands of slaves and captives, as had the ancient kings who built the huge constructions the ruins of which had now to be disinterred. With a hundred or two of hired workmen and very limited funds, the case was slightly different. The task really amounted to this: to achieve the greatest possible results at the least possible expense of labor and time, and this is how such excavations are carried out on a plan uniformly followed everywhere as the most practical and direct:

12. Trenches, more or less wide, are conducted from different sides towards the centre of the mound. This is obviously the surest and shortest way to arrive at whatever remains of walls may be im-

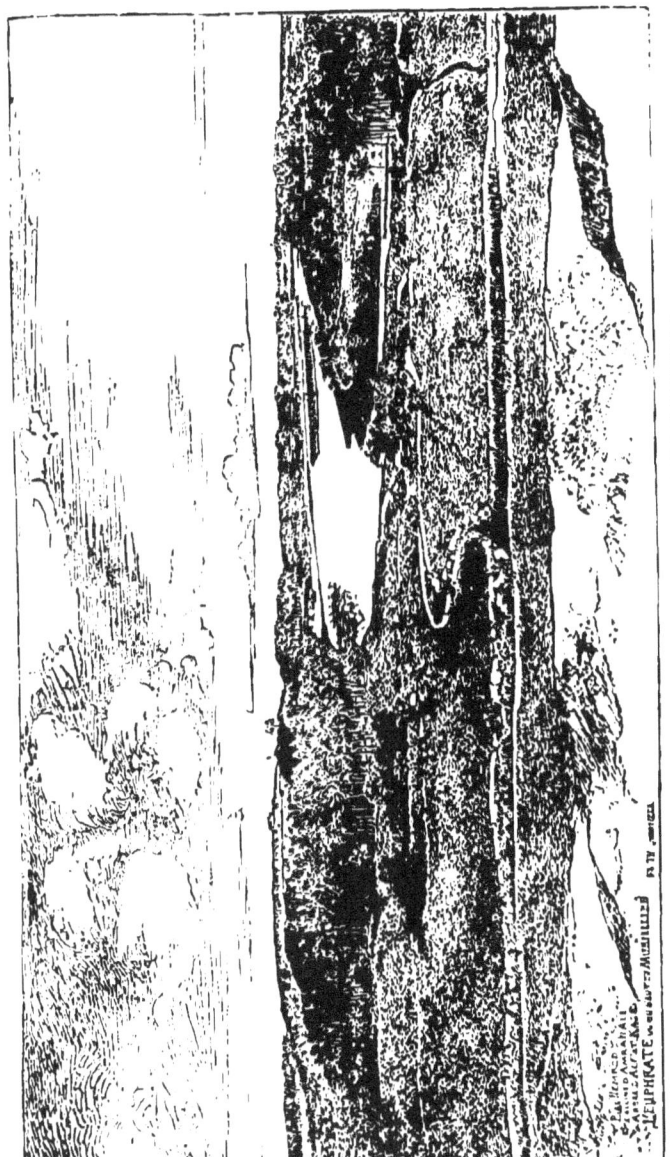

3.—VIEW OF EUPHRATES NEAR THE RUINS OF BABYLON.

(Lebelon.)

bedded in it. But even this preliminary operation has to be carried out with some judgment and discernment. It is known that the Chaldeans and Assyrians constructed their palaces and temples not upon the level, natural soil, but upon an artificial platform of brick and earth, at least thirty feet high. This platform was faced on all sides with a strong wall of solid burned brick, often moreover cased with stone. A trench dug straight from the plain into the lower part of the mound would consequently be wasted labor, since it could never bring to anything but that same blind wall, behind which there is only the solid mass of the platform. Digging therefore begins in the slope of the mound, at a height corresponding to the supposed height of the platform, and is carried on straight across its surface until a wall is reached,—a wall belonging to one of the palaces or temples. This wall has then to be followed, till a break in it is found, indicating an entrance or doorway.* The burrowing process becomes more and more complicated, and sometimes dangerous. Shafts have to be sunk from above at frequent intervals to introduce air and light into the long and narrow corridor; the sides and vault have to be propped by beams to prevent the soft earthy mass from falling in and crushing the diggers. Every shovelful of earth cleared away is removed in baskets which are passed from hand to hand till they are emptied outside the trench, or else lowered empty and sent up full, through the shafts by means of ropes and pulleys, to be emptied on the top. When a doorway is reached, it is cleared all

* See Figure 15, on p. 53.

4.—MOUND OF BABIL. (RUINS OF BABYLON.)
(Oppert.)

through the thickness of the wall, which is very great; then a similar tunnel is conducted all along the inside of the wall, the greatest care being needed not to damage the sculptures which generally line it, and which, as it is, are more or less injured and cracked, their upper parts sometimes entirely destroyed by the action of fire. When the tunnel has been carried along the four sides, every doorway or portal carefully noted and cleared, it is seen from the measurements,—especially the width—whether the space explored be an inner court, a hall or a chamber. If the latter, it is sometimes entirely cleared from above, when the rubbish frequently yields valuable finds in the shape of various small articles. One such chamber, uncovered by Layard, at Koyunjik, proved a perfect mine of treasures. The most curious relics were brought to light in it: quantities of studs and small rosettes in mother-of-pearl, ivory and metal, (such as were used to ornament the harness of the war-horses), bowls, cups and dishes of bronze,* besides caldrons, shields and other items of armor, even glass bowls, lastly fragments of a royal throne—possibly the very throne on which King Sennacherib sat to give audience or pronounce judgments, for the palace at Koyunjik where these objects were found was built by that monarch so long familiar to us only from the Bible, and the sculptures and inscriptions which cover its walls are the annals of his conquests abroad and his rule at home.

A description of the removal of the colossal bulls and lions which were shipped to England and now

---

* See Figures 5 6, and 7.

are safely housed in the British Museum, ought by rights to form the close of a chapter devoted to "Layard and his work." But the reference must

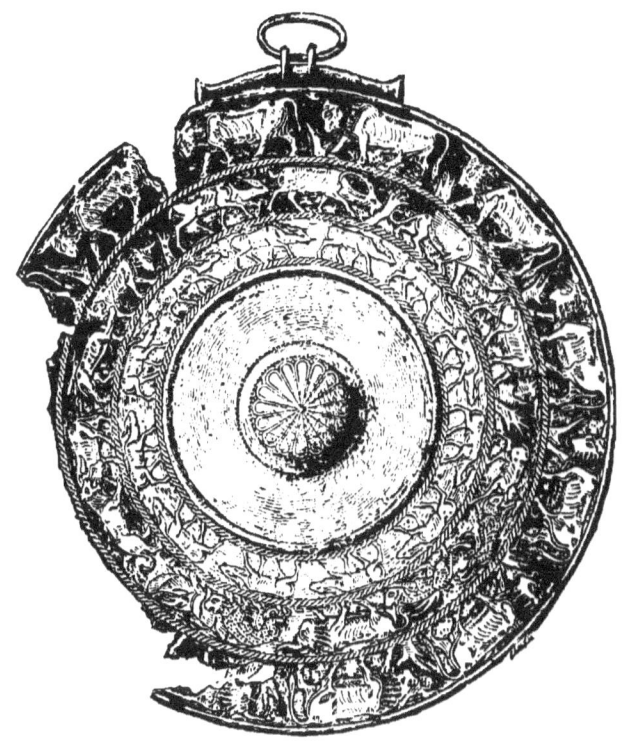

5.—BRONZE DISH.

suffice; the vivid and entertaining narrative should be read in the original, as the passages are too long for transcription, and would be marred by quoting.

III.

THE RUINS.

"And they said to one another, Go to, let us make brick, and burn them throughly. And they had brick for stone and slime for mortar."—*Gen.* xi. 3.

1. IT is a principle, long ago laid down and universally recognized, that every country *makes* its own people. That is, the mode of life and the intellectual culture of a people are shaped by the characteristic features of the land in which it dwells; or, in other words, men can live only in a manner suited to the peculiarities of their native country. Men settled along the sea-shore will lead a different life, will develop different qualities of mind and body from the owners of vast inland pasture-grounds or the holders of rugged mountain fastnesses. They will all dress differently, eat different food, follow different pursuits. Their very dwellings and public buildings will present an entirely different aspect, according to the material which they will have at hand in the greatest abundance, be it stone, wood or any other substance suitable for the purpose. Thus every country will create its own peculiar style of art, determined chiefly by its own natural productions. On these, architecture, the art of the

builder, will be even more dependent than any other.

2. It would seem as though Chaldea or Lower Mesopotamia, regarded from this point of view, could

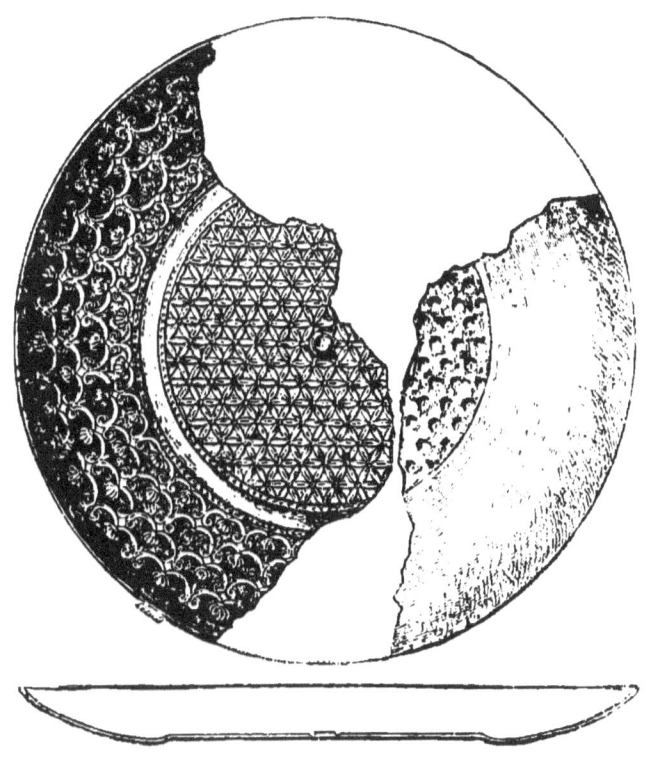

6.—BRONZE DISH (RUG-PATTERN).

never have originated any architecture at all, for it is, at first sight, absolutely deficient in building materials of any sort. The whole land is alluvial, that is, formed, gradually, through thousands of years, of the rich mud deposited by the two rivers, as they spread into vast marshy flats towards the end of their course. Such soil, when hardened into sufficient consistency, is the finest of all for cultivation, and a greater source of wealth than mines of the most precious ore; but it bears no trees and contains no stone. The people who were first tempted to settle in the lowlands towards the Persian Gulf by the extraordinary fertility of that region, found nothing at all available to construct their simple dwellings—nothing but reeds of enormous size, which grew there, as they do now, in the greatest profusion. These reeds "cover the marshes in the summer-time, rising often to the height of fourteen or fifteen feet. The Arabs of the marsh region form their houses of this material, binding the stems together and bending them into arches, to make the skeletons of their buildings; while, to form the walls, they stretch across from arch to arch mats made of the leaves." *

3. There can be no doubt that of such habitations consisted the villages and towns of those first settlers. They gave quite sufficient shelter in the very mild winters of that region, and, when coated with a layer of mud which soon dried and hardened in the sun, could exclude even the violent rains of that season. But they were in no way fitted for more ambitious and dignified purposes. Neither the palaces of the kings nor the temples of the gods could be constructed out of bent reeds. Something more

---

* Rawlinson's "Five Monarchies," Vol. I., p. 46.

durable must be found, some material that would lend itself to constructions of any size or shape. The mud coating of the cabins naturally suggested such a material. Could not this same mud or clay, of which an inexhaustible supply was always on hand, be moulded into cakes of even size, and after being left to dry in the sun, be piled into walls of

7.—SECTION OF BRONZE DISH.

the required height and thickness? And so men began to make bricks. It was found that the clay gained much in consistency when mixed with finely chopped straw—another article of which the country, abounding in wheat and other grains, yielded unlimited quantities. But even with this improvement the sun-dried bricks could not withstand the continued action of many rainy seasons, or many torrid summers, but had a tendency to crumble away when parched too dry, or to soak and dissolve back into mud, when too long exposed to rain. All these defects were removed by the simple expedient of baking the bricks in kilns or ovens, a process which gives them the hardness and solidity of stone. But as the cost of kiln-dried bricks is naturally very much greater than that of the original crude article, so the latter continued to be used in far greater quantities; the walls were made entirely of them and only protected by an outward casing of the hard baked bricks. These being so much more expensive, and calculated to last forever, great care was bestowed on their preparation; the best clay was selected and they were stamped with the names and titles of the king by whose order the palace or temple was built, for which they were to be used. This has been of great service in identifying the various ruins and assigning them dates, at least approximately. As is to be expected, there is a notable difference in the specimens of different periods. While on some bricks bearing the name of a king who lived about 3000 B.C. the inscription is uncouth and scarcely legible, and even their shape is rude and the material very inferior, those of the later Babylonian period (600 B.C.) are handsome and neatly made. As to the quality, all explorers agree in saying it is fully equal to that of the best modern English bricks. The excellence of these bricks for building purposes is a fact so well known that for now two thousand years—ever

8.—VIEW OF NEBBI YUNUS.

since the destruction of Babylon—its walls, temples and palaces have been used as quarries for the construction of cities and villages. The little town of HILLAH, situated nearest to the site of the ancient capital, is built almost entirely with bricks from one single mound, that of KASR—once the gorgeous and far-famed palace of Nebuchadnezzar, whose name and titles thus grace the walls of the most lowly Arab and Turkish dwellings. All the other mounds are similarly used, and so far is the valuable mine from being exhausted, that it furnishes forth, to this day, a brisk and flourishing trade. While a party of workmen is continually employed in digging for the available bricks, another is busy conveying them to Hillah; there they are shipped on the Euphrates and carried to any place where building materials are in demand, often even loaded on donkeys at this or that landing-place and sent miles away inland; some are taken as far as Baghdad, where they have been used for ages. The same thing is done wherever there are mounds and ruins. Both Layard and his successors had to allow their Arab workmen to build their own temporary houses out of ancient bricks, only watching them narrowly, lest they should break some valuable relic in the process or use some of the handsomest and best-preserved specimens.

4. No construction of bricks, either crude or kiln-dried, could have sufficient solidity without the help of some kind of cement, to make them adhere firmly together. This also the lowlands of Chaldea and Babylonia yield in sufficient quantity and of

9.—BUILDING IN BAKED BRICK (MODERN).
(Perrot and Chippiez.)

various qualities. While in the early structures a kind of sticky red clay or loam is used, mixed with chopped straw, bitumen or pitch is substituted at a later period, which substance, being applied hot, adheres so firmly to the bricks, that pieces of these are broken off when an attempt is made to procure a fragment of the cement. This valuable article was brought down by water from Is on the Euphrates (now called HIT,, where abundant springs of bitumen are to this day in activity. Calcareous earth—i.e., earth strongly mixed with lime—being very plentiful to the west of the lower Euphrates, towards the Arabian frontier, the Babylonians of the latest times learned to make of it a white mortar which, for lightness and strength, has never been surpassed.

5. All the essential materials for plain but durable constructions being thus procurable on the spot or in the immediate neighborhood, the next important point was the selection of proper sites for raising these constructions, which were to serve purposes of defence as well as of worship and royal majesty. A rocky eminence, inaccessible on one or several sides, or at least a hill, a knoll somewhat elevated above the surrounding plain, have usually been chosen wherever such existed. But this was not the case in Chaldea. There, as far as eye can see, not the slightest undulation breaks the dead flatness of the land. Yet there, more than anywhere else, an elevated position was desirable, if only as a protection from the unhealthy exhalations of a vast tract of swamps, and from the intolerable

10.—MOUND OF NIMRUD.
(Hommel.)

nuisance of swarms of aggressive and venomous insects, which infest the entire river region during the long summer season. Safety from the attacks of the numerous roaming tribes which ranged the country in every direction before it was definitely settled and organized, was also not among the last considerations. So, what nature had refused, the cunning and labor of man had to supply. Artificial hills or platforms were constructed, of enormous size and great height—from thirty to fifty, even sixty feet, and on their flat summits the buildings were raised. These platforms sometimes supported only one palace, sometimes, as in the case of the immense mounds of Koyunjik and Nimrud in Assyria, their surface had room for several, built by successive kings. Of course such huge piles could not be entirely executed in solid masonry, even of crude bricks. These were generally mixed with earth and rubbish of all kinds, in more or less regular, alternate layers, the bricks being laid in clay. But the outward facing was in all cases of baked brick. The platform of the principal mound which marks the place of ancient UR, (now called MUG-HEIR),* is faced with a wall ten feet thick, of red kiln-dried bricks, cemented with bitumen. In Assyria, where stone was not scarce, the sides of the platform were even more frequently "protected by massive stone-masonry, carried perpendicularly from the natural ground to a height somewhat exceeding that of the platform, and either made

---

* Ur of the Chaldees, from which Abraham went forth.

plain at the top, or else crowned into stone battlements cut into gradines."*

6. Some mounds are considerably higher than the others and of a peculiar shape, almost like a pyramid, that is, ending in a point from which it slopes

11.—MOUND OF MUGHEIR (ANCIENT UR).

down rapidly on all sides. Such is the pyramidal mound of Nimrud, which Layard describes as being so striking and picturesque an object as you approach the ruins from any point of the plain.† Such also is the still more picturesque mound of BOR-SIP (now BIRS NIMRUD) near Babylon, the larg-

* Rawlinson's "Five Monarchies," Vol. I., p. 349.
† Figure 10.

est of this kind.* These mounds are the remains of peculiar constructions, called ZIGGURATS, composed of several platforms piled one on the other, each square in shape and somewhat smaller than the preceding one; the topmost platform supported a temple or sanctuary, which by these means was raised far above the dwellings of men, a constant reminder not less eloquent than the exhortation in some of our religious services: "Lift up your hearts!" Of these heavenward pointing towers, which were also used as observatories by the Chaldeans, great lovers of the starry heavens, that of Borsip, once composed of seven stages, is the loftiest; it measures over 150 feet in perpendicular height.

7. It is evident that these artificial hills could have been erected only at an incredible cost of labor. The careful measurements which have been taken of several of the principal mounds have enabled explorers to make an accurate calculation of the exact amount of labor employed on each. The result is startling, even though one is prepared for something enormous. The great mound of Koyunjik—which represents the palaces of Nineveh itself—covers an area of one hundred acres, and reaches an elevation of 95 feet at its highest point. To heap up such a pile of brick and earth "would require the united exertions of 10,000 men for twelve years, or of 20,000 men for six years." † Then only could the construction of the palaces begin. The

* Figure 71, p. 281.
† Rawlinson's "Five Monarchies," Vol. I., pp. 317 and 318.

mound of Nebbi-Yunus, which has not yet been excavated, covers an area of forty acres and is loftier and steeper than its neighbor: "its erection would have given full employment to 10,000 men for the space of five years and a half." Clearly, none but conquering monarchs, who yearly took thousands of prisoners in battles and drove home into captivity a part of the population of every

12.—TERRACE WALL AT KHORSABAD.
(Perrot and Chipiez.)

country they subdued, could have employed such hosts of workmen on their buildings—not once, but continually, for it seems to have been a point of honor with the Assyrian kings that each should build a new palace for himself.

8. When one considers the character of the land along the upper course of the Tigris, where the Assyrians dwelt, one cannot help wondering why they went on building mounds and using nothing but

bricks in their constructions. There is no reason for it in the nature of the country. The cities of Assyria—NINEVEH (Koyunjik), KALAH (Nimrud), ARBELA, DUR-SHARRUKIN (Khorsabad) were built in the midst of a hilly region abounding in many varieties of stone, from soft limestone to hard basalt; some of them actually stood on rocky ground, their moats being in part cut through the rock. Had they wanted stone of better quality, they had only to get it from the Zagros range of mountains, which skirts all Assyria to the East, separating it from Media. Yet they never availed themselves of these resources, which must have led to great improvements in their architecture, and almost entirely reserved the use of stone for ornamental purposes. This would tend to show, at all events, that the Assyrians were not distinguished for inventive genius. They had wandered northward from the lowlands, where they had dwelt for centuries as a portion of the Chaldean nation. When they separated from it and went off to found cities for themselves, they took with them certain arts and tricks of handicraft learned in the old home, and never thought of making any change in them. It does not even seem to have occurred to them that by selecting a natural rocky elevation for their buildings they would avoid the necessity of an artificial platform and save vast amount of labor and time.

9. That they did put stone to one practical use—the outward casing of their walls and platforms—we have already seen. The blocks must have been cut in the Zagros mountains and brought by water—

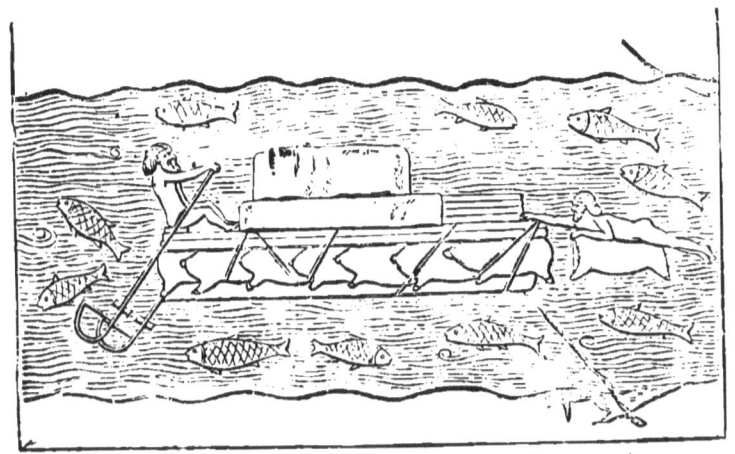

13.—RAFT BUOYED BY INFLATED SKINS. (ANCIENT.)
(Kaulen.)

14.—RAFT BUOYED BY INFLATED SKINS. (MODERN.)
(Kaulen.)

rafted down the Zab, or some other of the rivers which, springing from those mountains, flow into the Tigris. The process is represented with perfect clearness on some of the sculptures. That reproduced in Fig. 13 is of great interest, as showing a peculiar mode of transport,—rafts floated on inflated skins—which is at the present moment in as general and constant use as it appears to have been in the same parts three thousand years ago and probably more. When Layard wished to send off the bulls and lions which he had moved from Nimrud and Koyunjik down the Tigris to Baghdad and Busrah, (or Bassorah), there to be embarked for Europe, he had recourse to this conveyance, as no other is known for similar purposes. This is how he describes the primitive, but ingenious contrivance: "The skins of full-grown sheep and goats, taken off with as few incisions as possible, are dried and prepared, one aperture being left, through which the air is forced by the lungs. A framework of poplar beams, branches of trees, and reeds, having been constructed of the size of the intended raft, the inflated skins are tied to it by osier twigs. The raft is then complete and is moved to the water and launched. Care is taken to place the skins with their mouths upward, that, in case any should burst or require refilling, they can be easily reached. Upon the framework are piled bales of goods, and property belonging to merchants and travellers. . . . . The raftmen impel these rude vessels by long poles, to the ends of which are fastened a few pieces of split cane. (See Fig. 14.) . . . During the floods in spring, or after heavy rains, small rafts may float from Mosul to Baghdad in about eighty-four hours; but the larger are generally six or seven days in performing the voyage. In summer, and when the

15.—EXCAVATIONS AT MUGHEIR (UR).

river is low, they are frequently nearly a month in reaching their destination. When they have been unloaded, they are broken up, and the beams, wood and twigs sold at considerable profit. The skins are washed and afterward rubbed with a preparation, to keep them from cracking and rotting. They are then brought back, either on the shoulders of the raftmen or upon donkeys, to Mossul and Tekrit, where the men engaged in the navigation of the Tigris usually reside." Numerous sculptures show us that similar skins were also used by swimmers, who rode upon them in the water, probably when they intended to swim a greater distance than they could have accomplished by their unassisted efforts. (See Figure 16.)

10. Our imagination longs to reconstruct those gigantic piles as they must have struck the beholder in their towering hugeness, approached from the plain probably by several stairways and by at least one ascent of a slope gentle enough to offer a convenient access to horses and chariots. What an imposing object must have been, for instance, the palace of Sennacherib, on the edge of its battlemented platform (mound of Koyunjik), rising directly above the waters of the Tigris,—named in the ancient language "the Arrow" from the swiftness of its current—into the golden and crimson glory of an Eastern sunset! Although the sameness and unwieldy nature of the material used must have put architectural beauty of outline out of the question, the general effect must have been one of massive grandeur and majesty, aided as it was by the elaborate ornamentation lavished on every portion of the building. Unfortunately the work of reconstruction is left almost entirely to imagination, which derives but little help from the shapeless heaps into

16.—WARRIORS SWIMMING ON INFLATED SKINS.
(Babelon.)

which time has converted those ancient, mighty halls.

11. Fergusson, an English explorer and scholar whose works on subjects connected with art and especially architecture hold a high place, has attempted to restore the palace of Sennacherib such as he imagines it to have been, from the hints furnished by the excavations. He has produced a striking and most effective picture, of which, however, an entire half is simply guesswork. The whole nether part—the stone-cased, battlemented platform wall, the broad stairs, the esplanade handsomely paved with patterned slabs, and the lower part of the palace with its casing of sculptured slabs and portals guarded by winged bulls—is strictly according to the positive facts supplied by the excavations. For the rest, there is no authority whatever. We do not even positively know whether there was any second story to Assyrian palaces at all. At all events, no traces of inside staircases have been found, and the upper part of the walls of even the ground-floor has regularly been either demolished or destroyed by fire. As to columns, it is impossible to ascertain how far they may have been used and in what way. Such as were used could have been, as a rule, only of wood—trunks of great trees hewn and smoothed —and consequently every vestige of them has disappeared, though some round column bases in stone have been found.* The same remarks apply

---

* See Fig. 20, p. 63. There is but one exception, in the case of a recent exploration, during which one solitary broken column-shaft was discovered.

to the restoration of an Assyrian palace court, also after Fergusson, while that of a palace hall, after Layard, is not open to the same reproach and gives simply the result of actual discoveries. Without, therefore, stopping long to consider conjectures

17.—VIEW OF KOYUNJIK.
(Hommel.)

more or less unsupported, let us rather try to reproduce in our minds a clear perception of what the audience hall of an Assyrian king looked like from what we may term positive knowledge. We shall find that our materials will go far towards creating for us a vivid and authentic picture.

12. On entering such a hall the first thing to strike us would probably be the pavement, either of large alabaster slabs delicately carved in graceful patterns, as also the arched doorways leading into the adjacent rooms (see Figs. 24 and 25, pp. 69 and 71), or else covered with rows of inscriptions, the characters being deeply engraven and afterwards filled with a molten metallic substance, like brass or bronze, which would give the entire floor the appearance of being covered with inscriptions in gilt characters, the strange forms of cuneiform writing making the whole look like an intricate and fanciful design.

13. Our gaze would next be fascinated by the colossal human-headed winged bulls and lions keeping their silent watch in pairs at each of the portals, and we should notice with astonishment that the artists had allowed them each an extra leg, making the entire number five instead of four. This was not done at random, but with a very well-calculated artistic object—that of giving the monster the right number of legs, whether the spectator beheld it in front or in profile, as in both cases one of the three front legs is concealed by the others. The front view shows the animal standing, while it appears to be striding when viewed from the side. (See Figures 18 and 27, pp. 59 and 75.) The walls were worthy of these majestic door-keepers. The crude brick masonry disappeared up to a height of twelve to fifteen feet from the ground under the sculptured slabs of soft grayish alabaster which were solidly applied to the wall, and held together by strong iron cramps. Sometimes one subject or one gigan-

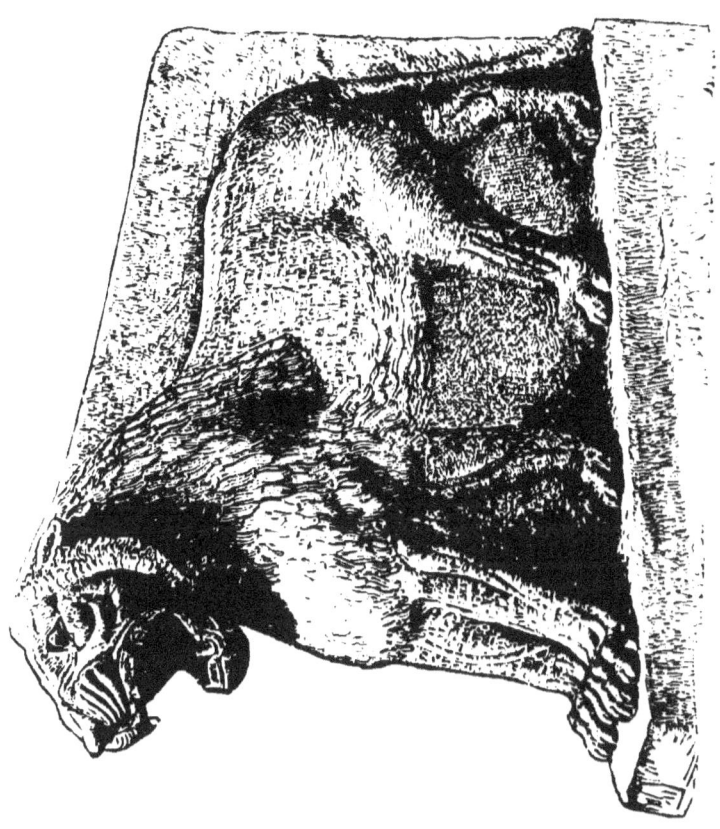

9.—STONE LION AT THE ENTRANCE OF A TEMPLE, NIMRUD
(Perrot and Chipiez.)

tic figure of king or deity was represented on one slab; often the same subject occupied several slabs, and not unfrequently was carried on along an entire wall. In this case the lines begun on one slab were continued on the next with such perfect smoothness, so absolutely without a break, as to warrant the conclusion that the slabs were sculptured *after* they had been put in their places, not before. Traces of paint show that color was to a certain extent employed to enliven these representations, probably not over plentifully and with some discrimination. Thus color is found in many places on the eyes, brows, hair, sandals, the draperies, the mitre or high head-dress of the kings, on the harness of horses and portions of the chariots, on the flowers carried by attendants, and sometimes on trees. Where a siege is portrayed, the flames which issue out of windows and roofs seem always to have been painted red. There is reason to believe, however, that color was but sparingly bestowed on the sculptures, and therefore they must have presented a pleasing contrast with the richness of the ornamentation which ran along the walls immediately above, and which consisted of hard baked bricks of large size, painted and glazed in the fire, forming a continuous frieze from three to five feet wide. Sometimes the painting represented human figures and various scenes, sometimes also winged figures of deities or fantastic animals,—in which case it was usually confined above and below by a simple but graceful running pattern; or it would consist wholly of a more or less elaborate continuous pat-

19.—COURT OF HAREM AT KHORSABAD. (RESTORED.)
(Perrot and Chipiez.)

tern like Fig. 22, 23, or 25, these last symbolical compositions with a religious signification. (See also Fig. 21, "Interior view," etc.) Curiously enough the remains—mostly very trifling fragments—which have been discovered in various ruins, show that these handsomely finished glazed tiles exhibited the very same colors which are nowadays in such high favor with ourselves for all sorts of decorative purposes: those used most frequently were a dark and a pale yellow, white and cream-color, a delicate pale green, occasionally orange and a pale lilac, very little blue and red; olive-green and brown are favorite colors for grounds. "Now and then an intense blue and a bright red occur, generally together; but these positive hues are rare, and the taste of the Assyrians seems to have led them to prefer, for their patterned walls, pale and dull hues. . . . The general tone of their coloring is quiet, not to say sombre. There is no striving after brilliant effects. The Assyrian artist seeks to please by the elegance of his forms and the harmony of his hues, not to startle by a display of bright and strongly contrasted colors.*"

14. It has been asked: how were those halls roofed and how were they lighted? questions which have given rise to much discussion and which can scarcely ever be answered in a positive way, since in no single instance has the upper part of the walls or any part whatever of the roofing been preserved. Still, the peculiar shape and dimensions of the princi-

---

* G. Rawlinson's "Five Monarchies," Vol. I., pp. 467, 468.

pal palace halls goes far towards establishing a sort of circumstantial evidence in the case. They are invariably long and narrow, the proportions in some being so striking as to have made them more like corridors than apartments—a feature, by the by, which must have greatly impaired their architectural beauty: they were three or four times as long as they were wide, and even more. The great hall of

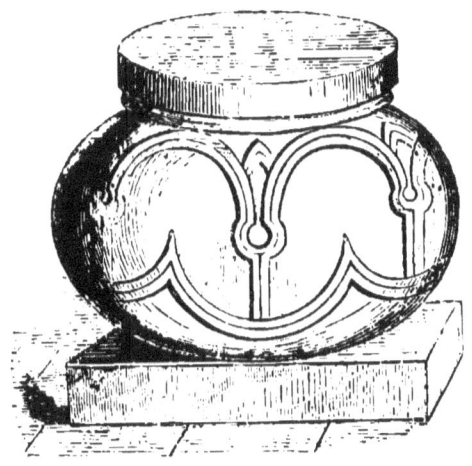

30.—CIRCULAR PILLAR-BASE.

the palace of Asshur-nazir-pal on the platform of the Nimrud mound (excavated by Layard, who calls it, from its position, "the North-West palace") is 160 feet long by not quite 40 wide. Of the five halls in the Khorsabad palace the largest measures 116 ft. by 33, the smallest 87 by 25, while the most imposing in size of all yet laid open, the great hall of Sennacherib at Koyunjik, shows a length of fully 180 ft. with a width of 40. It is scarcely probable that the old builders, who in other points have shown so much artistic taste, should have selected this uniform and unsatisfactory shape for their state apartments, unless they were forcibly held to it by some insuperable imperfection in the means at their disposal. That they knew how to use proportions more pleasing in their general effect, we see from the inner open courts, of which there were several in every palace, and which, in shape and dimensions are very much like those in our own castles and palaces,—nearly square, (about 180 ft. or 120 ft. each way) or slightly oblong: 93 ft. by 84, 124 ft. by 90, 150 ft. by 125. Only two courts have been found to lean towards the long-and-narrow shape, one being 250 ft. by 150, and the other 220 by 100. But even this is very different from those passage-like galleries. The only thing which entirely explains this awkward feature of all the royal halls, is the difficulty of providing them with a roof. It is impossible to make a flat roof of nothing but bricks, and although the Assyrians knew how to construct arches, they used them only for very narrow vaults or over gate-ways and doors, and could not have carried out the principle on any very extensive scale. The only obvious expedient consisted in simply spanning the width of the hall with wooden beams or rafters. Now no tree, not even the lofty cedar of Lebanon or the tall cypress of the East, will give a rafter, of equal thickness from end to end, more than 40 ft. in length, few even that. There was no getting over or around this necessity, and so the matter was set-

21.—INTERIOR VIEW OF ONE OF THE CHAMBERS OF THE HAREM AT KHORSABAD. (RESTORED.)

(Perrot and Chipiez.)

tied for the artists quite aside from their own wishes. This also explains the great value which was attached by all the Assyrian conquerors to fine timber. It was often demanded as tribute, nothing could be more acceptable as a gift, and expeditions were frequently undertaken into the distant mountainous regions of the Lebanon on purpose to cut some. The difficulty about roofing would naturally fall away in the smaller rooms, used probably as sleeping and dwelling apartments, and accordingly they vary freely from oblong to square; the latter being generally about 25 ft. each way, sometimes less, but never more. There were a great many such chambers in a palace; as many as sixty-eight have been discovered in Sennacherib's palace at Koyunjik, and a large portion of the building, be it remembered, is not yet fully explored. Some were as highly decorated as the great halls, some faced with plain slabs or plastered, and some had no ornaments at all and showed the crude brick. These differences probably indicate the difference of rank in the royal household of the persons to whom the apartments were assigned.

15. The question of light has been discussed by eminent explorers—Layard, Botta, Fergusson—at even greater length and with a greater display of ingenuity than that of roofing. The results of the learned discussion may be shortly summed up as follows: We may take it for granted that the halls were sufficiently lighted, for the builders would not have bestowed on them such lavish artistic labor had they not meant their work to be seen in all its details

22.—COLORED FRIEZE IN ENAMELLED TILES.

23.—COLORED FRIEZE IN ENAMELLED TILES.

and to the best advantage. This could be effected only in one of three ways, or in two combined: either by means of numerous small windows pierced at regular intervals above the frieze of enamelled bricks, between that and the roof,—or by means of one large opening in the roof of woodwork, as proposed by Layard in his own restoration, or by smaller openings placed at more frequent intervals. This latter contrivance is in general use now in Armenian houses, and Botta, who calls it a *louvre*, gives a drawing of it.* It is very ingenious, and would have the advantage of not admitting too great a mass of sunlight and heat, and of being easily covered with carpets or thick felt rugs to exclude the rain. The second method, though much the grandest in point of effect, would present none of these advantages and would be objectionable chiefly on account of the rain, which, pouring down in torrents—as it does, for weeks at a time, in those countries—must very soon damage the flooring where it is of brick, and eventually convert it into mud, not to speak of the inconvenience of making the state apartments unfit for use for an indefinite period. The small side windows just below the roof would scarcely give sufficent light by themselves. Who knows but they may have been combined with the *louvre* system, and thus something very satisfactory finally obtained.

16. The kings of Chaldea, Babylonia and Assyria seem to have been absolutely possessed with a mania for building. Scarcely one of them but left inscriptions telling how he raised this or that palace,

---

* See Fig. 33, p. 83.

this or that temple in one or other city, often in many cities. Few contented themselves with repairing the buildings left by their predecessors. This is easy to be ascertained, for they always mention all they did in that line. Vanity, which seems

24.—PAVEMENT SLAB.

to have been, together with the love of booty, almost their ruling passion, of course accounts for this in a great measure. But there are also other causes, of which the principal one was the very perishable nature of the constructions, all their heavy massiveness notwithstanding. Being made of comparatively soft and yielding material, their very weight would cause the mounds to settle and bulge out at the sides in some places, producing crevices in others, and of course disturbing the balance of the thick but loose masonry of the walls constructed on top of them. These accidents could not be guarded against by the outer casing of stone or burnt brick, or even by the strong buttresses which were used from a very early period to prop up the unwieldy piles: the pressure from within was too great to be resisted.

17. An outer agent, too, was at work, surely and steadily destructive: the long, heavy winter rains. Crude brick, when exposed to moisture, easily dissolves into its original element—mud; even burned brick is not proof against very long exposure to violent wettings; and we know that the mounds were half composed of loose rubbish. Once thoroughly permeated with moisture, nothing could keep these huge masses from dissolution. The builders were well aware of the danger and struggled against it to the best of their ability by a very artfully contrived and admirably executed system of drainage, carried through the mounds in all directions and pouring the accumulated waters into the plain out of mouths beautifully constructed in the shape of arched vaults.* Under the flooring of most of the halls have been found drains, running along the centre, then bending off towards a conduit in one of the corners, which carried the contents down into one of the principal channels.

---

* Figures 34 and 35, p. 84.

18. But all these precautions were, in the long run, of little avail, so that it was frequently a simpler and less expensive proceeding for a king to build a new palace, than to keep repairing and propping up an old one which crumbled to pieces, so to speak, under

25.—SECTION OF ORNAMENTAL DOORWAY (ENAMELLED BRICK OR TILES). KHORSABAD.
(Perrot and Chipiez.)

the workmen's hands. It is not astonishing that sometimes, when they had to give up an old mansion as hopeless, they proceeded to demolish it, in order to carry away the stone and use it in structures of their own, probably not so much as a matter of thrift, as with a view to quickening the work, stone-cutting in the quarries and transport down the river always being a lengthy operation. This explains why, in some later palaces, slabs were found with their sculptured face turned to the crude brick wall, and the other smoothed and prepared for the artist, or with the sculptures half erased, or piled up against the wall, ready to be put in place. The nature of the injuries which caused the ancient buildings to decay and lose all shape, is very faithfully described in an inscription of the Babylonian king Nebuchadnezzar, in which he relates how he constructed the Ziggurat of Borsip on the site of an ancient construction, which he repaired, as far as it went. This is what he says: "The temple of the Seven Spheres, the Tower of Borsip which a former king had built . . . . but had not finished its upper part, from remote days had fallen into decay. The channels for drawing off the water had not been properly provided; rain and tempest had washed away its bricks; the bricks of the roof were cracked; the bricks of the building were washed away into heaps of rubbish." All this sufficiently accounts for the peculiar aspect offered by the Mesopotamian ruins. Whatever process of destruction the buildings underwent, whether natural or violent, by conquerors' hands, whether through exposure to fire or to stress of weather, the upper part would be the first to suffer, but it would not disappear, from the nature of the material, which is not combustible. The crude bricks all through the enormous thickness of the walls, once thoroughly loosened, dislodged,

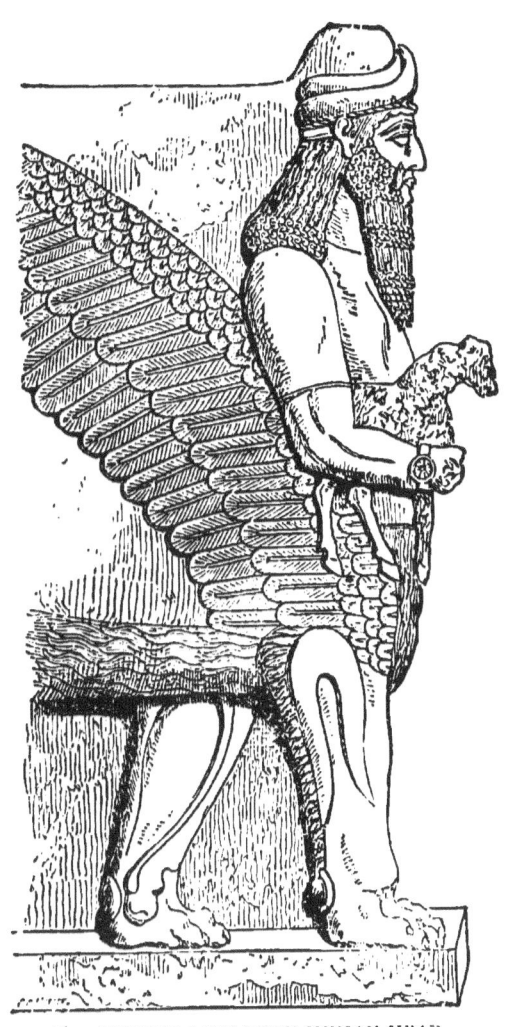

26.—WINGED LION WITH HUMAN HEAD.
(Perrot and Chipiez.)

dried up or soaked through, would lose their consistency and tumble down into the courts and halls, choking them up with the soft rubbish into which they crumbled, the surplus rolling down the sides and forming those even slopes which, from a distance, so deceivingly imitate natural hills. Time, accumulating the drift-sand from the desert and particles of fertile earth, does the rest, and clothes the mounds with the verdant and flowery garment which is the delight of the Arab's eyes.

19. It is to this mode of destruction the Assyrian kings allude in their annals by the continually recurring phrase: "I destroyed their cities, I overwhelmed them, I burned them in the fire, *I made heaps of them.*" However difficult it is to get at the treasures imbedded in these "heaps," we ought not to repine at the labor, since they owe their preservation entirely to the soft masses of earth, sand and loose rubbish which have protected them on all sides from the contact with air, rain and ignorant plunderers, keeping them as safely—if not as transparently—housed as a walnut in its lump of candied sugar. The explorers know this so well, that when they leave the ruins, after completing their work for the time, they make it a point to fill all the excavated spaces with the very rubbish that has been taken out of them at the cost of so much labor and time. There is something impressive and reverent in thus re-burying the relics of those dead ages and nations, whom the mysterious gloom of their self-erected tombs becomes better than the glare of the broad, curious daylight. When Layard, before his departure, after

once more wandering with some friends through all the trenches, tunnels and passages of the Nimrud mound, to gaze for the last time on the wonders on which no man had looked before him, found himself

27.—WINGED BULL.
(Perrot and Chipiez.)

once more on the naked platform and ordered the workmen to cover them up again, he was strongly moved by the contrast: "We look around in vain," says he, "for any traces of the wonderful remains we have just seen, and are half inclined to believe that we have dreamed a dream, or have been listening to some tale of Eastern romance. Some, who may hereafter tread on the spot when the grass again grows over the Assyrian palaces, may indeed suspect that I have been relating a vision."

20. It is a curious fact that in Assyria the ruins speak to us only of the living, and that of the dead there are no traces whatever. One might think people never died there at all. Yet it is well known that all nations have bestowed as much care on the interment of their dead and the adornment of their last resting-place as on the construction of their dwellings—nay, some even more, for instance, the Egyptians. To this loving veneration for the dead history owes half its discoveries; indeed we should have almost no reliable information at all on the very oldest races, who lived before the invention of writing, were it not for their tombs and the things we find in them. It is very strange, therefore, that nothing of the kind should be found in Assyria, a country which stood so high in culture. For the sepulchres which are found in such numbers in some mounds down to a certain depth, belong, as is shown by their very position, to later races, mostly even to the modern Turks and Arabs. This peculiarity is so puzzling that scholars almost incline to suppose that the Assyrians either made away with their dead in some manner unknown to us, or else took them somewhere to bury. The latter conjecture, though not entirely devoid of foundation, as we shall see, is unsupported by any positive facts, and therefore was never seriously discussed. The

28.—MAN-LION.
(Perrot and Chipiez.)

question is simply left open, until something happens to shed light on it.

21. It is just the contrary in Babylonia. It can boast few handsome ruins or sculptures. The platforms and main walls of many palaces and temples have been known from the names stamped on the bricks and the cylinders found in the foundations, but they present only shapeless masses, from which all traces of artistic work have disappeared. In compensation, there is no country in the world where so many and such vast cemeteries have been discovered. It appears that the land of Chaldea, —perhaps because it was the cradle of nations which afterwards grew to greatness, as the Assyrians and the Hebrews—was regarded as a place of peculiar holiness by its own inhabitants, and probably also by neighboring countries, which would explain the mania that seems to have prevailed through so many ages, for burying the dead there in unheard of numbers. Strangely enough, some portions of it even now are held sacred in the same sense. There are shrines in Kerbela and Nedjif (somewhat to the west of Babylon) where every caravan of pilgrims brings from Persia hundreds of dead bodies in their felt-covered coffins, for burial. They are brought on camels and horses. On each side of the animal swings a coffin, unceremoniously thumped by the rider's bare heels. These coffins are, like merchandise, unladen for the night—and sometimes for days too—in the khans or caravanseries (the enclosed halting-places), where men and beasts take their rest together. Under that tropical clime, it is easy

to imagine the results. It is in part to this disgusting custom that the great mortality in the caravans is to be attributed, one fifth of which leave their bones in the desert in *healthy* seasons. However that may be, the gigantic proportions of the Chaldean burying-grounds struck even the ancient

29.—FRAGMENT OF ENAMELLED BRICK.
(Perrot and Chipiez.)

Greek travellers with astonishment, and some of them positively asserted that the Assyrian kings used to be buried in Chaldea. If the kings, why not the nobler and wealthier of their subjects? The transport down the rivers presented no difficulties. Still, as already remarked, all this is mere conjecture.

22. Among the Chaldeans cities ERECH (now

WARKA) was considered from very old times one of the holiest. It had many extremely ancient temples and a college of learned priests, and around it gradually formed an immense "city of the dead" or Necropolis. The English explorer, Loftus, in 1854-5, specially turned his attention to it and his account is astounding. First of all, he was struck by the majestic desolation of the place. Warka and a few other mounds are raised on a slightly elevated tract of the desert, above the level of the yearly inundations, and accessible only from November to March, as all the rest of the time the surrounding plain is either a lake or a swamp. "The desolation and solitude of Warka," says Loftus, "are even more striking than the scene which is presented at Babylon itself. There is no life for miles around. No river glides in grandeur at the base of its mounds; no green date groves flourish near its ruins. The jackal and the hyæna appear to shun the dull aspect of its tombs. The king of birds never hovers over the deserted waste. A blade of grass or an insect finds no existence there. The shrivelled lichen alone, clinging to the weathered surface of the broken brick, seems to glory in its universal dominion over those barren walls. Of all the desolate pictures I have ever seen that of Warka incomparably surpasses all." Surely in this case it cannot be said that appearances are deceitful; for all that space, and much more, is a cemetery, and what a cemetery! "It is difficult," again says Loftus, "to convey anything like a correct idea of the piles upon piles of human remains which there utterly astound the

32.—BRONZE FORK AND SPOON.

31.—EBONY COMB.
(Perrot and Chipiez.)

30.—RAM'S HEAD IN ALABASTER.
(British Museum.)

beholder. Excepting only the triangular space between the three principal ruins, the whole remainder of the platform, the whole space between the walls and an unknown extent of desert beyond them, are everywhere filled with the bones and sepulchres of the dead. There is probably no other site in the world which can compare with Warka in this respect." It must be added that the coffins do not simply lie one next to the other, but in layers, down to a depth of 30-60 feet. Different epochs show different modes of burial, among which the following four are the most remarkable.

23. Perhaps the queerest coffin shape of all is that composed of two earthen jars (*a* and *b*), which accurately fit together, or one slightly fits into the other, the juncture being made air-tight by a coating of bitumen (*d, d*). The body can be placed in such a coffin only with slightly bent knees. At one end (*c*) there is an air-hole, left for the escape of the gases which form during the decomposition of the body and which might otherwise burst the jars—a precaution probably suggested by experience (fig. 36). Sometimes there is only one jar of much larger size, but of the same shape, with a similar cover, also made fast with bitumen, or else the mouth is closed with bricks. This is an essentially national mode of burial, perhaps the most ancient of all, yet it remained in use to a very late period. It is to be noted that this is the exact shape of the water jars now carried about the streets of Baghdad and familiar to every traveller.

24. Not much less original is the so-called "dish-

cover coffin," also very ancient and national. The illustrations sufficiently show its shape and arrangement.* In these coffins two skeletons are sometimes found, showing that when a widow or widower died, it was opened, to lay the newly dead by the side of the one who had gone before. The cover is all of

33.—ARMENIAN LOUVRE
(Botta.)

one piece—a very respectable achievement of the potter's art. In Mugheir (ancient Ur), a mound was found, entirely filled with this kind of coffins.

25. Much more elaborate, and consequently probably reserved for the noble and wealthy, is the sepulchral vault in brick, of nearly a man's height.† In these sepulchres, as in the preceding ones, the skele-

---
* Figs. 37 and 38, p. 87. † Fig. 39, p. 89.

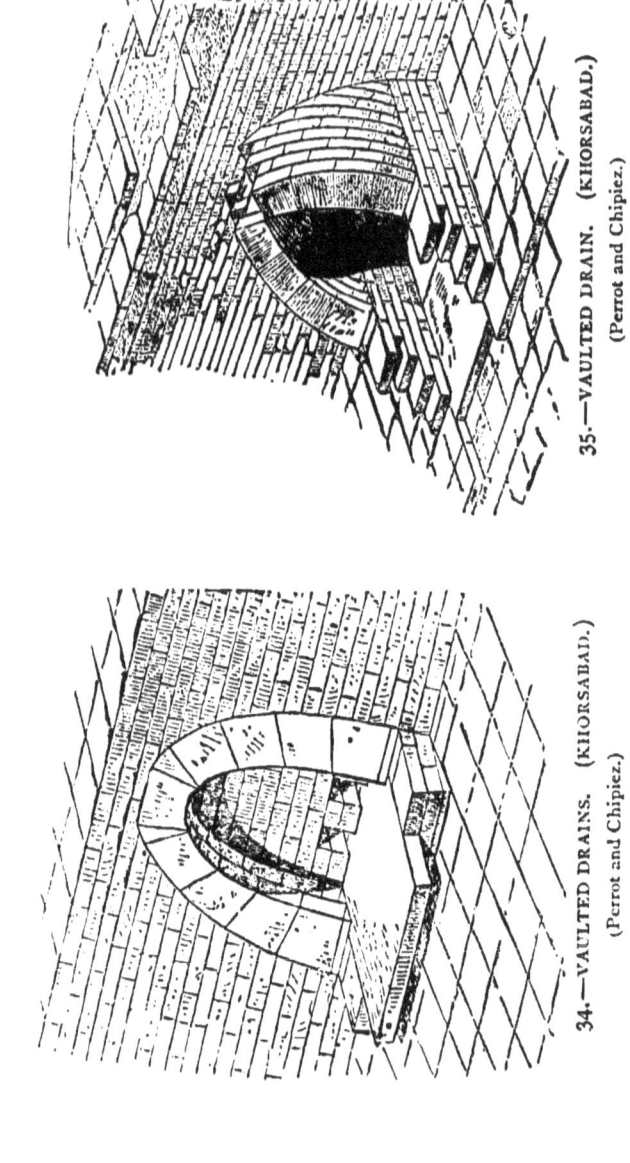

34.—VAULTED DRAINS. (KHORSABAD.)
(Perrot and Chipiez.)

35.—VAULTED DRAIN. (KHORSABAD.)
(Perrot and Chipiez.)

ton is always found lying in the same position, evidently dictated by some religious ideas. The head is pillowed on a large brick, commonly covered with a piece of stuff or a rug. In the tattered rags which sometimes still exist, costly embroideries and fringed golden tissue have more than once been recognized, while some female skeletons still showed handsome heads of hair gathered into fine nets. The body lies on a reed mat, on its left side, the right hand stretched out so as to reach with the tips of the fingers a bowl, generally of copper or bronze, and sometimes of fine workmanship, usually placed on the

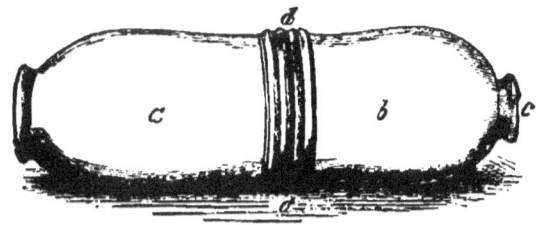

36.—CHALDEAN JAR-COFFIN.
(Taylor.)

palm of the left hand. Around are placed various articles—dishes, in some of which remnants of food are found, such as date stones,—jars for water, lamps, etc. Some skeletons wear gold and silver bangles on their wrists and ankles. These vaults were evidently family sepulchres, for several skeletons are generally found in them; in one there were no less than eleven. (Fig. 39, p. 89.)

26. All these modes of burial are very old and peculiarly Chaldean. But there is still another, which belongs to more recent times, even as late as the first centuries after Christ, and was used by a differ-

ent and foreign race, the Parthians, one of those who came in turns and conquered the country, stayed there awhile, then disappeared. These coffins are, from their curious form, known under the name of "slipper-shaped." They are glazed, green on the outside and blue on the inside, but of very inferior make: poor clay, mixed with straw, and only half baked, therefore very brittle. It is thought that they were put in their place empty, then the body was laid in, the lid put down, and the care of covering them with sand left to the winds. The lid is fastened with the same mortar which is used in the brick masonry surrounding the coffin, where such a receptacle has been made for it; but they more usually lie pell-mell, separated only by thin layers of loose sand. There are mounds which are, as one may say, larded with them: wherever you begin to dig a trench, the narrow ends stick out from both sides. In these coffins also various articles were buried with the dead, sometimes valuable ones. The Arabs know this; they dig in the sand with their hands, break the coffins open with their spears, and grope in them for booty. The consequence is that it is extremely difficult to procure an entire coffin. Loftus succeeded, however, in sending some to the British Museum, having first pasted around them several layers of thick paper, without which precaution they could not have borne the transport.

27. On the whole, the ancient Chaldean sepulchres of the three first kinds are distinguished by greater care and tidiness. They are not only sepa-

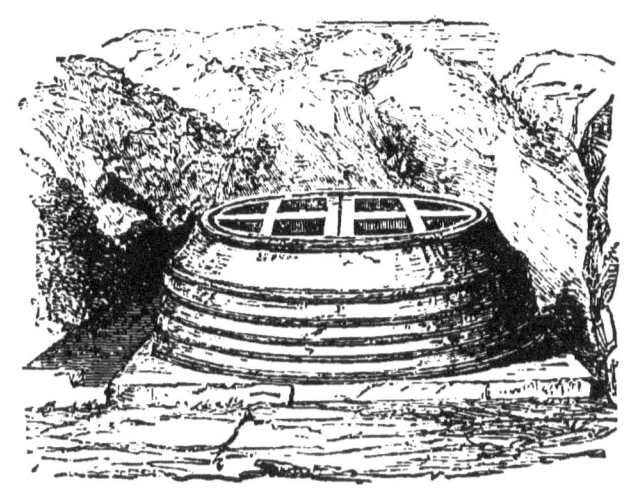

37.—" DISH-COVER" TOMB AT MUGHEIR.
(Taylor.)

38.—" DISH-COVER " TOMB.
(Taylor.)

rated by brick partitions on the sides, and also above and below by a thin layer of brick masonry, but the greatest care was taken to protect them against dampness. The sepulchral mounds are pierced through and through, from top to bottom, by drainage pipes or shafts, consisting of a series of rings, solidly joined together with bitumen, about one foot in diameter. These rings are made of baked clay. The top one is shaped somewhat like a funnel, of which the end is inserted in perforated bricks, and which is provided with small holes, to receive any infiltration of moisture. Besides all this the shafts, which are sunk in pairs, are surrounded with broken pottery. How ingenious and practical this system was, we see from the fact that both the coffins and their contents are found in a state of perfect dryness and preservation. (Fig. 41, p. 90.)

28. In fact the Chaldeans, if they could not reach such perfection as the Assyrians in slab-sculpture, on account of not having stone either at home or within easy reach, seem to have derived a greater variety of architectural ornaments from that inexhaustible material of theirs—baked clay or terra-cotta. We see an instance of it in remnants—unfortunately very small ones, of some walls belonging to that same city of Erech. On one of the mounds Loftus was puzzled by the large quantity of small terra-cotta cones, whole and in fragments, lying about on the ground. The thick flat end of them was painted red, black or white. What was his amazement when he stumbled on a piece of wall (some seven feet in height and not more than thirty

39.—SEPULCHRAL VAULT AT MUGHEIR.
(Taylor.)

40.—STONE JARS FROM GRAVES. (LARSAM.)
(Hommel.)

in length), which showed him what their use had been. They were grouped into a variety of patterns to decorate the entire wall, being stuck with their thin end into a layer of soft clay with which it was coated for the purpose. Still more original and even rather incomprehensible is a wall decoration consisting of several bands, composed each of three rows of small pots or cups—about four inches in diameter—stuck into the soft clay coating in the same manner, with the mouth turned outward of

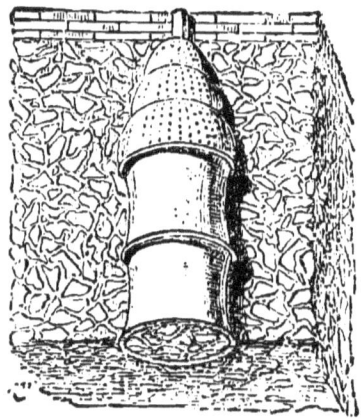

41.—DRAIN IN MOUND.
(Perrot and Chipiez.)

course! Loftus found such a wall, but unfortunately has given no design of it. (Figures 43 and 44.)

29. As to the ancient Babylonian, or rather Chaldean, art in sculpture, the last word has by no means been said on that subject. Discoveries crowd in every year, constantly leading to the most unexpected conclusions. Thus, it was long an accepted fact that Assyria had very few statues and Babylonia none at all, when a few years ago (1881),

42.—WALL WITH DESIGNS IN TERRA-COTTA CONES, AT WARKA (ERECH).
(Loftus.)

43.—TERRA-COTTA CONE, NATURAL SIZE.
(Loftus.)

what should a French explorer, Mr. E. De Sarzec, French consul in Basra, bring home but nine magnificent statues made of a dark, nearly black stone as hard as granite, called diorite.* Unfortunately they are all headless; but, as though to make up for this mutilation, one head was found separate,— a shaved and turbaned head beautifully preserved and of remarkable workmanship, the very pattern of the turban being plain enough to be reproduced by any modern loom.† These large prizes were accompanied by a quantity of small works of art representing both men and animals, of a highly artistic design and some of them of exquisite finish of execution. This astounding find, the result of several years' indefatigable work, now gracing the Assyrian rooms of the Louvre in Paris, comes from one of the Babylonian mounds which had not been opened before, the ruins of a mighty temple at a place now called TELL-LOH, and supposed to be the site of SIR-BURLA, or SIRGULLA, one of the most ancient cities of Chaldea. This "Sarzec-collection," as it has come to be generally called, not only entirely upsets the ideas which had been formed on Old-Chaldean art, but is of immense historical importance from the inscriptions which cover the back of every statue, (not to speak of the cylinders and other small objects,) and which, in connection with the monuments of other ruins, enable scholars to fix, at least approximately, the date at which flourished the city and rulers who have left such extraordinary memorials of their artistic gifts. Some place them at about 4500 B.C., others about 4000.

---

* See Fig. 59, p. 217.   † See Figs. 44 and 45, p. 101.

However overwhelming such a valuation may be at first sight, it is not an unsupported fancy, but proofs concur from many sides to show that the builders and sculptors of Sirgulla could in no case have lived and worked much later than 4000 B.C. It is impossible to indicate in a few lines all the points, the conjectures, the vexed questions, on which this discovery sheds light more or less directly, more or less decisively; they come up continually as the study of those remote ages proceeds, and it will be years before the materials supplied by the Sarzec-Collection are exhausted in all their bearings.

IV.

THE BOOK OF THE PAST.—THE LIBRARY OF NINEVEH.

1. WHEN we wish to learn the great deeds of past ages, and of mighty men long dead, we open a book and read. When we wish to leave to the generations who will come long after us a record of the things that were done by ourselves or in our own times, we take pen, ink and paper, and write a book. What we have written is then printed, published in several hundreds—or thousands—of copies, as the case may be, and quickly finds its way to all the countries of the world inhabited by people who are trained from childhood to thought and study. So that we have the satisfaction of knowing that the information which we have labored to preserve will be obtainable any number of years or centuries after we shall have ceased to exist, at no greater trouble than procuring the book from the shelves of a bookstore, a public or a private library. It is all very simple. And there is not a small child who does not perfectly know a book by its looks, and even has not a pretty correct idea of how a book is made and what it is good for.

2. But books are not always of the shape and material so familiar to us. Metal, stone, brick, walls and pillars, nay, the very rocks of nature's own making, can be books, conveying information as plainly as our volumes of paper sheets covered with written or printed lines. It only needs to know how to read them, and the necessary knowledge and skill may be acquired by processes as simple as the art of ordinary reading and writing, though at the cost of a somewhat greater amount of time and pains.

3. There are two natural cravings, which assert themselves strongly in every mind not entirely absorbed by the daily work for bread and by the anxious care how to procure that work: these are the wish, on the one hand, to learn how the people who came before us lived and what they did, on the other—to transmit our own names and the memory of our deeds to those who will come after us. We are not content with our present life; we want to stretch it both backward and forward—to live both in the past and the future, as it were. This curiosity and this ambition are but parts of the longing for immortality which was never absent from any human soul. In our own age they are satisfied mainly by books; indeed they were originally the principal causes why books began to be made at all. And how easy to satisfy these cravings in our time, when writing materials have become as common as food and far cheaper, and reading may be had for nothing or next to nothing! For, a very few dollars will supply a writer with as much paper as he can possibly use up in a year, while the public libra-

ries, the circulating and college libraries and the reading-rooms make study a matter more of love and perseverance than of money.

4. Yet if the papermill and the printing press were the only material aid to our researches into the past, these researches would stop short very soon, seeing that printing was invented in Europe scarce four hundred years ago, and paper has not been manufactured for more than six hundred years at the outside. True, other materials have been used to write on before paper: bark of trees, skins of animals—(parchment)—cunningly worked fibres of plants—(papyrus, byblos)—even wooden tablets covered with a thin layer of wax, on which characters were engraved with a pointed instrument or " style,"—and these contrivances have preserved for us records which reach back many hundreds of years beyond the introduction of paper. But our curiosity, when once aroused, is insatiable, and an area of some twenty, or thirty, or forty centuries seems to it but a narrow field. Looking back as far as that— and no kind of manuscript information takes us much further—we behold the world wondrously like what it is now. With some differences in garb, in manners, and a much greater one in the range of knowledge, we find men living very nearly as we do and enacting very nearly the same scenes: nations live in families clustered within cities, are governed by laws, or ruled by monarchs, carry on commerce and wars, extend their limits by conquest, excel in all sorts of useful and ornamental arts. Only we notice that larger regions are unknown, vaster portions of

the earth, with their populations, are unexplored, than in our days. The conclusion is clearly forced on us, that so complicated and perfect an organization of public and private life, a condition of society implying so many discoveries and so long a practice in thought and handicraft, could not have been an early stage of existence. Long vistas are dimly visible into a past far vaster than the span as yet laid open to our view, and we long to pierce the tantalizing gloom. There, in that gloom, lurk the beginnings of the races whose high achievements we admire, emulate, and in many ways surpass; there, if we could but send a ray of light into the darkness of ages, we must find the solution of numberless questions which suggest themselves as we go: Whence come those races? What was the earlier history of other races with which we find them contending, treating, trading? When did they learn their arts, their songs, their forms of worship? But here our faithful guide, manuscript literature, forsakes us; we enter on a period when none of the ancient substitutes for paper were yet invented. But then, there were the stones. *They* did not need to be invented—only hewn and smoothed for the chisel.

5. Fortunately for us, men, twenty-five, and forty, and fifty centuries ago, were actuated by the same feelings, the same aspirations as they are now, and of these aspirations, the passionate wish of perpetuating their names and the memory of their deeds has always been one of the most powerful. This wish they connected with and made subservient to

the two things which were great and holy in their eyes: their religion and the power of their kings. So they built, in brick and stone, at an almost incalculable expense of time, human labor and human life, palaces and temples. On these huge piles they lavished treasures untold, as also all the resources of their invention and their skill in art and ornament; they looked on them with exulting pride, not only because they thought them, by their vastness and gorgeousness, fit places for public worship and dwellings worthy of their kings, but because these constructions, in their towering grandeur, their massive solidity, bid fair to defy time and outlast the nations which raised them, and which thus felt assured of leaving behind them traces of their existence, memorials of their greatness. That a few defaced, dismantled, moss-grown or sand-choked fragments of these mighty buildings would one day be the *only* trace, the sole memorial of a rule and of nations that would then have past away forever, even into nothingness and oblivion, scarcely was anticipated by the haughty conquerors who filled those halls with their despotic presence, and entered those consecrated gates in the pomp of triumph to render thanks for bloody victories and warlike exploits which elated their souls in pride till they felt themselves half divine. Nothing doubting but that those walls, those pillars, those gateways would stand down to the latest ages, they confided to them that which was most precious to their ambition, the record of their deeds, the praises of their names, thus using those stony surfaces as so many blank pages, which they covered with row after row of wondrous characters, carefully engraved or chiselled, and even with painted or sculptured representations of their own persons and of the scenes, in war or peace, in which they had been leaders and actors.

6. Thus it is that on all the points of the globe where sometime great and flourishing nations have held their place, then yielded to other nations or to absolute devastation—in Egypt, in India, in Persia, in the valley of the Tigris and Euphrates, in the sandy, now desert plains of Syria, in the once more populous haunts of ancient Rome and Greece —the traveller meets clusters of great ruins, lofty still in their utter abandonment, with a strange, stern beauty hovering around their weather-beaten, gigantic shafts and cornices, wrapt in the pathetic silence of desolation, and yet not dumb—for their pictured faces eloquently proclaim the tale of buoyant life and action entrusted to them many thousands of years ago. Sometimes, it is a natural rock, cut and smoothed down at a height sufficient to protect it from the wantonly destructive hand of scoffing invaders, on which a king of a deeper turn of thought, more mindful than others of the law which dooms all the works of men to decay, has caused a relation of the principal events of his reign to be engraved in those curious characters which have for centuries been a puzzle and an enigma. Many tombs also, besides the remains of the renowned or wealthy dead, for whom they have been erected at a cost as extravagant and with art as

elaborate as the abodes of the living, contain the full description of their inmate's lineage, his life, his habits and pursuits, with prayers and invocations to the divinities of his race and descriptions or portrayed representations of religious ceremonies. Or, the walls of caves, either natural, or cut in the rock for purposes of shelter or concealment, yield to the explorer some more chapters out of the old, old story, in which our interest never slackens. This story man has himself been writing, patiently, laboriously, on every surface on which he could trace words and lines, ever since he has been familiar with the art of expressing his thoughts in visible signs,—and so each such surviving memorial may truly be called a stray leaf, half miraculously preserved to us, out of the great Book of the Past, which it has been the task of scholars through ages, and especially during the last eighty years, to decipher and teach others how to read.

7. Of this venerable book the walls of the Assyrian palaces, with their endless rows of inscriptions, telling year for year through centuries the history of the kings who built them, are so many invaluable pages, while the sculptures which accompany these annals are the illustrations, lending life and reality to what would otherwise be a string of dry and unattractive records. But a greater wonder has been brought to light from amidst the rubbish and dust of twenty-five centuries: a collection of literary and scientific works, of religious treatises, of private and public documents, deposited in rooms constructed on purpose to contain them, arranged

44.—HEAD OF ANCIENT CHALDEAN. FROM TELL-LOH (SIRGULLA)
SARZEC COLLECTION.
(Perrot and Chipiez.)

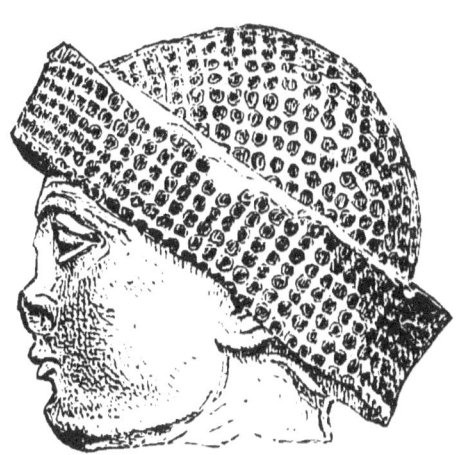

45.—SAME, PROFILE VIEW.

in admirable order, in short —a LIBRARY. Truly and literally a library, in the sense in which we use the word. Not the only one either, nor the first by many hundred years, although the volumes are of singular make and little like those we are used to.

8. When Layard was at work for the second time amidst the ruins along the Tigris, he devoted much of his labor to the great mound of Koyunjik, in which the remains of two sumptuous palaces were distinctly discerned, one of them the royal residence of Sennacherib, the other that of his grandson Asshurbanipal, who lived some 650 years before Christ—two of the mightiest conquerors and most magnificent sovereigns of the Eastern world. In the latter palace he came upon two comparatively small chambers, the floor of which was entirely littered with fragments—some of considerable size, some very small—of bricks, or rather baked-clay tablets, covered on both sides with cuneiform writing. It was a layer more than a foot in height which must have been formed by the falling in of the upper part of the edifice. The tablets, piled in good order along the walls, perhaps in an upper story—if, as many think, there was one—must have been precipitated promiscuously into the apartment and shattered by the fall. Yet, incredible as it may appear, several were found entire. Layard filled many cases with the fragments and sent them off to the British Museum, fully aware of their probable historical value.

9. There they lay for years, heaped up at random, a mine of treasures which made the mouths of schol-

ars water, but appalled them by the amount of labor, nay, actual drudgery, needful only to sift and sort them, even before any study of their contents could be begun. At length a young and ambitious archæologist, attached to the British Museum, George Smith, undertook the long and wearisome task. He was not originally a scholar, but an engraver, and was employed to engrave on wood cuneiform texts for the magnificent atlas edited by the British Museum under the title of "Cuneiform Inscriptions of Western Asia." Being endowed with a quick and enquiring mind, Smith did not content himself, like most of his colleagues, with a conscientious and artistic, but merely technical reproduction; he wished to know *what* he was doing and he learned the language of the inscriptions. When he took on himself the sorting of the fragments, it was in the hope of distinguishing himself in this new field, and of rendering a substantial service to the science which had fascinated him. Nor was he deceived in this hope. He succeeded in finding and uniting a large quantity of fragments belonging together, and thus restoring pages of writing, with here and there a damaged line, a word effaced, a broken corner, often a larger portion missing, but still enough left to form continuous and readable texts. In some cases it was found that there was more than one copy of this or that work or document, and then sometimes the parts which were hopelessly injured in one copy, would be found whole or nearly so in another.

10. The results accomplished by this patient me-

chanical process were something astonishing. And when he at length restored in this manner a series of twelve tablets containing an entire poem of the greatest antiquity and highest interest, the occasion seemed important enough to warrant the enterprising owners of the London *Daily Telegraph* in sending the young student to resume excavations and try to complete some missing links. For of some of the tablets restored by him only portions could be found among the fragments of the British Museum. Of course he made his way straight to the Archive Chambers at Koyunjik, had them opened again and cleared them of another large instalment of their valuable contents, among which he had the inconceivable good fortune to find some of the very pieces which were missing in his collection. Joyfully he returned to England twice with his treasures, and hopefully set out on a third expedition of the same kind. He had reason to feel buoyant; he had already made his name famous by several works which greatly enriched the science he loved, and had he not half a life-time before him to continue the work which few could do as well? Alas, he little knew that his career was to be cut short suddenly by a loathsome and brutal foe: he died of the plague in Syria, in 1876—just thirty-six years old. He was faithful to the end. His diary, in which he made some entries even within a very few days before his death, shows that at the last, when he knew his danger and was fast losing hope, his mind was equally divided between thoughts of his family and of his work. The following lines, almost the last intelligible ones he wrote, are deeply touching in their simple, single-minded earnestness: —" Not so well. If Doctor present, I should recover, but he has not come, very doubtful case ; if fatal farewell to. . . . *My work has been entirely for the science I study*. . . . There is a large field of study in my collection. I intended to work it out, but desire now that my antiquities and notes may be thrown open to all students. I have done my duty thoroughly. I do not fear the change but desire to live for my family. Perhaps all may be well yet."—George Smith's death was a great loss, which his brother-scholars of all countries have not ceased to deplore. But the work now proceeds vigorously and skilfully. The precious texts are sorted, pieced, and classified, and a collection of them, carefully selected, is reproduced by the aid of the photographer and the engraver, so that, should the originals ever be lost or destroyed, (not a very probable event), the Museum indeed would lose one of its most precious rarities, but science would lose nothing.

11. An eminent French scholar and assyriologist, Joachim Ménant, has the following picturesque lines in his charming little book "*La Bibliothèque du Palais de Ninive*": "When we reflect that these records have been traced on a substance which neither fire nor water could destroy, we can easily comprehend how those who wrote them thus thirty or forty centuries ago, believed the monuments of their history to be safe for all future times,—much safer than the frail sheets which printing scatters

with such prodigious fertility. . . . Of all the nations who have bequeathed to us written records of their past life, we may assert that none has left monuments more imperishable than Assyria and Chaldea. Their number is already considerable; it is daily increased by new discoveries. It is not possible to foresee what the future has in store for us in this respect; but we can even now make a valuation of the entire material which we possess. . . . . The number of the tablets from the Nineveh Library alone passes ten thousand. . . . If we compare these texts with those left us by other nations, we can easily become convinced that the history of the Assyro-Chaldean civilization will soon be one of the best known of antiquity. It has a powerful attraction for us, for we know that the life of the Jewish people is mixed up with the history of Nineveh and Babylon. . . ."

12. It will be seen from this that throughout the following pages we shall continually have to refer to the contents of Asshurbanipal's royal library. We must therefore dispense in this place with any details concerning the books, more than a general survey of the subjects they treated. Of these, religion and science were the chief. Under "science" we must understand principally mathematics and astronomy, two branches in which the old Chaldeans reached great perfection and left us many of our own most fundamental notions and practices, as we shall see later on. Among the scientific works must also be counted those on astrology, i.e., on the influence which the heavenly bodies were supposed to

40.—CUNEIFORM INSCRIPTION. (ARCHAIC CHARACTERS.)
(Perrot and Chipiez.)

exert on the fate of men, according to their positions and combinations, for astrology was considered a real science, not only by the Chaldeans, but by much later nations too; also hand-books of geography, really only lists of the seas, mountains and rivers, nations and cities then known, lastly lists of plants and animals with a very rude and defective attempt at some sort of classification. History is but scantily represented; it appears to have been mostly confined to the great wall inscriptions and some other objects, of which more hereafter. But —what we should least expect—grammars, dictionaries, school reading-books, occupy a prominent place. The reason is that, when this library was founded, the language in which the venerable books of ancient sages were written not only was not spoken any longer, but had for centuries been forgotten by all but the priests and those who made scholarship their chief pursuit, so that it had to be taught in the same way that the so-called "dead languages," Latin and Greek, are taught at our colleges. This was the more necessary as the prayers had to be recited in the old language called the Accadian, that being considered more holy—just as, in Catholic countries, the common people are even now made to learn and say their prayers in Latin, though they understand not a word of the language. The ancient Accadian texts were mostly copied with a modern Assyrian translation, either interlinear or facing it, which has been of immense service to those who now decipher the tablets.

13. So much for what may be called the classical

and reference department of the library. Important as it is, it is scarcely more so than the documentary department or Archive proper, where documents and deeds of all kinds, both public and private, were deposited for safe keeping. Here by the side of treatises, royal decrees and despatches, lists of tribute, reports from generals and governors, also those daily sent in by the superintendents of the royal observatories,—we find innumerable private documents: deeds of sale duly signed, witnessed and sealed, for land, houses, slaves—any kind of property,—of money lent, of mortgages, with the rate of interest, contracts of all sorts. The most remarkable of private documents is one which has been called the "will of King Sennacherib," by which he entrusts some valuable personal property to the priests of the temple of Nebo, to be kept for his favorite son,—whether to be delivered after his (the king's) death or at another time is not stated.

47.—INSCRIBED CLAY TABLET.
(Smith's "Assyria.")

14. It requires some effort to bear in mind the nature and looks of the things which we must represent to ourselves when we talk of Assyrian "*books.*" The above (Fig. 47) is the portrait of a "*volume*" in perfect condition. But it is seldom indeed that one such is found. Layard, in his first description of his startling "find," says: "They (the tablets) were of different sizes; the largest were flat, and measured nine inches by six and a half; the smaller were slightly

convex, and some were not more than an inch long, with but one or two lines of writing. The cuneiform characters on most of them were singularly sharp and well-defined, but so minute in some instances as to be illegible without a magnifying glass." Most curiously, glass lenses have been found among the ruins, which may have been used for the purpose. Specimens have also been found of the very instruments which were employed to trace the cuneiform characters, and their form sufficiently accounts for the peculiar shape of these characters which was imitated by the engravers on stone. It is a little iron rod—(or *style*, as the ancients used to call such implements)—not sharp, but *triangular* at the end : ▽. By slightly pressing this end on the cake of soft moist clay held in the left hand no other shape of sign could be obtained than a wedge, ▼, the direction being determined by a turn of the wrist, presenting the instrument in different positions. When one side of the tablet was full, the other was to be filled. If it was small, it was sufficient to turn it over, continuing to hold the edges between the thumb and third finger of the left hand. But if the tablet was large and had to be laid on a table to be written on, the face that was finished would be pressed to the hard surface, and the clay being soft, the writing would be effaced. This was guarded against by a contrivance as ingenious as it was simple. Empty places were left here and there in the lines, in which were stuck small pegs, like matches. On these the tablet was supported when turned over, and also while baking in the oven.

On many of the tablets that have been preserved are to be seen little holes or dints, where the pegs have been stuck. Still, it should be mentioned that

48.—CLAY TABLET IN ITS CASE.
(Hommel.)

these holes are not confined to the large tablets and not found on all large tablets. When the tablet was full, it was allowed to dry, then generally, but not always, baked. Within the last few years several thousands unbaked tablets have been found in Babylonia; they crumbled into dust under the finders' fingers. It was then proposed to bake such of them as could at all bear handling. The experiment was successful, and numbers of valuable documents were thus preserved and transported to the great repository of the British Museum. The tablets are covered with writing on both sides and most accurately classed and numbered, when they form part of a series, in which case they are all of the same shape and size. The poem discovered by George Smith is written out on twelve tablets, each of which is a separate book or chapter of the whole. There is an astronomical work in over seventy tablets. The first of them begins with the words: "*When the gods Anu and* . . . ." These words are taken as the title of the entire series. Each tablet bears the notice: First, second, third tablet of "*When the gods Anu and* . . . ." To guard against all chance of confusion, the last line of one tablet is repeated as the first line of the following one—a fashion which we still see in old books, where the last word or two at the bottom of a page is repeated at the top of the next.

15. The clay tablets of the ancient Chaldeans are distinguished from the Assyrian ones by a curious peculiarity: they are sometimes enclosed in a case

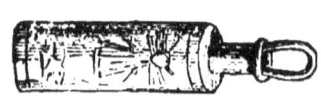

49.—ANTIQUE BRONZE SETTING OF CYLINDER.
(Perrot and Chipiez.)

of the same material, with exactly the same inscription and seals as on the inner tablet, even more carefully executed.* It is evidently a sort of duplicate document, made in the prevision that the outer

50.—CHALDEAN CYLINDER AND IMPRESSION.
(Perrot and Chipiez.)

51.—ASSYRIAN CYLINDER.
(Perrot and Chipiez.)

one might be injured, when the inner record would remain. Rows of figures across the tablet are impressed on it with seals called from their shape cylinders, which were rolled over the soft moist clay. These cylinders were generally of some valuable

* See Fig. 48, p. 111.

hard stone—jasper, amethyst, cornelian, onyx, agate, etc.,—and were used as signet rings were later and are still. They are found in great numbers, being from their hardness well-nigh indestructible. They were generally bored through, and through the hole was passed either a string to wear them on, or a metal axis, to roll them more easily.* There is a large and most valuable collection of seal cylinders at the British Museum. Their size ranges from a quarter of an inch to two inches or a little more. But cylinders were also made of baked clay and larger size, and then served a different purpose, that of historical documents. These are found in the foundations of palaces and temples, mostly in the four corners, in small niches or chambers, generally produced by leaving out one or more bricks. These tiny monuments range from a couple of inches to half a foot in height, seldom more; they are sometimes shaped like a prism with several faces (mostly six), sometimes like a barrel, and covered with that compact and minute writing which it often requires a magnifying glass to make out. Owing to their sheltered position, these singular records are generally very well preserved. Although their original destination is only to tell by whom and for what purpose the building has been erected, they frequently proceed to give a full though condensed account of the respective kings' reigns, so that, should the upper structure with its engraved annals be destroyed by the vicissitudes of war or in the course of natural decay, some memorial of their deeds should still be preserved—a prevision which, in several cases, has

---

* See above, Figs. 49 and 50.

52.—PRISM OF SENNACHERIB, ALSO CALLED "TAYLOR CYLINDER."

been literally fulfilled. Sometimes the manner and material of these records were still more fanciful. At Khorsabad, at the very interior part of the construction, was found a large stone chest, which enclosed several inscribed plates in various materials. .... In this only extant specimen of an Assyrian foundation stone were found one little golden tablet, one of silver, others of copper, lead and tin; a sixth text was engraved on alabaster, and the seventh document was written on the chest itself." * Unfortunately the heavier portion of this remarkable find was sent with a collection which foundered on the Tigris and was lost. Only the small plates, —gold, silver, copper and tin (antimonium scholars now think it to be)—survived, and the inscriptions on them have been read and translated. They all commemorate, in very nearly the same terms, the foundation and erection of a new city and palace by a very famous king and conqueror, generally (though not correctly) called Sargon, and three of them end with a request to the kings his successors to keep the building in good repair, with a prayer for their welfare if they do and a heavy curse if they fail in this duty: "Whoever alters the works of my hand, destroys my constructions, pulls down the walls which I have raised,—may Asshur, Nineb, Raman and the great gods who dwell there, pluck his name and seed from the land and let him sit bound at the feet of his foe." Most inscriptions end with invocations of the same kind, for, in the words of

---

* Dr. Julius Oppert, " Records of the Past," Vol. XI., p. 31.

Ménant: "it was not mere whim which impelled the kings of Assyria to build so assiduously. Palaces had in those times a destination which they have no longer in ours. Not only was the palace indeed *the dwelling of royalty*, as the inscriptions have it,—it was also the BOOK, which each sovereign

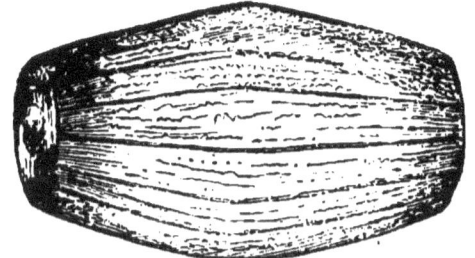

53—INSCRIBED CYLINDER FROM BORSIP.

began at his accession to the throne and in which he was to record the history of his reign."*

And each such book of brick and stone we can with perfect truth call a chapter—or a volume—of the great Book of the Past whose leaves are scattered over the face of the earth.

* "Les Écritures Cunéiformes," of Joachim Ménant: page 198 (2d edition, 1864).

THE STORY OF CHALDEA.

I.

NOMADS AND SETTLERS.—THE FOUR STAGES OF CULTURE.

1. MEN, whatever their pursuit or business, can live only in one of two ways: they can stay where they are, or they can go from one place to another. In the present state of the world, we generally do a little of both. There is some place—city, village, or farm—where we have our home and our work. But from time to time we go to other places, on visits or on business, or travel for a certain length of time to great distances and many places, for instruction and pleasure. Still, there is usually some place which we think of as home and to which we return. Wandering or roving is not our natural or permanent condition. But there are races for whom it is. The Bedouin Arabs are the principal and best known of such races. Who has not read with delight accounts of their wild life in the deserts of Arabia and Northern Africa, so full of adventure and romance,—of their wonderful, priceless horses

who are to them as their own children,—of their noble qualities, bravery, hospitality, generosity, so strangely blended with love of booty and a passion for robbing expeditions? They are indeed a noble race, and it is not their choice, but their country which has made them robbers and rovers—Nomads, as such wandering races are called in history and geography. They cannot build cities on the sand of the desert, and the small patches of pasture and palm groves, kept fresh and green by solitary springs and called "oases," are too far apart, too distant from permanently peopled regions to admit of comfortable settlement. In the south of Arabia and along the sea-shore, where the land is fertile and inviting, they live much as other nations do, and when, a thousand years ago, Arabs conquered vast and wealthy countries both in Europe and Asia, and in Africa too, they not only became model husbandmen, but built some of the finest cities in the world, had wise and strictly enforced laws and took the lead in literature and science. Very different are the scattered nomadic tribes which still roam the steppes of Eastern Russia, of Siberia and Central Asia. They are not as gifted by far as the Arabs, yet would probably quickly settle down to farming, were it not that their wealth consists in flocks of sheep and studs of horses, which require the pasture yielded so abundantly by the grassy steppes, and with which they have to move from one place, when it is browsed bare, to another, and still another, carrying their felt-tents and simple utensils with them, living on the milk of their mares and the meat of their sheep. The Red Indian tribes of the far West present still another aspect of nomadic life— that of the hunter, fierce and entirely untamed, the simplest and wildest of all.

2. On the whole, however, nomadic life is at the present day the exception. Most of the nations that are not savages live in houses, not in portable tents, in cities, not encampments, and form compact, solidly bound communities, not loose sets of tribes, now friendly, now hostile to one another. But it has not always been so. There have been times when settled life was the exception and nomadic life the rule. And the older the times, the fewer were the permanent communities, the more numerous the roving tribes. For wandering in search of better places must have been among the first impulses of intelligent humanity. Even when men had no shelter but caves, no pursuit but hunting the animals, whose flesh was their food and in whose skins they clothed themselves, they must frequently have gone forth, in families or detachments, either to escape from a neighborhood too much infested with the gigantic wild beasts which at one time peopled the earth more thickly than men, or simply because the numbers of the original cave-dwellers had become too great for the cave to hold them. The latter must have been a very usual occurrence: families stayed together until they had no longer room enough, or quarrelled, when they separated. Those who went never saw again the place and kindred they left, although they carried with them memories of both, the few simple arts

they had learned there and the customs in which they had been trained. They would stop at some congenial halting-place, when, after a time, the same process would be repeated—and so again and again.

3. How was the first horse conquered, the first wild-dog tamed and conciliated? How were cattle first enticed to give man their milk, to depend on his care and follow his movements? Who shall tell? However that may have happened, it is certain that the transition from a hunter's wild, irregular and almost necessarily lawless existence to the gentler pursuits of pastoral life must have been attended by a great change in manners and character. The feeling of ownership too, one of the principal promoters of a well-regulated state of society, must have quickly developed with the possession of rapidly increasing wealth in sheep and horses,—the principal property of nomadic races. But it was not a kind of property which encouraged to settling, or uniting in close communities; quite the contrary. Large flocks need vast pasture-grounds. Besides, it is desirable to keep them apart in order to avoid confusion and disputes about wells and springs, those rare treasures of the steppes, which are liable to exhaustion or drying up, and which, therefore, one flock-owner is not likely to share with another, though that other were of his own race and kin. The Book of Genesis, which gives us so faithful and lively a picture of this nomadic pastoral life of ancient nations, in the account of the wanderings of Abraham and the other Hebrew patriarchs, has pre-

served such an incident in the quarrel between the herdsmen of Abraham and his nephew Lot, which led to their separation. This is what Abraham said to Lot: "Is not the whole land before thee? Separate thyself, I pray thee, from me: if thou wilt take the left hand, then I will go to the right; or if thou depart to the right hand, then I will go to the left."* So also it is said of Esau that he "went into the country from the face of his brother Jacob: for their riches were more than they might dwell together, and the land wherein they were strangers could not bear them because of their cattle."† This was a facility offered by those immense plains, unclaimed as yet by any one people in particular, and which must ofttimes have averted strife and bloodshed, but which ceased from the moment that some one tribe, tired of wandering or tempted by some more than usually engaging spot, settled down on it, marking that and the country around it, as far as its power reached, for its own. There is even now in the East something very similar to this mode of occupation. In the Turkish Empire, which is, in many places, thinly peopled, there are large tracts of waste land, sometimes very fertile, accounted as nobody's property, and acknowledged to belong, legally and forever, to the first man who takes possession of them, provided he cultivates them. The government asks no purchase price for the land, but

---

* Genesis, xiii. 7–11. † Genesis, xxxvi. 6–7.

demands taxes from it as soon as it has found an owner and begins to yield crops.

4. The pastoral nomad's life is, like the hunter's, a singularly free one,—free both from restraint, and, comparatively, from toil. For watching and tending flocks is not a laborious occupation, and no authority can always reach or weigh very heavily on people who are here to-day and elsewhere to-morrow. Therefore, it is only with the third stage of human existence, the agricultural one, that civilization, which cannot subsist without permanent homes and authority, really commences. The farmer's homestead is the beginning of the State, as the hearth or fireplace was the beginning of the family. The different labors of the fields, the house, and the dairy require a great number of hands and a well-regulated distribution of the work, and so keep several generations of the settler's family together, on the same farm. Life in common makes it absolutely necessary to have a set of simple rules for home government, to prevent disputes, keep up order and harmony, and settle questions of mutual rights and duties. Who should set down and enforce these rules but the head of the family, the founder of the race—the patriarch? And when the family has become too numerous for the original homestead to hold it, and part of it has to leave it, to found a new home for itself, it does not, as in the primitive nomadic times, wander off at random and break all ties, but settles close by on a portion of the family land, or takes possession of a new piece of ground somewhat further off, but still within easy reach. In

the first case the land which had been common property gets broken up into lots, which, though belonging more particularly to the members who separate from the old stock, are not for that withdrawn from the authority of the patriarch. There are several homesteads now, which form a village, and, later on, several villages; but the bond of kindred, of tradition and custom is religiously preserved, as well as subordination to the common head of the race, whose power keeps increasing as the community grows in numbers and extent of land, as the greater complications of relationships, property, inheritance, demand more laws and a stricter rule,—until he becomes not so much Father as King. Then naturally come collisions with neighboring similar settlements, friendly or hostile, which result in alliances or quarrels, trade or war, and herewith we have the State complete, with inner organization and foreign policy.

5. This stage of culture, in its higher development, combines with the fourth and last—city-building, and city-life, when men of the same race, and conscious of a common origin, but practically strangers to each other, form settlements on a large scale, which, being enclosed in walls, become places of refuge and defence, centres of commerce, industry and government. For, when a community has become very numerous, with wants multiplied by continual improvements and increasing culture, each family can no longer make all the things it needs, and a portion of the population devotes itself to manufacture and arts, occupations best pursued in

cities, while the other goes on cultivating the land and raising cattle, the two sets of produces—those of nature and those of the cunning hand and brain —being bartered one for the other, or, when coin is invented, exchanged through that more convenient medium. In the same manner, the task of government having become too manifold and complicated for one man, the former Patriarch, now King, is obliged to surround himself with assistants—either the elders of the race, or persons of his own choice, —and send others to different places, to rule in his name and under his authority. The city in which the King and his immediate ministers and officers reside, naturally becomes the most important one— the Capital of the State.

6. It does not follow by any means that a people, once settled, never stirred from its adopted country. The migratory or wandering instinct never quite died out—our own love of travelling sufficiently proves that—and it was no unfrequent occurrence in very ancient times for large tribes, even portions of nations, to start off again in search of new homes and to found new cities, compelled thereto either by the gradual overcrowding of the old country, or by intestine discords, or by the invasion of new nomadic tribes of a different race who drove the old settlers before them to take possession of their settlements, massacred them if they resisted and reduced those who remained to an irksome subjection. Such invasions, of course, might also be perpetrated with the same results by regular armies, led by kings and generals from some other settled and organized

country. The alternative between bondage and emigration must have been frequently offered, and the choice in favor of the latter was helped not a little by the spirit of adventure inborn in man, tempted by so many unexplored regions as there were in those remote ages.

7. Such have been the beginnings of all nations. There can be no other. And there is one more observation which will scarcely ever prove wrong. It is that, however far we may go back into the past, the people whom we find inhabiting any country at the very dawn of tradition, can always be shown to have come from somewhere else, and not to have been the first either. Every swarm of nomads or adventurers who either pass through a country or stop and settle there, always find it occupied already. Now the older population was hardly ever entirely destroyed or dislodged by the new-comers. A portion at least remained, as an inferior or subject race, but in time came to mix with them, mostly in the way of intermarriage. Then again, if the new-comers were peaceable and there was room enough—which there generally was in very early times—they would frequently be suffered to form separate settlements, and dwell in the land; when they would either remain in a subordinate condition, or, if they were the finer and better gifted race, they would quickly take the upper hand, teach the old settlers their own arts and ideas, their manners and their laws. If the new settlement was effected by conquest, the arrangement was short and simple: the conquerors, though less numerous, at

once established themselves as masters and formed a ruling nobility, an aristocracy, while the old owners of the land, those at least that did not choose to emigrate, became what may be called "the common people," bound to do service and pay tribute or taxes to their self-instituted masters. Every country has generally experienced, at various times, all these modes of invasion, so that each nation may be said to have been formed gradually, in successive layers, as it were, and often of very different elements, which either finally amalgamated or kept apart, according to circumstances.

The early history of Chaldea is a particularly good illustration of all that has just been said.

II.

THE GREAT RACES.—CHAPTER X. OF GENESIS.

1. THE Bible says (Genesis xi. 2): "And it came to pass, as they journeyed in the east, that they found a plain in the land of Shinar; and they dwelt there."

Shinar—or, more correctly, Shineâr—is what may be called Babylonia proper, that part of Mesopotamia where Babylon was, and south of it, almost to the Gulf. "They" are descendants of Noah, long after the Flood. They found the plain and dwelt there, but they did not find the whole land desert; it had been occupied long before them. How long? For such remote ages an exact valuation of time in years is not to be thought of.

2. What people were those whom the descendants of Noah found in the land to which they came from the East? It seems a simple question, yet no answer could have been given to it even as lately as fifteen or sixteen years ago, and when the answer was first suggested by unexpected discoveries made in the Royal Library at Nineveh, it startled the discoverers extremely. The only indication on the subject then known was this, from a Chaldean writer of a late period: "There was originally at

Babylon " (i.e., in the land of Babylon, not the city alone) " a multitude of men of foreign race who had settled in Chaldea." This is told by Berosus, a learned priest of Babylon, who lived immediately after Alexander the Great had conquered the country, and when the Greeks ruled it (somewhat after 300 B.C.). He wrote a history of it from the most ancient times, in which he gave an account of the oldest traditions concerning its beginnings. As he wrote his book in Greek, it is probable that his object was to acquaint the new masters with the history and religion of the land and people whom they had come to rule. Unfortunately the work was lost—as so many valuable works have been, as long as there was no printing, and books existed only in a few manuscript copies—and we know of it only some short fragments, quoted by later writers, in whose time Berosus' history was still accessible. The above lines are contained in one such fragment, and naturally led to the question: who were these men of foreign race who came from somewhere else and settled in Chaldea in immemorial times?

3. One thing appears clear: they belonged to none of the races classed in the Bible as descended from Noah, but probably to one far older, which had not been included in the Flood.

4. For it begins to be pretty generally understood nowadays that the Flood may not have been absolutely universal, but have extended over the countries *which the Hebrews knew*, which made *their* world, and that not literally all living beings except those who are reported to have been in the Ark may

have perished in it. From a negligent habit of reading Chap. VI.–IX. of Genesis without reference to the texts of other chapters of the same Book, it has become a general habit to understand it in this literal manner. Yet the evidence is by no means so positive. The question was considered an open one by profounder students even in antiquity, and freely discussed both among the Jews themselves and the Fathers of the early Christian Church. The following are the statements given in the Book of Genesis; we have only to take them out of their several places and connect them.

5. When Cain had killed his brother Abel, God banished him from the *earth* which had received his brother's blood and laid a curse on him: "a fugitive and a vagabond shalt thou be in the *earth*"—using another word than the first time, one which means earth in general (*êrêç*), in opposition to *the* earth (*adâmâh*), or fruitful land to the east of Eden, in which Adam and Eve dwelt after their expulsion. Then Cain went forth, still further East, and dwelt in a land which was called "the land of Nod," *i.e.*, "of wandering" or "exile." He had a son, Enoch, after whom he named the city which he built,—the first city,—and descendants. Of these the fifth, Lamech, a fierce and lawless man, had three sons, two of whom, Jabal and Jubal, led a pastoral and nomadic life; but the third, Tubalcain, invented the use of metals: he was "the forger of every cutting instrument of brass and iron." This is what the Chap. IV. of Genesis tells of Cain, his crime, his exile and immediate posterity. After that they are heard of

no more. Adam, meanwhile, has a third son, born after he had lost the first two and whom he calls Seth (more correctly *Sheth*). The descendants of this son are enumerated in Chap. V.; the list ends with Noah. These are the parallel races: the accursed and the blest, the proscribed of God and the loved of God, the one that "goes out of the presence of the Lord" and the one that "calls on the name of the Lord," and "walks with God." Of the latter race the last-named, Noah, is "a just man, perfect in his generation," and "finds grace in the eyes of the Lord."

6. Then comes the narrative of the Flood (Chap. VI.-VIII.), the covenant of God with Noah and re-peopling of the earth by his posterity (Chap. IX.). Lastly Chap. X. gives us the list of the generations of Noah's three sons, Shem, Ham and Japheth;—"of these were the nations divided in the earth after the flood.

7. Now this tenth chapter of Genesis is the oldest and most important document in existence concerning the origins of races and nations, and comprises all those with whom the Jews, in the course of their early history, have had any dealings, at least all those who belonged to the great white division of mankind. But in order properly to understand it and appreciate its value and bearing, it must not be forgotten that EACH NAME IN THE LIST IS THAT OF A RACE, A PEOPLE OR A TRIBE, NOT THAT OF A MAN. It was a common fashion among the Orientals—a fashion adopted also by ancient European nations—to express in this manner the

kindred connections of nations among themselves and their differences. Both for brevity and clearness, such historical genealogies are very convenient. They must have been suggested by a proceeding most natural in ages of ignorance, and which consists in a tribe's explaining its own name by taking it for granted that it was that of its founder. Thus the name of the Assyrians is really Asshur. Why? Clearly, they would answer, if asked the question, because their kingdom was founded by one whose name was Asshur. Another famous nation, the Aramæans, are supposed to be so called because the name of their founder was Aram; the Hebrews name themselves from a similarly supposed ancestor, Heber. These three nations,—and several more, the Arabs among others—spoke languages so much alike that they could easily understand each other, and had generally many common features in looks and character. How account for that? By making their founders, Asshur, and Aram, and Heber, etc., sons or descendants of one great head or progenitor, Shem, a son of Noah. It is a kind of parable which is extremely clear once one has the key to it, when nothing is easier than to translate it into our own sober, positive forms of speech. The above bit of genealogy would read thus: A large portion of humanity is distinguished by certain features more or less peculiar to itself; it is one of several great races, and has been called for more than a hundred years the Semitic, (better Shemitic) race, the race of Shem. This race is composed of many different tribes and nations, who have gone each its own way, have each its own name and history, speak dialects of the same original language, and have preserved many common ideas, customs and traits of character, —which all shows that the race was once united and dwelt together, then, as it increased in numbers, broke up into fractions, of which some rose to be great and famous nations and some remained comparatively insignificant tribes. The same applies to the subdivisions of the great white race (the whitest of all) to which nearly all the European nations belong, and which is personified in the Bible under the name of Japhet, third son of Noah,—and to those of a third great race, also originally white, which is broken up into very many fractions, both great nations and scattered tribes, all exhibiting a decided likeness to each other. The Bible gives the names of all these most carefully, and sums up the whole of them under the name of the second son of Noah, Ham, whom it calls their common progenitor.

8. That the genealogies of Chap. X. of Genesis should be understood in this sense, has long been admitted by scientists and churchmen. St. Augustine, one of the greatest among the Fathers of the early church, pointedly says that the names in it represent "nations, not men."* On the other hand there is also literal truth in them, in this way, that, if all mankind is descended from one human couple, every fraction of it must necessarily have had some one particular father or ancestor, only in so remote a

---

* "*Gentes non homines.*" (*De Civitate Dei*, XVII., 3.)

past that his individuality or actual name cannot possibly have been remembered, when every people, as has been remarked above, naturally gave him its own name. Of these names many show by their very nature that they could not have belonged to individuals. Some are plural, like MIZRAIM, "the Egyptians;" some have the article: "*the* AMORITE, *the* HIVITE;" one even is the name of a city: SIDON is called "the first-born of Canaan;" now Sidon was long the greatest maritime city of the Canaanites, who held an undisputed supremacy over the rest, and therefore "the first-born." The name means "fisheries"—an appropriate one for a city on the sea, which must of course have been at first a settlement of fishermen. "CANAAN" really is the name of a vast region, inhabited by a great many nations and tribes, all differing from each other in many ways, yet manifestly of one race, wherefore they are called "the sons of Canaan," Canaan being personified in a common ancestor, given as one of the four sons of Ham. Modern science has, for convenience' sake, adopted a special word for such imaginary personages, invented to account for a nation's, tribe's, or city's name, while summing up, so to speak, its individuality: they are called EPONYMS. The word is Greek, and means "one from whom or for whom somebody or something is named," a "namesake." It is not too much to say that, while popular tradition always claims that the eponymous ancestor or city-founder gave his name to his family, race, or city, the contrary is in reality invariably the case, the name of the race or city being transferred to him. Or, in other words, the eponym is really only that name, transformed into a traditional person by a bold and vivid poetical figure of speech, which, if taken for what it is, makes the beginnings of political history wonderfully plain and easy to grasp and classify.

9. Yet, complete and correct as is the list of Chap. X., within the limits which the writer has set to himself, it by no means exhausts the nations of the earth. The reason of the omissions, however, is easily seen. Among the posterity of Japhet the Greeks indeed are mentioned, (under the name of JAVAN, which should be pronounced *Yavan*, and some of his sons), but not a single one of the other ancient peoples of Europe,—Germans, Italians, Celts, etc.,—who also belonged to that race, as we, their descendants, do. But then, at the time Chap. X. was written, these countries, from their remoteness, were outside of the world in which the Hebrews moved, beyond their horizon, so to speak. They either did not know them at all, or, having nothing to do with them, did not take them into consideration. In neither case would they have been given a place in the great list. The same may be said of another large portion of the same race, which dwelt to the far East and South of the Hebrews—the Hindoos, (the white conquerors of India), and the Persians. There came a time indeed, when the latter not only came into contact with the Jews, but were their masters; but either that was after Chap. X. was written or the Persians were identified by the writers with a kindred nation, the Per-

sians' near neighbor, who had flourished much earlier and reacted in many ways on the countries westward of it; this nation was the MEDES, who, under the name of MADAI, are mentioned as one of the sons of Japhet, with Javan the Greek.

10. More noticeable and more significant than these partial omissions is the determination with which the authors of Chap. X. consistently ignore all those divisions of mankind which do not belong to one of the three great *white* races. Neither the Black nor the Yellow races are mentioned at all; they are left without the pale of the Hebrew brotherhood of nations. Yet the Jews, who staid three or four hundred years in Egypt, surely learned there to know the real negro, for the Egyptians were continually fighting with pure-blood black tribes in the south and south-west, and bringing in thousands of black captives, who were made to work at their great buildings and in their stone-quarries. But these people were too utterly barbarous and devoid of all culture or political importance to be taken into account. Besides, the Jews could not be aware of the vast extent of the earth occupied by the black race, since the greater part of Africa was then unknown to the world, and so were the islands to the south of India, also Australia and its islands—all seats of different sections of that race.

11. The same could not be said of the Yellow Race. True, its principal representatives, the nations of the far East of Asia—the Chinese, the Mongols and the Mandchous,—could not be known to the Hebrews at any time of antiquity, but there

were more than enough representatives of it who could not be *un*known to them.* For it was both a very old and extremely numerous race, which early spread over the greater part of the earth and at one time probably equalled in numbers the rest of mankind. It seems always to have been broken up into a great many tribes and peoples, whom it has been found convenient to gather under the general designation of TURANIANS, from a very ancient name,— TUR or TURA—which was given them by the white population of Persia and Central Asia, and which is still preserved in that of one of their principal surviving branches, the TURKS. All the different members of this great family have had very striking features in common,—the most extraordinary being an incapability of reaching the highest culture, of progressing indefinitely, improving continually. A strange law of their being seems to have condemned them to stop short, when they had attained a certain, not very advanced, stage. Thus their speech has remained extremely imperfect. They spoke, and such Turanian nations as now exist still speak, languages, which, however they may differ, all have this peculiarity, that they are composed either entirely of monosyllables, (the most rudimentary form of speech), or of monosyllables pieced into words in the stiffest, most unwieldy manner, stuck

---

* If, as has been suggested, the "land of Sinim" in Isaiah xlix., 12, is meant for China, such a solitary, incidental and unspecified mention of a country the name of which may have been vaguely used to express the remotest East, cannot invalidate the scheme so evidently and persistently pursued in the composition of Chap. X.

together, as it were, with nothing to join them, wherefore this kind of language has been called *agglutinative*. Chinese belongs to the former class of languages, the "monosyllabic," Turkish to the latter, the "agglutinative." Further, the Turanians were probably the first to invent writing, but never went in that art beyond having one particular sign for every single word—(such is Chinese writing with its forty thousand signs or thereabouts, as many as words in the language)—or at most a sign for every syllable. They had beautiful beginnings of poetry, but in that also never went beyond beginnings. They were also probably the first who built cities, but were wanting in the qualities necessary to organize a society, establish a state on solid and lasting foundations. At one time they covered the whole of Western Asia, dwelt there for ages before any other race occupied it,— fifteen hundred years, according to a very trustworthy tradition,—and were called by the ancients "the oldest of men;" but they vanish and are not heard of any more the moment that white invaders come into the land; these drive the Turanians before them, or bring them into complete subjection, or mix with them, but, by force of their own superiorly gifted nature, retain the dominant position, so that the others lose all separate existence. Thus it was everywhere. For wherever tribes of the three Biblical races came, they mostly found Turanian populations who had preceded them. There are now a great number of Turanian tribes, more or less numerous—Kirghizes, Bashkirs, Ostiaks, Tunguzes, etc., etc.—scattered over the vast expanse of Siberia and Eastern Russia, where they roam at will with their flocks and herds of horses, occasionally settling down,—fragmentary remnants of a race which, to this latest time, has preserved its original peculiarities and imperfections, whose day is done, which has long ceased to improve, unless it assimilates with the higher white race and adopts their culture, when all that it lacked is supplied by the nobler element which mixes with it, as in the case of the Hungarians, one of the most high-spirited and talented nations of Europe, originally of Turanian stock. The same may be said, in a lesser degree, of the Finns—the native inhabitants of the Russian principality of Finland.

12. All this by no means goes to show that the Yellow Race has ever been devoid of fine faculties and original genius. Quite the contrary; for, if white races everywhere stepped in, took the work of civilization out of their hands and carried it on to a perfection of which they were incapable, still they, the Turanians, had everywhere *begun* that work, it was their inventions which the others took up and improved : and we must remember that it is very much easier to improve than to invent. Only there is that strange limitation to their power of progress and that want of natural refinement, which are as a wall that encloses them around. Even the Chinese, who, at first sight, are a brilliant exception, are not so on a closer inspection. True, they have founded and organized a great empire which still endures; they have a vast literature,

they have made most important inventions—printing, manufacturing paper out of rags, the use of the compass, gunpowder—centuries before European nations made them in their turn. Yet the latter do all those things far better; they have improved these, to them, new inventions more in a couple of hundred years than the Chinese in a thousand. In fact it is a good many centuries since the Chinese have ceased to improve anything at all. Their language and writing are childishly imperfect, though the oldest in existence. In government, in the forms of social life, in their ideas generally, they follow rules laid down for them three thousand years ago or more and from which to swerve a hair's breadth were blasphemy. As they have always stubbornly resisted foreign influences, and gone the length of trying actually to erect material walls between themselves and the rest of the world, their empire is a perfectly fair specimen of what the Yellow Race can do, if left entirely to itself, and quite as much of what it can*not* do, and now they have for centuries presented that unique phenomenon—a great nation at a standstill.

13. All this obviously leads us to a very interesting and suggestive question : what is this great race which we find everywhere at the very roots of history, so that not only ancient tradition calls them " the oldest of men," but modern science more and more inclines to the same opinion? Whence came it? How is it not included in the great family of nations, of which Chap. X. of Genesis gives so clear and comprehensive a scheme? Parallel to this

question arises another: what became of Cain's posterity? What, above all, of the descendants of those three sons of Lamech, whom the writer of Genesis clearly places before us as heads of nations and thinks of sufficient importance to specify what their occupations were? (See Genesis iv. 19-22.) Why do we never hear any more of this entire half of humanity, severed in the very beginning from the other half—the lineage of the accursed son from that of the blest and favored son? And may not the answer to this series of questions be the answer to the first series also?

14. With regard to the second series this answer is plain and decisive. The descendants of Cain were necessarily out of the pale of the Hebrew world. The curse of God, in consequence of which their forefather is said to have gone "out of the presence of the Lord," at once and forever separated them from the posterity of the pious son, from those who "walked with God." The writer of Genesis tells us that they lived in the "Land of Exile" and multiplied, then dismisses them. For what could the elect, the people of God, or even those other nations who went astray, who were repeatedly chastised, but whose family bond with the righteous race was never entirely severed—what could they have in common with the banished, the castaway, the irretrievably accursed? These did not count, they were not of humanity. What more probable, therefore, than that, being excluded from all the other narratives, they should not be included in that of the Flood? And in that case, who should

they be but that most ancient race, set apart by its color and several striking peculiarities, which everywhere preceded their white brethren, but were invariably supplanted by them and not destined to supremacy on the earth? This supposition has been hazarded by men of great genius, and if bold, still has much to support it; if confirmed it would solve many puzzles, throw strong and unexpected light on many obscure points. The very antiquity of the Yellow Race tallies admirably with the Biblical narrative, for of the two Biblical brothers Cain was the eldest. And the doom laid on the race, " a fugitive and a vagabond shalt thou be on the earth," has not been revoked through all ages. Wherever pure Turanians are—they are nomads. And when, fifteen hundred years ago and later, countless swarms of barbarous people flooded Europe, coming from the east, and swept all before them, the Turanian hordes could be known chiefly by this, that they destroyed, burned, laid waste— and passed, vanished: whereas the others, after treating a country quite as savagely, usually settled in it and founded states, most of which exist even now—for, French, German, English, Russian, we are all descended from some of those barbarous invaders. And this also would fully explain how it came to pass that, although the Hebrews and their forefathers—let us say the Semites generally —everywhere found Turanians on their way, nay, dwelt in the same lands with them, the sacred historian ignores them completely, as in Gen. xi. 2.

15. For they were Turanians, arrived at a, for them, really high state of culture, who peopled the land of Shinar, when "*they*"—descendants of Noah, —journeying in the East, found that plain where they dwelt for many years.

III.

TURANIAN CHALDEA.—SHUMIR AND ACCAD.—THE BEGINNINGS OF RELIGION.

1. IT is not Berosus alone who speaks of the "multitudes of men of foreign race" who colonized Chaldea "in the beginning." It was a universally admitted fact throughout antiquity that the population of the country had always been a mixed one, but a fact known vaguely, without particulars. On this subject, as on so many others, the discoveries made in the royal library of Nineveh shed an unexpected and most welcome light. The very first, so to speak preliminary, study of the tablets showed that there were amongst them documents in two entirely different languages, of which one evidently was that of an older population of Chaldea. The other and later language, usually called Assyrian, because it was spoken also by the Assyrians, being very like Hebrew, an understanding of it was arrived at with comparative ease. As to the older language there was absolutely no clue. The only conjecture which could be made with any certainty was, that it must have been spoken by a double people, called the people of Shumir and Accad, because later kings of

Babylon, in their inscriptions, always gave themselves the title of "Kings of Shumir and Accad," a title which the Assyrian sovereigns, who at times conquered Chaldea, did not fail to take also. But who and what were these people might never have been cleared up, but for the most fortunate discovery of dictionaries and grammars, which, the texts being supplied with Assyrian translations, served our modern scholars, just as they did Assyrian students 3000 years ago, to decipher and learn to understand the oldest language of Chaldea. Of course, it was a colossal piece of work, beset with difficulties which it required an almost fierce determination and superhuman patience to master. But every step made was so amply repaid by the results obtained, that the zeal of the laborers was never suffered to flag, and the effected reconstruction, though far from complete even now, already enables us to conjure a very suggestive and life-like picture of those first settlers of the Mesopotamian Lowlands, their character, religion and pursuits.

2. The language thus strangely brought to light was very soon perceived to be distinctly of that peculiar and primitive type—partly monosyllables, partly words rudely pieced together,—which has been described in a preceding chapter as characteristic of the Turanian race, and which is known in science by the general name of *agglutinative*, i.e., "glued or stuck together," without change in the words, either by declension or conjugation. The people of Shumir and Accad, therefore, were one and the same Turanian nation, the difference in the name

being merely a geographical one. SHUMIR is Southern or Lower Chaldea, the country towards and around the Persian Gulf,—that very land of Shinar which is mentioned in Genesis xi. 2. Indeed "Shinar" is only the way in which the Hebrews pronounced and spelt the ancient name of Lower Chaldea. ACCAD is Northern or Upper Chaldea. The most correct way, and the safest from all misunderstanding, is to name the people the Shumiro-Accads and their language, the Shumiro-Accadian; but for brevity's sake, the first name is frequently dropped, and many say simply "the Accads" and "the Accadian language." It is clear, however, that the royal title must needs unite both names, which together represented the entire country of Chaldea. Of late it has been discovered that the Shumiro-Accads spoke two slightly differing dialects of the same language, that of Shumir being most probably the older of the two, as culture and conquest seem to have been carried steadily northward from the Gulf.

3. That the Accads themselves came from somewhere else, is plain from several circumstances, although there is not the faintest symptom or trace of any people whom they may have found in the country. They brought into it the very first and most essential rudiments of civilization, the art of writing, and that of working metals; it was probably also they who began to dig those canals without which the land, notwithstanding its fabulous fertility, must always be a marshy waste, and who began to make bricks and construct buildings out of

them. There is ground to conclude that they came down from mountains in the fact that the name "Accad" means "Mountains" or "Highlands," a name which they could not possibly have taken in the dead flats of Lower Chaldea, but must have retained as a relic of an older home. It is quite possible that this home may have been in the neighboring wild and mountainous land of SHUSHAN (Susiana on the maps), whose first known population was also Turanian. These guesses take us into a past, where not a speck of positive fact can be discerned. Yet even that must have been only a station in this race's migration from a far more northern centre. Their written language, even after they had lived for centuries in an almost tropical country, where palms grew in vast groves, almost forests, and lions were common game, as plentiful as tigers in the jungles of Bengal, contained no sign to designate either the one or the other, while it was well stocked with the signs of metals,—of which there is no vestige, of course, in Chaldea,—and all that belongs to the working thereof. As the ALTAI range, the great Siberian chain, has always been famous for its rich mines of every possible metal ore, and as the valleys of the Altaï are known to be the nests from which innumerable Turanian tribes scattered to the north and south, and in which many dwell to this day after their own nomadic fashion, there is no extravagance in supposing that *there* may have been our Accads' original point of departure. Indeed the Altaï is so indissolubly connected with the origin of most Turanian nations, that many scientists prefer to call the entire Yellow Race, with all its gradations of color, "the Altaïc." Their own traditions point the same way. Several of them have a pretty legend of a sort of paradise, a secluded valley somewhere in the Altaï, pleasant and watered by many streams, where their forefathers either dwelt in the first place or whither they were providentially conducted to be saved from a general massacre. The valley was entirely enclosed with high rocks, steep and pathless, so that when, after several hundred years, it could no longer hold the number of its inhabitants, these began to search for an issue and found none. Then one among them, who was a smith, discovered that the rocks were almost entirely of iron. By his advice, a huge fire was made and a great many mighty bellows were brought into play, by which means a path was *melted* through the rocks. A tradition, by the by, which, while confirming the remark that the invention of metallurgy belongs originally to the Yellow Race in its earliest stages of development, is strangely in accordance with the name of the Biblical Tubalcain, "the forger of every cutting instrument of brass and iron." That the Accads were possessed of this distinctive accomplishment of their race is moreover made very probable by the various articles and ornaments in gold, brass and iron which are continually found in the very oldest tombs.

4. But infinitely the most precious acquisition secured to us by the unexpected revelation of this stage of remotest antiquity is a wonderfully exten-

sive collection of prayers, invocations and other sacred texts, from which we can reconstruct, with much probability, the most primitive religion in the world—for such undoubtedly was that of the Accads. As a clear and authentic insight into the first manifestation of the religious instinct in man was just what was wanting until now, in order to enable us to follow its development from the first, crudest attempts at expression to the highest aspirations and noblest forms of worship, the value of this discovery can never be overrated. It introduces us moreover into so strange and fantastical a world as not the most imaginative of fictions can surpass.

5. The instinct of religion—" religiosity," as it has been called—is inborn to man; like the faculty of speech, it belongs to man, and to man only, of all living beings. So much so, that modern science is coming to acknowledge these two faculties as *the* distinctive characteristics which mark man as a being apart from and above the rest of creation. Whereas the division of all that exists upon the earth has of old been into three great classes or realms—the "mineral realm," the "vegetable realm" and the "animal realm," in which latter man was included—it is now proposed to erect the human race with all its varieties into a separate "realm," for this very reason: that man has all that animals have, and two things more which they have not—speech and religiosity, which assume a faculty of abstract thinking, observing and drawing general conclusions, solely and distinctively human. Now

the very first observations of man in the most primitive stage of his existence must necessarily have awakened in him a twofold consciousness—that of power and that of helplessness. He could do many things. Small in size, weak in strength, destitute of natural clothing and weapons, acutely sensitive to pain and atmospheric changes as all higher natures are, he could kill and tame the huge and powerful animals which had the advantage of him in all these things, whose numbers and fierceness threatened him at every turn with destruction, from which his only escape would seem to have been constant cowering and hiding. He could compel the earth to bear for him choicer food than for the other beings who lived on her gifts. He could command the service of fire, the dread visitor from heaven. Stepping victoriously from one achievement to another, ever widening his sphere of action, of invention, man could not but be filled with legitimate pride. But on the other hand, he saw himself surrounded with things which he could neither account for nor subdue, which had the greatest influence on his well-being, either favorable or hostile, but which were utterly beyond his comprehension or control. The same sun which ripened his crop sometimes scorched it; the rain which cooled and fertilized his field, sometimes swamped it; the hot winds parched him and his cattle; in the marshes lurked disease and death. All these and many, many more, were evidently POWERS, and could do him great good or work him great harm, while he was unable to do either to them. These things existed, he felt their action every day of his life, consequently they were to him living Beings, alive in the same way that he was, possessed of will, for good or for evil. In short, to primitive man everything in nature was alive with an individual life, as it is to the very young child, who would not beat the chair against which he has knocked himself, and then kiss it to make friends, did he not think that it is a living and feeling being like himself. The feeling of dependence and absolute helplessness thus created must have more than balanced that of pride and self-reliance. Man felt himself placed in a world where he was suffered to live and have his share of what good things he could get, but which was not ruled by him,—in a spirit-world. Spirits around him, above him, below him, —what could he do but humble himself, confess his dependence, and pray to be spared? For surely, if those spirits existed and took enough interest in him to do him good or evil, they could hear him and might be moved by supplication. To establish a distinction between such spirits which did only harm, were evil in themselves, and those whose action was generally beneficial and only on rare occasions destructive, was the next natural step, which led as naturally to a perception of divine displeasure as the cause of such terrible manifestations and a seeking of means to avert or propitiate it. While fear and loathing were the portion of the former spirits, the essentially evil ones, love and gratitude, were the predominant feelings inspired by the latter,—feelings which, together with the ever present consciousness of dependence, are the very essence of religion, just as praise and worship are the attempts to express them in a tangible form.

6. It is this most primitive, material and unquestioning stage in the growth of religious feeling, which a large portion of the Shumiro-Accadian documents from the Royal Library at Nineveh brings before us with a force and completeness which, however much room there may still be for uncertainty in details, on the whole really amounts to more than conjecture. Much will, doubtless, be discovered yet, much will be done, but it will only serve to fill in a sketch, of which the outlines are already now tolerably fixed and authentic. The materials for this most important reconstruction are almost entirely contained in a vast collection of two hundred tablets, forming one consecutive work in three books, over fifty of which have been sifted out of the heap of rubbish at the British Museum and first deciphered by Sir Henry Rawlinson, one of the greatest, as he was the first discoverer in this field, and George Smith, whose achievements and too early death have been mentioned in a former chapter. Of the three books into which the collection is divided, one treats "of evil spirits," another of diseases, and the third contains hymns and prayers—the latter collection showing signs of a later and higher development. Out of these materials the lately deceased French scholar, Mr. François Lenormant, whose name has for the last fifteen years or so of his life stood in the very front of this branch of Oriental research, has been the first to reconstruct

an entire picture in a book not very voluminous indeed, but which must always remain a corner-stone in the history of human culture. This book shall be our guide in the strange world we now enter.*

7. To the people of Shumir and Accad, then, the universe was peopled with Spirits, whom they distributed according to its different spheres and regions. For they had formed a very elaborate and clever, if peculiar idea of what they supposed the world to be like. According to the ingenious expression of a Greek writer of the 1st century A.D. they imagined it to have the shape of an inverted round boat or bowl, the thickness of which would represent the mixture of land and water (*ki-a*) which we call the crust of the earth, while the hollow beneath this inhabitable crust was fancied as a bottomless pit or abyss (*ge*), in which dwelt many powers. Above the convex surface of the earth (*ki-a*) spread the sky (*ana*), itself divided into two regions :—the highest heaven or firmament, which, with the fixed stars immovably attached to it, revolved, as round an axis or pivot, around an immensely high mountain, which joined it to the earth as a pillar, and was situated somewhere in the far North-East—some say North—and the lower heaven, where the planets—a sort of resplendent animals, seven in number, of beneficent nature— wandered forever on their appointed path. To these were opposed seven evil demons, sometimes

---

* "La Magie et la Divination chez les Chaldéens," 1874-5. German translation of it, 1878.

called "the Seven Fiery Phantoms." But above all these, higher in rank and greater in power, is the Spirit (*Zi*) of heaven (*ana*), ZI-ANA, or, as often, simply ANA—"Heaven." Between the lower heaven and the surface of the earth is the atmospheric region, the realm of IM or MERMER, the Wind, where he drives the clouds, rouses the storms, and whence he pours down the rain, which is stored in the great reservoir of Ana, in the heavenly Ocean. As to the earthly Ocean, it is fancied as a broad river, or watery rim, flowing all round the edge of the imaginary inverted bowl; in its waters dwells ÊA (whose name means "the House of Waters"), the great Spirit of the Earth and Waters (*Zi-ki-a*), either in the form of a fish, whence he is frequently called "Êa the fish," or "the Exalted Fish," or on a magnificent ship, with which he travels round the earth, guarding and protecting it. The minor spirits of earth (*Anunna-ki*) are not much spoken of except in a body, as a sort of host or legion. All the more terrible are the seven spirits of the abyss, the MASKIM, of whom it is said that, although their seat is in the depths of the earth, yet their voice resounds on the heights also: they reside at will in the immensity of space, "not enjoying a good name either in heaven or on earth." Their greatest delight is to subvert the orderly course of nature, to cause earthquakes, inundations, ravaging tempests. Although the Abyss is their birth-place and proper sphere, they are not submissive to its lord and ruler MUL-GE ("Lord of the Abyss"). In that they are like their brethren of the lower heaven who do not acknowledge Ana's supremacy, in fact are called "spirits of rebellion," because, being originally Ana's messengers, they once "secretly plotted a wicked deed," rose against the heavenly powers, obscured the Moon, and all but hurled him from his seat. But the Maskim are ever. more feared and hated, as appears from the following description, which has become celebrated for its real poetical force:

8. "They are seven! they are seven!—Seven they are in the depths of Ocean,—seven they are, disturbers of the face of Heaven.—They arise from the depths of Ocean, from hidden lurking-places.— They spread like snares.—Male they are not, female they are not.—Wives they have not, children are not born to them.—Order they know not, nor beneficence;—prayers and supplication they hear not.— Vermin grown in the bowels of the mountains— foes of Êa—they are the throne-bearers of the gods —they sit in the roads and make them unsafe.— The fiends! the fiends!—They are seven, they are seven, seven they are!

"Spirit of Heaven (*Zi-ana, Ana*), be they conjured! "Spirit of Earth (*Zi-ki-a, Êa*), be they conjured!"

9. Besides these regular sets of evil spirits in sevens—seven being a mysterious and consecrated number—there are the hosts untold of demons which assail man in every possible form, which are always on the watch to do him harm, not only bodily, but moral in the way of civil broils and family dissensions; confusion is their work; it is they who "steal the child from the father's knee," who "drive

the son from his father's house," who withhold from the wife the blessing of children; they have stolen days from heaven, which they have made evil days, that bring nothing but ill-luck and misfortune,— and nothing can keep them out : " They fall as rain from the sky, they spring from the earth,—they steal from house to house,—doors do not stop them, —bolts do not shut them out,—they creep in at the doors like serpents,—they blow in at the roof like winds." Various are their haunts: the tops of mountains, the pestilential marshes by the sea, but especially the desert. Diseases are among the most dreaded of this terrible band, and first among these NAMTAR or DIBBARA, the demon of Pestilence, IDPA (Fever), and a certain mysterious disease of the head, which must be insanity, of which it is said that it oppresses the head and holds it tight like a tiara (a heavy headdress) or "like a dark prison," and makes it confused, that " it is like a violent tempest; no one knows whence it comes, nor what is its object."

10. All these evil beings are very properly classed together under the general name of "creations of the Abyss," births of the nether world, the world of the dead. For the unseen world below the habitable earth was naturally conceived as the dwelling place of the departed spirits after death. It is very remarkable as characteristic of the low standard of moral conception which the Shumiro-Accads had attained at this stage of their development, that, although they never admitted that those who died ceased to exist altogether, there is very

little to show that they imagined any happy state for them after death, not even as a reward for a righteous life, nor, on the other hand, looked to a future state for punishment of wrongs committed in this world, but promiscuously consigned their dead to the ARALI, a most dismal region which is called the "support of chaos," or, in phrase no less vague and full of mysterious awe, "the Great Land" (*Ki-gal*), "the Great City" (*Uru-gal*), "the spacious dwelling," "where they wander in the dark,"—a region ruled by a female divinity called by different names, but most frequently "Lady of the Great Land" (*Nin-ki-gal*), or "Lady of the Abyss" (*Nin-ge*), who may the rather be understood as Death personified, that Namtar (Pestilence) is her chief minister. The Shumiro-Accads seem to have dimly fancied that association with so many evil beings whose proper home the Arali was, must convert even the human spirits into beings almost as noxious, for one or two passages appear to imply that they were afraid of ghosts, at least on one occasion it is threatened to send the dead back into the upper world, as the direst calamity that can be inflicted.

11. As if all these terrors were not sufficient to make life a burden, the Shumiro-Accads believed in sorcerers, wicked men who knew how to compel the powers of evil to do their bidding and thus could inflict death, sickness or disasters at their pleasure. This could be done in many ways—by a look, by uttering certain words, by drinks made of herbs prepared under certain conditions and ceremonies.

Nay, the power of doing harm sometimes fatally belonged even to innocent persons, who inflicted it unintentionally by their look—for the effect of "the evil eye" did not always depend on a person's own will.

12. Existence under such conditions must have been as unendurable as that of poor children who have been terrified by silly nurses into a belief in ogres and a fear of dark rooms, had there not existed real or imaginary defences against this array of horrible beings always ready to fall on unfortunate humanity in all sorts of inexplicable ways and for no other reason but their own detestable delight in doing evil. These defences could not consist in rational measures dictated by a knowledge of the laws of physical nature, since they had no notion of such laws; nor in prayers and propitiatory offerings, since one of the demons' most execrable qualities was, as we have seen, that they "knew not beneficence" and "heard not prayer and supplication." Then, if they cannot be coaxed, they must be compelled. This seems a very presumptuous assumption, but it is strictly in accordance with human instinct. It has been very truly said * that " man was so conscious of being called to exercise empire over the powers of nature, that, the moment he entered into any relations with them, it was to try and subject them to his will. Only instead of studying the phenomena, in order to grasp their laws and apply

---

* Alfred Maury, "La Magie et l'Astrologie dans l'Antiquité et au Moyen-âge." Introduction, p. 1.

them to his needs, he fancied he could, by means of peculiar practices and consecrated forms, compel the physical agents of nature to serve his wishes and purposes.... This pretension had its root in the notion which antiquity had formed of the natural phenomena. It did not see in them the consequence of unchangeable and necessary laws, always active and always to be calculated upon, but fancied them to depend on the arbitrary and varying will of the spirits and deities it had put in the place of physical agents." It follows that in a religion which peoples the universe with spirits of which the greater part are evil, magic—i.e., conjuring with words and rites, incantations, spells—must take the place of worship, and the ministers of such a religion are not priests, but conjurers and enchanters. This is exactly the state of things revealed by the great collection of texts discovered by Sir H. Rawlinson and G. Smith. They contain forms for conjuring all the different kinds of demons, even to evil dreams and nightmares, the object of most such invocations being to drive them away from the habitations of men and back to where they properly belong—the depth of the desert, the inaccessible mountain tops, and all remote, waste and uninhabited places generally, where they can range at will, and find nobody to harm.

13. Yet there are also prayers for protection and help addressed to beings conceived as essentially good and beneficent—a step marking a great advance in the moral feeling and religious consciousness of the people. Such beings—gods, in fact—

were, above all, Ana and Êa, whom we saw invoked in the incantation of the Seven Maskim as "Spirit of Heaven," and "Spirit of Earth." The latter especially is appealed to as an unfailing refuge to ill-used and terrified mortals. He is imagined as possessed of all knowledge and wisdom, which he uses only to befriend and protect. His usual residence is the deep,—(hence his name, *Ê-a*, "the House of Waters")—but he sometimes travels round the earth in a magnificent ship. His very name is a terror to the evil ones. He knows the words, the spells that will break their power and compel their obedience. To him, therefore, the people looked in their need with infinite trust. Unable to cope with the mysterious dangers and snares which, as they fancied, beset them on all sides, ignorant of the means of defeating the wicked beings who, they thought, pursued them with abominable malice and gratuitous hatred, they turned to Êa. *He* would know. *He* must be asked, and he would tell.

14. But, as though bethinking themselves that Êa was a being too mighty and exalted to be lightly addressed and often disturbed, the Shumiro-Accads imagined a beneficent spirit, MERI-DUG (more correctly MIRRI-DUGGA), called son of Êa and DAM-KINA, (a name of Earth). Meridug's only office is to act as mediator between his father and suffering mankind. It is he who bears to Êa the suppliant's request, exposes his need sometimes in very moving words, and requests to know the remedy—if illness be the trouble—or the counter-

spell, if the victim be held in the toils of witchcraft. Êa tells his son, who is then supposed to reveal the secret to the chosen instrument of assistance— of course the conjuring priest, or better, soothsayer. As most incantations are conceived on this principle, they are very monotonous in form, though frequently enlivened by the supposed dialogue between the father and son. Here is one of the more entertaining specimens. It occupies an entire tablet, but unfortunately many lines have been hopelessly injured, and have to be omitted. The text begins:

"The Disease of the Head has issued from the Abyss, from the dwelling of the Lord of the Abyss."

Then follow the symptoms and the description of the sufferer's inability to help himself. Then "Meridug has looked on his misery. He has entered the dwelling of his father Êa, and has spoken unto him:

"'My father, the Disease of the Head has issued from the Abyss.'

"A second time he has spoken unto him:

"'What he must do against it the man knows not. How shall he find healing?'

"Êa has replied to his son Meridug:

"'My son, how dost thou not know? What should I teach thee? What I know, thou also knowest. But come hither, my son Meridug. Take a bucket, fill it with water from the mouth of the rivers; impart to this water thy exalted magic power; sprinkle with it the man, son of his god, ... wrap up his head, ... and on the highway pour it out. May insanity be dispelled! that the disease of his head vanish like a phantom of the night. May Êa's word drive it out! May Damkina heal him.'"

15. Another dialogue of the same sort, in which Ea is consulted as to the means of breaking the power of the Maskim, ends by his revealing that

"The white cedar is the tree which breaks the Maskim's noxious might."

In fact the white cedar was considered an infallible defence against all spells and evil powers. Any action or ceremony described in the conjuration must of course be performed even as the words are spoken. Then there is a long one, perhaps the best preserved of all, to be recited by the sufferer, who is supposed to be under the effects of an evil spell, and from which it is evident that the words are to accompany actions performed by the conjurer. It is divided into parallel verses, of which the first runs thus:

"As this onion is being peeled of its skins, thus shall it be of the spell. The burning fire shall consume it; it shall no more be planted in a row, ... the ground shall not receive its root, its head shall contain no seed and the sun shall not take care of it;—it shall not be offered at the feast of a god or a king.—The man who has cast the evil spell, his eldest son, his wife,—the spell, the lamentations, the transgressions, the written spells, the blasphemies, the sins,—the evil which is in my body, in my flesh, in my sores,—may they all be destroyed as this onion, and may the burning fire consume them this day! May the evil spell go far away, and may I see the light again!"

Then the destruction of a date is similarly described:

"It shall not return to the bough from which it has been plucked."

The untying of a knot:

"Its threads shall not return to the stem which has produced them.'

The tearing up of some wool:

"It shall not return to the back of its sheep."

The tearing of some stuff, and after each act the second verse:

"The man who has cast the spell," etc.

is repeated.

16. It is devoutly to be hoped, for the patients' sake, that treatments like these took effect on the disease, for they got no other. Diseases being conceived as personal demons who entered a man's body of their own accord or under compulsion from powerful sorcerers, and illness being consequently considered as a kind of possession, clearly the only thing to do was to drive out the demon or break the spell with the aid of the beneficent Êa and his son. If this intervention was of no avail, nothing remained for the patient but to get well as he could, or to die. This is why there never was a science of medicine in the proper sense in Chaldea, even as late as three or four hundred years B.C., and the Greek travellers who then visited Babylon must have been not a little shocked at the custom they found there of bringing desperately sick persons out of the houses with their beds and exposing them in the streets, when any passer-by could approach them, inquire into the disease and suggest some remedy—which was sure to be tried as a last chance. This extraordinary experiment was of course not resorted to until all known forms of conjuration had been gone through and had proved inefficient.

17. The belief that certain words and impreca-

tions could break the power of demons or sorcerers must have naturally led to the notion that to wear such imprecations, written on some substance or article, always about one's person must be a continual defence against them; while on the other hand, words of invocation to the beneficent spirits and images representing them, worn in the same way, must draw down on the wearer those spirits' protection and blessing. Hence the passion for talismans. They were of various kinds : strips of stuff, with the magic words written on them, to be fastened to the body, or the clothes, or articles of household furniture, were much used; but small articles of clay or hard stone were in greater favor on account of their durability. As houses could be possessed by evil spirits just as well as individuals, talismans were placed in different parts of them for protection, and this belief was so enduring that small clay figures of gods were found in Assyrian palaces under thresholds—as in the palace of Khorsabad, by Botta—placed there "to keep from it fiends and enemies." It has been discovered in this manner that many of the sculptures which adorned the Assyrian palaces and temples were of talismanic nature. Thus the winged bulls placed at the gateways were nothing but representations of an Accadian class of guardian spirits,—the *Kirûbu*, Hebrew *Kerubim*, of which we have made *Cherub*, *Cherubim*—who were supposed to keep watch at entrances, even at that of the Arali, while some sculptures on which demons, in the shape of hideous monsters, are seen fighting

54.—DEMONS FIGHTING.
(From the British Museum.)

each other, are, so to speak, imprecations in stone, which, if translated into words, would mean : " May the evil demons stay outside, may they assail and fight each other,"—as, in that case, they would clearly have no leisure to assail the inhabitants of the dwelling. That these sculptures really were regarded as talismans and expected to guard the inmates from harm, is abundantly shown by the manner in which they are mentioned in several inscriptions, down to a very late date. Thus Esarhaddon, one of the last kings of Assyria (about 700 B.C.), says, after describing a very sumptuous palace which he had built :—"'I placed in its gates bulls and colossi, who, according to their fixed command, against the wicked turn themselves; they protect the footsteps, making peace to be upon the path of the king their creator."

18. The cylinder seals with their inscriptions and engraved figures were mostly also talismans of like nature ; which must be the reason why so many are found in graves, tied to the dead person's wrist by a string—evidently as a protection against the fiends which the departed spirit was expected to meet. The magic power was of course conferred on all talismans by the words which the conjurer spoke over them with the necessary ceremonies. One such long incantation is preserved entire. It is designed to impart to the talisman the power of keeping the demons from all parts of the dwelling, which are singly enumerated, with the consequences to the demons who would dare to trespass: those who steal into gutters, remove bolts or

hinges, shall be broken like an earthen jug, crushed like clay; those who overstep the wooden frame of the house shall be clipped of their wings; those who stretch their neck in at the window, the window shall descend and cut their throat. The most original in this class of superstitions was that which, according to Lenormant, consisted in the notion that all these demons were of so unutterably ugly a form and countenance, that they must fly away terrified if they only beheld their own likeness. As an illustration of this principle he gives an incantation against "the wicked Namtar." It begins with a highly graphic description of the terrible demon, who is said to "take man captive like an enemy," to "burn him like a flame," to "double him up like a bundle," to "assail man, although having neither hand nor foot, like a noose." Then follows the usual dialogue between Êa and Meridug, (in the identical words given above), and Êa at length reveals the prescription: "Come hither, my son Meridug. Take mud of the Ocean and knead out of it a likeness of him, (the Namtar.) Lay down the man, after thou hast purified him; lay the image on his bare abdomen, impart to it my magic power and turn its face westward, that the wicked Namtar, who dwells in his body, may take up some other abode. Amen." The idea is that the Namtar, on beholding his own likeness, will flee from it in dismay!

19. To this same class belongs a small bronze statuette, which is to be seen in the Louvre. Mr. Lenormant thus describes it: "It is the image of a

horrible demon, standing, with the body of a dog, the talons of an eagle, arms ending in a lion's paws, the tail of a scorpion, the head of a skeleton, but with eyes, and a goat's horns, and with four large wings at the back, unfolded. A ring placed at the back of the head served to hang the figure up. Along the back is an inscription in the Accadian language, informing us that this pretty creature is the Demon of the South-west Wind, and is to be placed at the door or window. For in Chaldea the South-west Wind comes from the deserts of Arabia, its burning breath consumes everything and produces the same ravages as the Simoon in Africa. Therefore this particular talisman is most frequently met with. Our museums contain many other figures of demons, used as talismans to frighten away the evil spirits they were supposed to represent. One has the head of a goat on a disproportionately long neck; another shows a hyena's head, with huge open mouth, on a bear's body with lion's paws." On the principle that possession is best guarded against by the presence of beneficent spirits, the exorcisms—i.e., forms of conjuring designed to drive the evil demons out of a man or dwelling—are usually accompanied with a request to good spirits to enter the one or the other, instead of the wicked ones who have been ejected. The supreme power which breaks that of all incantations, talismans, conjuring rites whatever, is, it would appear, supposed to reside in a great, divine name,—possibly a name of Êa himself. At all events, it is Êa's own secret. For even in his dialogues with

55.—DEMON OF THE SOUTH-WEST WIND
(Perrot and Chipiez.)

Meridug, when entreated for this supreme aid in desperate cases, he is only supposed to impart it to his son to use against the obdurate demons and thereby crush their power, but it is not given, so that the demons are only threatened with it, but it is not actually uttered in the course of the incantations.

20. Not entirely unassisted did Êa pursue his gigantic task of protection and healing. Along with him invocations are often addressed to several other spirits conceived as essentially good divine beings, whose beneficent influence is felt in many ways. Such was Im, the Storm-Wind, with its accompanying vivifying showers; such are the purifying and wholesome Waters, the Rivers and Springs which feed the earth; above all, such were the Sun and Fire, als the Moon, objects of double reverence and gratitude because they dispel the darkness of night, which the Shumiro-Accads loathed and feared excessively, as the time when the wicked demons are strongest and the power of bad men for weaving deadly spells is greatest. The third Book of the Collection of Magic Texts is composed almost entirely of hymns to these deities—as well as to Êa and Meridug—which betray a somewhat later stage in the nation's religious development, by the

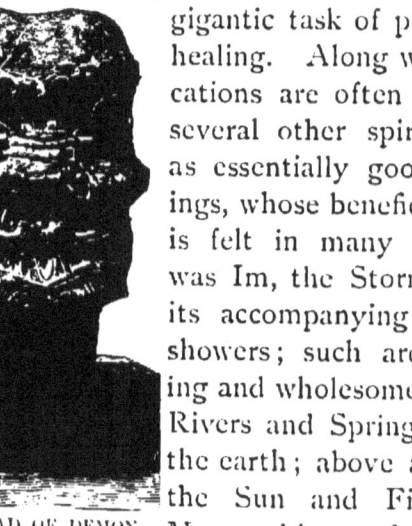

56.—HEAD OF DEMON.

poetical beauty of some of the fragments, and especially by a purer feeling of adoration and a higher perception of moral goodness, which are absent from the oldest incantations.

21. At noon, when the sun has reached the highest point in its heavenly course, the earth lies before it without a shadow; all things, good or bad, are manifest; its beams, after dispelling the unfriendly gloom, pierce into every nook and cranny, bringing into light all ugly things that hide and lurk; the evil-doer cowers and shuns its all-revealing splendor, and, to perform his accursed deeds, waits the return of his dark accomplice, night. What wonder then that to the Shumiro-Accads UD, the Sun in all its midday glory, was a very hero of protection, the source of truth and justice, the "supreme judge in Heaven and on earth," who "knows lie from truth," who knows the truth that is in the soul of man. The hymns to Ud that have been deciphered are full of beautiful images. Take for instance the following:—

"O Sun,* I have called unto thee in the bright heavens. In the shadow of the cedar art thou;" (i.e., it is thou who makest the cedar to cast its shadow, holy and auspicious as the tree itself.) "Thy feet are on the summits. . . . The countries have wished for thee, they have longed for thy coming, O Lord! Thy radiant light illumines all countries. . . . Thou makest lies to vanish, thou destroyest the noxious influence of portents, omens, spells, dreams and evil apparitions; thou turnest wicked plots to a happy issue. . . ."

---

* "UD" not being a proper name, but the name of the sun in the language of Shumir and Accad, it can be rendered in translation by "Sun," with a capital.

This is both true and finely expressed. For what most inveterate believer in ghosts and apparitions ever feared them by daylight? and the last touch shows much moral sense and observation of the mysterious workings of a beneficent power which often not merely defeats evil but even turns it into good. There is splendid poetry in the following fragment describing the glory of sunrise:—

"O Sun! thou hast stepped forth from the background of heaven, thou hast pushed back the bolts of the brilliant heaven,—yea, the gate of heaven. O Sun! above the land thou hast raised thy head! O Sun! thou hast covered the immeasurable space of heaven and countries!"

Another hymn describes how, at the Sun's appearance in the brilliant portals of the heavens, and during his progress to their highest point, all the great gods turn to his light, all the good spirits of heaven and earth gaze up to his face, surround him joyfully and reverently, and escort him in solemn procession. It needs only to put all these fragments into fine verse to make out of them a poem which will be held beautiful even in our day, when from our very childhood we learn to know the difference between good and poor poetry, growing up, as we do, on the best of all ages and all countries.

22. When the sun disappeared in the West, sinking rapidly, and diving, as it were, into the very midst of darkness, the Shumiro-Accads did not fancy him as either asleep or inactive, but on the contrary as still engaged in his everlasting work. Under the name of NIN-DAR, he travels through

the dreary regions ruled by Mulge and, his essence being *light*, he combats the powers of darkness in their own home, till He comes out of it, a triumphant hero, in the morning. Nin-dar is also the keeper of the hidden treasures of the earth—its metals and precious stones, because, according to Mr. Lenormant's ingenious remark, "they only wait, like him, the moment of emerging out of the earth, to emit a bright radiancy." This radiancy of precious stones, which is like a concentration of light in its purest form, was probably the reason why they were in such general use as talismans, quite as much as their hardness and durability.

23. But while the Sun accomplishes his nightly underground journey, men would be left a prey to mortal terrors in the upper world, deprived of light, their chief defence against the evil brood of darkness, were it not for his substitute, Fire, who is by nature also a being of light, and, as such, the friend of men, from whose paths and dwellings he scares not only wild beasts and foes armed with open violence, but the far more dangerous hosts of unseen enemies, both demons and spells cast by wicked sorcerers. It is in this capacity of protector that the god GIBIL (Fire) is chiefly invoked. In one very complete hymn he is addressed thus :—

"Thou who drivest away the evil Maskim, who furtherest the well-being of life, who strikest the breast of the wicked with terror,—Fire, the destroyer of foes, dread weapon which drivest away Pestilence."

This last attribute would show that the Shumiro-Accads had noticed the hygienic properties of fire, which does indeed help to dispel miasmas on account of the strong ventilation which a great blaze sets going. Thus at a comparatively late epoch, some 400 years B.C., a terrible plague broke out at Athens, the Greek city, and Hippocrates, a physician of great genius and renown, who has been called " the Father of Medicine," tried to diminish the contagion by keeping huge fires continually blazing at different points of the city. It is the same very correct idea which made men invoke Gibil as he who purifies the works of man. He is also frequently called " the protector of the dwelling, of the family," and praised for " creating light in the house of darkness," and for bringing peace to all creation. Over and above these claims to gratitude, Gibil had a special importance in the life of a people given to the works of metallurgy, of which fire is the chief agent: "It is thou," says one hymn, " who mixest tin and copper, it is thou who purifiest silver and gold." Now the mixture of tin and copper produces bronze, the first metal which has been used to make weapons and tools of, in most cases long before iron, which is much more difficult to work, and as the quality of the metal depends on the proper mixture of the two ingredients, it is but natural that the aid of the god Fire should have been specially invoked for the operation. But Fire is not only a great power on earth, it is also, in the shape of Lightning, one of the dreadest and most mysterious powers of the skies, and as such sometimes called son of Ana (Heaven), or, in a more roundabout way, "the Hero, son of the Ocean"—

meaning the celestial Ocean, the great reservoir of rains, from which the lightning seems to spring, as it flashes through the heavy showers of a Southern thunder storm. In whatever shape he appear, and whatever his functions, Gibil is hailed as an invariably beneficent and friendly being.

24. When the feeling of helplessness forced on man by his position in the midst of nature takes the form of a reverence for and dependence on beings whom he conceives of as essentially good, a far nobler religion and far higher moral tone are the immediate consequence. This conception of absolute goodness sprang from the observation that certain beings or spirits—like the Sun, Fire, the Thunderstorm—though possessing the power of doing both good and harm, used it almost exclusively for the benefit of men. This position once firmly established, the conclusion naturally followed, that if these good beings once in awhile sent down a catastrophe or calamity,—if the Sun scorched the fields or the Thunderstorm swamped them, if the wholesome North Wind swept away the huts and broke down the trees—it must be in anger, as a mark of displeasure—in punishment. By what could man provoke the displeasure of kind and beneficent beings? Clearly by not being like them, by doing not good, but evil. And what is evil? That which is contrary to the nature of the good spirits: doing wrong and harm to men; committing sins and wicked actions. To avoid, therefore, provoking the anger of those good but powerful spirits, so terrible in its manifestations, it is neces-

sary to try to please them, and that can be done only by being like them,—good, or at least striving to be so, and, when temptation, ignorance, passion or weakness of will have betrayed man into a transgression, to confess it, express regret for the offence and an intention not to offend again, in order to obtain forgiveness and be spared. A righteous life, then, prayer and repentance are the proper means of securing divine favor or mercy. It is evident that a religion from which such lessons naturally spring is a great improvement on a belief in beings who do good or evil indiscriminately, indeed prefer doing evil, a belief which cannot teach a distinction between moral right and wrong, or a rational distribution of rewards or punishment, nor consequently inculcate the feeling of duty and responsibility, without which goodness as a matter of principle is impossible and a reliable state of society unattainable.

25. This higher and therefore later stage of moral and religious development is very perceptible in the third book of the Magic Collection. With the appreciation of absolute goodness, conscience has awakened, and speaks with such insistence and authority that the Shumiro-Accad, in the simplicity of his mind, has earnestly imagined it to be the voice of a personal and separate deity, a guardian spirit belonging to each man, dwelling within him and living his life. It is a god—sometimes even a divine couple, both "god and goddess, pure spirits"—who protects him from his birth, yet is not proof against the spells of sorcerers and the attacks of the

demons, and even can be compelled to work evil in the person committed to its care, and frequently called therefore "the son of his god," as we saw above, in the incantation against the Disease of the Head. The conjuration or exorcism which drives out the demon, of course restores the guardian spirit to its own beneficent nature, and the patient not only to bodily well-being, but also to peace of mind. That is what is desired, when a prayer for the cure of a sick or possessed person ends with the words: "May he be placed again in the gracious hands of his god!" When therefore a man is represented as speaking to "his god" and confessing to him his sin and distress, it is only a way of expressing that silent self-communing of the soul, in which it reviews its own deficiencies, forms good resolutions and prays to be released from the intolerable burden of sin. There are some most beautiful prayers of this sort in the collection. They have been called "the Penitential Psalms," from their striking likeness to some of those psalms in which King David confesses his iniquities and humbles himself before the Lord. The likeness extends to both spirit and form, almost to words. If the older poet, in his spiritual groping, addresses "his god and goddess," the higher, better self which he feels within him and feels to be divine —his Conscience, instead of the One God and Lord, his feeling is not less earnest, his appeal not less pure and confiding. He confesses his transgression, but pleads ignorance and sues for mercy. Here are some of the principal verses, of which each is repeated twice, once addressed to "my god," and the second time to "my goddess." The title of the Psalm is: "The complaints of the repentant heart. Sixty-five verses in all."

26. "My Lord, may the anger of his heart be allayed! May the fool attain understanding! The god who knows the unknown, may he be conciliated! The goddess who knows the unknown, may she be conciliated!—I eat the food of wrath and drink the waters of anguish. . . . O my god, my transgressions are very great, very great my sins. . . . I transgress, and know it not. I sin, and know it not. I feed on transgressions, and know it not. I wander on wrong paths, and know it not.—The Lord, in the wrath of his heart, has overwhelmed me with confusion. . . . I lie on the ground, and none reaches a hand to me. I am silent and in tears, and none takes me by the hand. I cry out, and there is none that hears me. I am exhausted, oppressed, and none releases me. . . . My god, who knowest the unknown, be merciful! . . . . My goddess, who knowest the unknown, be merciful! . . . . How long, O my god? . . . . How long, O my goddess? . . . . Lord, thou wilt not repulse thy servant. In the midst of the stormy waters, come to my assistance, take me by the hand! I commit sins—turn them into blessedness! I commit transgressions—let the wind sweep them away! My blasphemies are very many—rend them like a garment! . . . . God who knowest the unknown,* my sins are seven times seven,—forgive my sins! . . . ."

27. The religious feeling once roused to this extent, it is not to be wondered at that in some invocations the distress or disease which had formerly been taken as a gratuitous visitation, begins to be considered in the light of a divine punishment, even though the afflicted person be the king himself. This is very evident from the concluding passage of

---

* Another and more recent translator renders this line: "God who knowest I knew not." Whichever rendering is right, the thought is beautiful and profound.

a hymn to the Sun, in which it is the conjurer who speaks on behalf of the patient, while presenting an offering:—

"O Sun, leave not my uplifted hands unregarded!—Eat his food, refuse not his sacrifice, bring back his god to him, to be a support unto his hand!—May his sin, at thy behest, be forgiven him, his misdeed be forgotten!—May his trouble leave him! May he recover from his illness!—Give to the king new vital strength. . . . Escort the king, who lies at thy feet!—Also me, the conjurer, thy respectful servant!"

28. There is another hymn of the same kind, not less remarkable for its artistic and regular construction than for its beauty of feeling and diction. The penitent speaks five double lines, and the priest adds two more, as though endorsing the prayer and supporting it with the weight of his own sacred character. This gives very regular strophes, of which, unfortunately, only two have been well preserved:—

Penitent.—"I, thy servant, full of sighs, I call to thee. Whoever is beset with sin, his ardent supplication thou acceptest. If thou lookest on a man with pity, that man liveth. Ruler of all, mistress of mankind! Merciful one, to whom it is good to turn, who dost receive sighs!" *Priest.*—"While his god and his goddess are wroth with him he calls on thee. Thy countenance turn on him, take hold of his hand."

Penitent.—"Besides thee there is no deity to lead in righteousness. Kindly look on me, accept my sighs. Speak: how long? and let thine heart be appeased. When, O Lady, will thy countenance turn on me? Even like doves I moan, I feed on sighs." *Priest.*—"His heart is full of woe and trouble, and full of sighs. Tears he sheds and breaks out into lamentation."[*]

---

[*] This hymn is given by H. Zimmern, as the text to a dissertation on the language and grammar.

29. Such is a not incomplete outline of this strange and primitive religion, the religion of a people whose existence was not suspected twenty-five years ago, yet which claims, with the Egyptians and the Chinese, the distinction of being one of the oldest on earth, and in all probability was older than both. This discovery is one of the most important conquests of modern science, not only from its being highly interesting in itself, but from the light it throws on innumerable hitherto obscure points in the history of the ancient world, nay, on many curious facts which reach down to our own time. Thus, the numerous Turanian tribes which exist in a wholly or half nomadic condition in the immense plains of Eastern and South-eastern Russia, in the forests and wastes of Siberia, on the steppes and highlands of Central Asia, have no other religion now than this of the old Shumiro-Accads, in its earliest and most material shape. Everything to them is a spirit or has a spirit of its own ; they have no worship, no moral teaching, but only conjuring, sorcerers, not priests. These men are called *Shamans* and have great influence among the tribes. The more advanced and cultivated Turanians, like the Mongols and Mandchous, accord to one great Spirit the supremacy over all others and call that Spirit which they conceive as absolutely good, merciful and just, " Heaven," just as the Shumiro-Accads invoked " Ana." This has been and still is the oldest national religion of the Chinese. They say " Heaven " wherever we would say " God," and

with the same idea of loving adoration and reverent dread, which does not prevent them from invoking the spirit of every hill, river, wind or forest, and numbering among this host also the souls of the deceased. This clearly corresponds to the second and higher stage of the Accadian religion, and marks the utmost limit which the Yellow Race have been able to attain in spiritual life. True, the greater part of the Chinese now have another religion ; they are Buddhists ; while the Turks and the great majority of the Tatars, Mongols and Mandchous, not to speak of other less important divisions, are Mussulmans. But both Buddhism and Mahometanism are foreign religions, which they have borrowed, adopted, not worked out for themselves. Here then we are also met by that fatal law of limitation, which through all ages seems to have said to the men of yellow skin and high cheek-bones, "Thus far shalt thou go, and no further." Thus it was in Chaldea. The work of civilization and spiritual development begun by the people of Shumir and Accad was soon taken out of their hands and carried on by newcomers from the east, those descendants of Noah, who " found a plain in the land of Shinar and dwelt there."

APPENDIX TO CHAPTER III.

Professor Louis Dyer, of Harvard University, has attempted a rendering into English verse of the famous incantation of the Seven Maskim. The result of the experiment is a translation most faithful in the spirit and main features, if not always literal; and which, by his kind permission, we here offer to our readers.

A CHARM.

I.

Seven are they, they are seven;
   In the caverns of ocean they dwell,
They are clothed in the lightnings of heaven,
   Of their growth the deep waters can tell;
Seven are they, they are seven.

II.

Broad is their way and their course is wide,
   Where the seeds of destruction they sow,
O'er the tops of the hills where they stride,
   To lay waste the smooth highways below,—
Broad is their way and their course is wide.

III.

Man they are not, nor womankind,
   For in fury they sweep from the main,
And have wedded no wife but the wind,
   And no child have begotten but pain,—
Man they are not, nor womankind.

IV.

Fear is not in them, not awe;
   Supplication they heed not, nor prayer.
For they know no compassion nor law,
   And are deaf to the cries of despair,—
Fear is not in them, not awe.

V.

Cursèd they are, they are cursèd,
   They are foes to wise Ēa's great name:
By the whirlwind are all things dispersèd
   On the paths of the flash of their flame,—
Cursèd they are, they are cursèd.

VI.

Spirit of Heaven, oh, help! Help, oh, Spirit of Earth!
They are seven, thrice said they are seven;
For the gods they are Bearers of Thrones,
But for men they are Breeders of Dearth
And the authors of sorrows and moans.
They are seven, thrice said they are seven.
Spirit of Heaven, oh, help! Help, oh, Spirit of Earth!

IV.

CUSHITES AND SEMITES.—EARLY CHALDEAN HISTORY.

1. WE have just seen that the hymns and prayers which compose the third part of the great Magic Collection really mark a later and higher stage in the religious conceptions of the Turanian settlers of Chaldea, the people of Shumir and Accad. This improvement was not entirely due to a process of natural development, but in a great measure to the influence of that other and nobler race, who came from the East. When the priestly historian of Babylon, Berosus, calls the older population "men of foreign race," it is because he belonged himself to that second race, who remained in the land, introduced their own superior culture, and asserted their supremacy to the end of Babylon. The national legends have preserved the memory of this important event, which they represent as a direct divine revelation. Êa, the all-wise himself, it was believed, had appeared to men and taught them things human and divine. Berosus faithfully reports the legend, but seems to have given the God's name "Êa-Han" ("Êa the Fish") under the corrupted

Greek form of OANNES. This is the narrative, of which we already know the first line:

"There was originally at Babylon a multitude of men of foreign race who had colonized Chaldea, and they lived without order, like animals. But in the first year" (meaning the first year of the new order of things, the new dispensation) "there appeared, from out of the Erythrean Sea (the ancient Greek name for the Persian Gulf) where it borders upon Babylonia, an animal endowed with reason, who was called OANNES. The whole body of the animal was that of a fish, but under the fish's head he had another head, and also feet below, growing out of his fish's tail, similar to those of a man; also human speech, and his image is preserved to this day. This being used to spend the whole day amidst men, without taking any food, and he gave them an insight into letters, and sciences, and every kind of art; he taught them how to found cities, to construct temples, to introduce laws and to measure land; he showed them how to sow seeds and gather in crops; in short, he instructed them in everything that softens manners and makes up civilization, so that from that time no one has invented anything new. Then, when the sun went down, this monstrous Oannes used to plunge back into the sea and spend the night in the midst of the boundless waves, for he was amphibious."

2. The question, *Who* were the bringers of this advanced civilization? has caused much division among the most eminent scholars. Two solutions are offered. Both being based on many and serious

grounds and supported by illustrious names, and the point being far from settled yet, it is but fair to state them both. The two greatest of German assyriologists, Professors Eberhard Schrader and Friedrich Delitzsch, and the German school which acknowledges them as leaders, hold that the bringers of the new and more perfect civilization were Semites—descendants of Shem, i.e., people of the same race as the Hebrews—while the late François Lenormant and his followers contend that they were Cushites in the first instance,—i.e., belonged to that important family of nations which we find grouped, in Chapter X. of Genesis, under the name of Cush, himself a son of Ham—and that the Semitic immigration came second. As the latter hypothesis puts forward, among other arguments, the authority of the Biblical historians, and moreover involves the destinies of a very numerous and vastly important branch of ancient humanity, we will yield to it the right of precedence.

3. The name "HAM" signifies "brown, dark" (not "black"). Therefore, to speak of certain nations as "sons of Ham," is to say that they belonged to "the Dark Race." Yet, originally, this great section of Noah's posterity was as white of color as the other two. It seems to have first existed as a separate race in a region not very distant from the high table-land of Central Asia, the probable first cradle of mankind. That division of this great section which again separated and became the race of Cush, appears to have been drawn southwards by reasons which it is, of course, impossible to ascertain. It

57.—OANNES.
(Smith's "Chaldean Genesis.")

is easier to guess at the route they must have taken along the HINDU CUSH,* a range of mountains which must have been to it a barrier in the west, and which joins the western end of the Himâlaya, the mightiest mountain-chain in the world. The break between the Hindu-Cush and the Himâlaya forms a mountain pass, just at the spot where the river INDUS (most probably the PISCHON of Gen., Ch. II.) turns abruptly to the south, to water the rich plains of India. Through this pass, and following the course of the river, further Cushite detachments must have penetrated into that vast and attractive peninsula, even to the south of it, where they found a population mostly belonging to the Black branch of humanity, so persistently ignored by the writer of Chap. X. Hundreds of years spent under a tropical clime and intermarriage with the Negro natives altered not only the color of their skin, but also the shape of their features. So that when Cushite tribes, with the restless migratory spirit so characteristic of all early ages, began to work their way back again to the north, then to the west, along the shores of the Indian Ocean and the Persian Gulf, they were both dark-skinned and thick-lipped, with a decided tendency towards the Negro type, lesser or greater according to the degree of mixture with the inferior race. That this type was foreign to them is proved by the facility with which their features resumed the nobler cast of the white races wherever they stayed long enough among these, as was the case in Chaldea, in Arabia, in the

* Names are often deceptive. That of the Hindu-Cush is now thought to mean " Killers of Hindus," probably in allusion to robber tribes of the mountains, and to have nothing to do with the Cushite race.

countries of Canaan, whither many of these tribes wandered at various times.

4. Some Cushite detachments, who reached the straits of Bab-el-Mandeb, crossed over into Africa, and settling there amidst the barbarous native negro tribes, formed a nation which became known to its northern neighbors, the Egyptians, to the Hebrews, and throughout the ancient East under its own proper name of CUSH, and whose outward characteristics came, in the course of time, so near to the pure Negro type as to be scarcely recognizable from it. This is the same nation which, to us moderns, is better known under the name of ETHIOPIANS, given to it by the Greeks, as well as to the eastern division of the same race. The Egyptians themselves were another branch of the same great section of humanity, represented in the genealogy of Chap. X. by the name of MIZRAIM, second son of Ham. These must have come from the east along the Persian Gulf, then across Northern Arabia and the Isthmus of Suez. In the color and features of the Egyptians the mixture with black races is also noticeable, but not enough to destroy the beauty and expressiveness of the original type, at all events far less than in their southern neighbors, the Ethiopians, with whom, moreover, they were throughout on the worst of terms, whom they loathed and invariably designated under the name of "vile Cush."

5. A third and very important branch of the Hamite family, the CANAANITES, after reaching the Persian Gulf, and probably sojourning there some

time, spread, not to the south, but to the west, across the plains of Syria, across the mountain chain of LEBANON and to the very edge of the Mediterranean Sea, occupying all the land which later became Palestine, also to the north-west, as far as the mountain chain of TAURUS. This group was very numerous, and broken up into a great many peoples, as we can judge from the list of nations given in Chap. X. (v. 15-18) as "sons of Canaan." In its migrations over this comparatively northern region, Canaan found and displaced not black natives, but Turanian nomadic tribes, who roamed at large over grassy wildernesses and sandy wastes and are possibly to be accounted as the representatives of that portion of the race which the biblical historian embodies in the pastoral names of Jabal and Jubal—(Gen. iv., 20-22)—" The father of such as dwell in tents and have cattle," and "the father of all such as handle the harp and pipe." In which case the Turanian settlers and builders of cities would answer to Tubalcain, the smith and artificer. The Canaanites, therefore, are those among the Hamites who, in point of color and features, have least differed from their kindred white races, though still sufficiently bronzed to be entitled to the name of "sons of Ham," i.e., "belonging to the dark-skinned race."

6. Migrating races do not traverse continents with the same rapidity as marching armies. The progress is slow, the stations are many. Every station becomes a settlement, sometimes the beginning of a new nation—so many landmarks along the way.

And the distance between the starting-point and the furthest point reached by the race is measured not only by thousands of miles, but also by hundreds and hundreds of years; only the space can be actually measured, while the time can be computed merely by conjecture. The route from the south of India, along the shore of Malabar, the Persian Gulf, across the Arabian deserts, then down along the Red Sea and across the straits into Africa, is of such tremendous length that the settlements which the Cushite race left scattered along it must have been more than usually numerous. According to the upholders of a Cushite colonization of Chaldea, one important detachment appears to have taken possession of the small islands along the eastern shore of the Persian Gulf and to have stayed there for several centuries, probably choosing these island homes on account of their seclusion and safety from invasion. There, unmolested and undisturbed, they could develop a certain spirit of abstract speculation to which their natural bent inclined them. They were great star-gazers and calculators—two tastes which go well together, for Astronomy cannot exist without Mathematics. But star-gazing is also favorable to dreaming, and the Cushite islanders had time for dreams. Thoughts of heavenly things occupied them much; they worked out a religion beautiful in many ways and full of deep sense; their priests dwelt in communities or colleges, probably one on every island, and spent their time not only in scientific study and religious contemplation, but also in the more practical art of government, for there do not appear as yet to have been any kings among them.

7. But there came a time when the small islands were overcrowded with the increased population, and detachments began to cross the water and land at the furthest point of the Gulf, in the land of the great rivers. Here they found a people not unpractised in several primitive arts, and possessed of some important fundamental inventions—writing, irrigation by means of canals—but deplorably deficient in spiritual development, and positively barbarous in the presence of an altogether higher culture. The Cushites rapidly spread through the land of Shumir and Accad, and taught the people with whom they afterwards, as usual, intermarried, until both formed but one nation—with this difference, that towards the north of Chaldea the Cushite element became predominant, while in the south numbers remained on the side of the Turanians. Whether this result was attained altogether peacefully or was preceded by a period of resistance and fighting, we have no means of ascertaining. If there was such a period, it cannot have lasted long, for intellect was on the side of the newcomers, and that is a power which soon wins the day. At all events the final fusion must have been complete and friendly, since the old national legend reported by Berosus cleverly combines the two elements, by attributing the part of teacher and revealer to the Shumiro-Accad's own favorite divine being Êa, while it is not impossible that it alludes to the coming of the Cushites in making the amphibious

Oannes rise out of the Persian Gulf, "where it borders on Chaldea." The legend goes on to say that Oannes set down his revelations in books which he consigned into the keeping of men, and that several more divine animals of the same kind continued to appear at long intervals. Who knows but the latter strange detail may have been meant to allude fantastically to the arrival of successive Cushite colonies? In the long run of time, of course all such meaning would be forgotten and the legend remain as a miraculous and inexplicable incident.

8. It would be vain to attempt to fix any dates for events which took place in such remote antiquity, in the absence of any evidence or document that might be grasped. Yet, by close study of facts, by laborious and ingenious comparing of later texts, of every scrap of evidence furnished by monuments, of information contained in the fragments of Berosus and of other writers, mostly Greek, it has been possible, with due caution, to arrive at some approximative dates, which, after all, are all that is needed to classify things in an order intelligible and correct in the main. Even should further discoveries and researches arrive at more exact results, the gain will be comparatively small. At such a distance, differences of a couple of centuries do not matter much. When we look down a long line of houses or trees, the more distant ones appear to run together, and we do not always see where it ends—yet we can perfectly well pursue its direction. The same with the so-called double stars in astronomy: they are stars which, though really separated by thousands

of miles, appear as one on account of the immense distance between them and our eye, and only the strongest telescope lenses show them to be separate bodies, though still close together. Yet this is sufficient to assign them their place so correctly on the map of the heavens, that they do not disturb the calculations in which they are included. The same kind of perspective applies to the history of remote antiquity. As the gloom which has covered it so long slowly rolls back before the light of scientific research, we begin to discern outlines and landmarks, at first so dim and wavering as rather to mislead than to instruct; but soon the searcher's eye, sharpened by practice, fixes them sufficiently to bring them into connection with the later and more fully illumined portions of the eternally unrolling picture. Chance, to which all discoverers are so much indebted, frequently supplies such a landmark, and now and then one so firm and distinct as to become a trustworthy centre for a whole group.

9. The annals of the Assyrian king Asshurbanipal (the founder of the great Library at Nineveh) have established beyond a doubt the first positive date that has been secured for the History of Chaldea. That king was for a long time at war with the neighboring kingdom of ELAM, and ended by conquering and destroying its capital, SHUSHAN (Susa), after carrying away all the riches from the royal palace and all the statues from the great temple. This happened in the year 645 B.C. In the inscriptions in which he records this event, the king informs us that in that temple he found a statue of

the Chaldean goddess NANA, which had been carried away from her own temple in the city of UR-UKH (Erech, now Warka) by a king of Elam of the name of KHUDUR-NANKHUNDI, who invaded the land of Accad 1635 years before, and that he, Asshurbanipal, by the goddess's own express command, took her from where she had dwelt in Elam, "a place not appointed her," and reinstated her in her own sanctuary "which she had delighted in." 1635 added to 645 make 2280, a date not to be disputed. Now if a successful Elamite invasion in 2280 found in Chaldea famous sanctuaries to desecrate, the religion to which these sanctuaries belonged, that of the Cushite, or Semitic colonists, must have been established in the country already for several, if not many, centuries. Indeed, quite recent discoveries show that it had been so considerably over a thousand years, so that we cannot possibly accept a date later than 4000 B.C. for the foreign immigration. The Shumiro-Accadian culture was too firmly rooted then and too completely worked out—as far as it went—to allow less than about 1000 years for its establishment. This takes us as far back as 5000 B.C.—a pretty respectable figure, especially when we think of the vista of time which opens behind it, and for which calculation fairly fails us. For if the Turanian settlers brought the rudiments of that culture from the highlands of Elam, how long had they sojourned there before they descended into the plains? And how long had it taken them to reach that station on their way from the race's mountain home in the far Northeast, in the Altai valleys?

10. However that may be, 5000 B.C. is a moderate and probable date. But ancient nations were not content with such, when they tried to locate and classify their own beginnings. These being necessarily obscure and only vaguely shadowed out in traditions which gained in fancifulness and lost in probability with every succeeding generation that received them and handed them down to the next, they loved to magnify them by enshrouding them in the mystery of innumerable ages. The more appalling the figures, the greater the glory. Thus we gather from some fragments of Berosus that, according to the national Chaldean tradition, there was an interval of over 259,000 years between the first appearance of Oannes and the first king. Then come ten successive kings, each of whom reigns a no less extravagant number of years (one 36,000, another 43,000, even 64,000; 10,800 being the most modest figure), till the aggregate of all these different periods makes up the pretty sum total of 691,-200 years, supposed to have elapsed from the first appearance of Oannes to the Deluge. It is so impossible to imagine so prodigious a number of years or couple with it anything at all real, that we might just as well substitute for such a figure the simpler "very, very long ago," or still better, the approved fairy tale beginning, "There was once upon a time. . . ." It conveys quite as definite a notion, and would, in such a case, be the more appropriate,

that all a nation's most marvellous traditions, most fabulous legends, are naturally placed in those stupendously remote ages which no record could reach, no experience control. Although these traditions and legends generally had a certain body of actual truth and dimly remembered fact in them, which might still be apparent to the learned and the cultivated few, the ignorant masses of the people swallowed the thing whole, as real history, and found things acknowledged as impossible easy to believe, for the simple reason that "it was so very long ago!" A Chaldean of Alexander's time certainly did not expect to meet a divine Man-Fish in his walks along the sea-shore, but—there was no knowing what might or might not have happened seven hundred thousand years ago! In the legend of the six successive apparitions under the first ten long-lived kings, he would not have descried the simple sense so lucidly set forth by Mr. Maspero, one of the most distinguished of French Orientalists:— "The times preceding the Deluge represented an experimental period, during which mankind, being as yet barbarous, had need of divine assistance to overcome the difficulties with which it was surrounded. Those times were filled up with six manifestations of the deity, doubtless answering to the number of sacred books in which the priests saw the most complete expression of revealed law."* This presents another and more probable explanation of the legend than the one suggested above,

---

* "Histoire Ancienne des Peuples de l'Orient," 1878, p. 160.

(end of § 7); but there is no more actual *proof* of the one than of the other being the correct one.

11. If Chaldea was in after times a battle-ground of nations, it was in the beginning a very nursery and hive of peoples. The various races in their migrations must necessarily have been attracted and arrested by the exceeding fertility of its soil, which it is said, in the times of its highest prosperity and under proper conditions of irrigation, yielded two hundredfold return for the grain it received. Settlement must have followed settlement in rapid succession. But the nomadic element was for a long time still very prevalent, and side by side with the builders of cities and tillers of fields, shepherd tribes roamed peacefully over the face of the land, tolerated and unmolested by the permanent population, with which they mixed but warily, occasionally settling down temporarily, and shifting their settlements as safety or advantage required it, —or wandering off altogether from that common halting-place, to the north, and west, and southwest. This makes it very plain why Chaldea is given as the land where the tongues became confused and the second separation of races took place.

12. Of those principally nomadic tribes the greatest part did not belong, like the Cushites or Canaanites, to the descendants of Ham, "the Dark," but to those of SHEM, whose name, signifying "Glory, Renown," stamps him as the eponymous ancestor of that race which has always firmly believed itself to be the chosen one of God. They were Semites.

When they arrived on the plains of Chaldea, they were inferior in civilization to the people among whom they came to dwell. They knew nothing of city arts and had all to learn. They did learn, for superior culture always asserts its power,—even to the language of the Cushite settlers, which the latter were rapidly substituting for the rude and poor Turanian idiom of Shumir and Accad. This language, or rather various dialects of it, were common to most Hamitic and Semitic tribes, among whom that from which the Hebrews sprang brought it to its greatest perfection. The others worked it into different kindred dialects—the Assyrian, the Aramaic or Syrian, the Arabic—according to their several peculiarities. The Phœnicians of the seashore, and all the Canaanite nations, also spoke languages belonging to the same family, and therefore classed among the so-called Semitic tongues. Thus it has come to pass that philology,—or the Science of Languages,—adopted a wrong name for that entire group, calling the languages belonging to it, "Semitic," while, in reality, they are originally "Hamitic." The reason is that the Hamitic origin of those important languages which have been called Semitic these hundred years had not been discovered until very lately, and to change the name now would produce considerable confusion.

13. Most of the Semitic tribes who dwelt in Chaldea adopted not only the Cushite language, but the Cushite culture and religion. Asshur carried all three northward, where the Assyrian kingdom arose out of a few Babylonian colonies,

and Aram westward to the land which was afterwards called Southern Syria, and where the great city of Damascus long flourished and still exists. But there was one tribe of higher spiritual gifts than the others. It was not numerous, for through many generations it consisted of only one great family governed by its own eldest chief or patriarch. It is true that such a family, with the patriarch's own children and children's children, its wealth of horses, camels, flocks of sheep, its host of servants and slaves, male and female, represented quite a respectable force; Abraham could muster three hundred eighteen armed and *trained* servants who had been born in his own household. This particular tribe seems to have wandered for some time on the outskirts of Chaldea and in the land itself, as indicated by the name given to its eponym in Chap. X.: ARPHAXAD (more correctly ARPHAKSHAD), corrupted from AREPH-KASDÎM, which means, "bordering on the Chaldeans," or perhaps "boundaries"—in the sense of "land"—of the Chaldeans. Generation after generation pushed further westward, traversed the land of Shinar, crossed the Euphrates and reached the city of Ur, in or near which the tribe dwelt many years.

14. Ur was then the greatest city of Southern Chaldea. The earliest known kings of Shumir resided in it, and besides that, it was the principal commercial mart of the country. For, strange as it may appear when we look on a modern map, Ur, the ruins of which are now 150 miles from the sea, **was then a maritime city, with harbor and ship**

docks. The waters of the Gulf reached much further inland than they do now. There was then a distance of many miles between the mouths of the Tigris and Euphrates, and Ur lay very near the mouth of the latter river. Like all commercial and maritime cities, it was the resort not only of all the different races which dwelt in the land itself, but also of foreign traders. The active intellectual life of a capital, too, which was at the same time a great religious centre and the seat of a powerful priesthood, must of necessity have favored interchange of ideas, and have exerted an influence on that Semitic tribe of whom the Bible tells us that it "went forth from Ur of the Chaldees, to go into the land of Canaan," led by the patriarch Terah and his son Abraham (Genesis xi. 31). The historian of Genesis here, as throughout the narrative, does not mention any date whatever for the event he relates; nor does he hint at the cause of this removal. On the first of these points the study of Chaldean cuneiform monuments throws considerable light, while the latter does not admit of more than guesses—of which something hereafter.

15. Such is a broad and cursory outline of the theory according to which Cushite immigrations preceded the arrival of the Semites in the land of Shumir and Accad. Those who uphold it give several reasons for their opinion, such as that the Bible several times mentions a Cush located in the East and evidently different from the Cush which has been identified as Ethiopia; that, in Chap. X. of Genesis (8-12), Nimrod, the legendary hero,

whose empire at first was in "the land of Shinar," and who is said to have "gone forth out of that land into Assyria," is called a son of Cush; that the most ancient Greek poets knew of "Ethiopians" in the far East as opposed to those of the South—and several more. Those scholars who oppose this theory dismiss it wholesale. They will not admit the existence of a Cushite element or migration in the East at all, and put down the expressions in the Bible as simple mistakes, either of the writers or copyists. According to them, there was only one immigration in the land of Shumir and Accad, that of the Semites, achieved through many ages and in numerous instalments. The language which superseded the ancient Shumiro-Accadian idiom is to them a Semitic one in the directest and most exclusive sense; the culture grafted on that of the earlier population is by them called purely "Semitic;" while their opponents frequently use the compound designation of "Cushito-Semitic," to indicate the two distinct elements of which, to them, it appears composed. It must be owned that the anti-Cushite opinion is gaining ground. Yet the Cushite theory cannot be considered as disposed of, only "not proven,"—or not sufficiently so, and therefore in abeyance and fallen into some disfavor. With this proviso we shall adopt the word "Semitic," as the simpler and more generally used.

16. It is only with the rise of Semitic culture in Southern Mesopotamia that we enter on a period which, however remote, misty, and full of

blanks, may still be called, in a measure, "historical," because there is a certain number of facts, of which contemporary monuments give positive evidence. True, the connection between those facts is often not apparent; their causes and effects are frequently not to be made out save by more or less daring conjectures; still there are numerous landmarks of proven fact, and with these real history begins. No matter if broad gaps have to be left open or temporarily filled with guesses. New discoveries are almost daily turning up, inscriptions, texts, which unexpectedly here supply a missing link, there confirm or demolish a conjecture, establish or correct dates which had long been puzzles or suggested on insufficient foundations. In short, details may be supplied as yet brokenly and sparingly, but the general outline of the condition of Chaldea may be made out as far back as forty centuries before Christ.

17. Of one thing there can be no doubt: that our earliest glimpse of the political condition of Chaldea shows us the country divided into numerous small states, each headed by a great city, made famous and powerful by the sanctuary or temple of some particular deity, and ruled by a *patesi*, a title which is now thought to mean *priestking*, i.e., priest and king in one. There can be little doubt that the beginning of the city was everywhere the temple, with its college of ministering priests, and that the surrounding settlement was gradually formed by pilgrims and worshippers. That royalty developed out of the priesthood is

also more than probable, and consequently must have been, in its first stage, a form of priestly rule, and, in a great measure, subordinate to priestly influence. There comes a time when for the title of *patesi* is substituted that of "king" simply—a change which very possibly indicates the assumption by the kings of a more independent attitude towards the class from which their power originally sprang. It is noticeable that the distinction between the Semitic newcomers and the indigenous Shumiro-Accadians continues long to be traceable in the names of the royal temple-builders, even after the new Semitic idiom, which we call the Assyrian, had entirely ousted the old language—a process which must have taken considerable time, for it appears, and indeed stands to reason, that the newcomers, in order to secure the wished for influence and propagate their own culture, at first not only learned to understand but actually used themselves the language of the people among whom they came, at least in their public documents. This it is that explains the fact that so many inscriptions and tablets, while written in the dialect of Shumir or Accad, are Semitic in spirit and in the grade of culture they betray. Furthermore, even superficial observation shows that the old language and the old names survive longest in Shumir,—the South. From this fact it is to be inferred with little chance of mistake that the North,—the land of Accad,—was earlier Semitized, that the Semitic immigrants established their first headquarters in that part of the country, that their power and influence thence spread to the South.

18. Fully in accordance with these indications, the first grand historical figure that meets us at the threshold of Chaldean history, dim with the mists of ages and fabulous traditions, yet unmistakably real, is that of the Semite SHARRUKIN, king of Accad—or AGADÊ, as the great Northern city came to be called—more generally known in history under the corrupt modern reading of SARGON, and called Sargon I., "the First," to distinguish him from another monarch of the same name who was found to have reigned many centuries later. As to the city of Agadê, it is no other than the city of Accad mentioned in Genesis x., 10. It was situated close to the Euphrates on a wide canal just opposite Sippar, so that in time the two cities came to be considered as one double city, and the Hebrews always called it "the two Sippars"—SEPHARVAIM, which is often spoken of in the Bible. It was there that Sharrukin established his rule, and a statue was afterwards raised to him there, the inscription on which, making him speak, as usual, in the first person, begins with the proud declaration: "Sharrukin, the mighty king, the king of Agadê, am I." Yet, although his reforms and conquests were of lasting importance, and himself remained one of the favorite heroes of Chaldean tradition, he appears to have been an adventurer and usurper. Perhaps he was, for this very reason, all the dearer to the popular fancy, which, in the absence of positive facts concerning his birth and origin, wove around them a halo of

romance, and told of him a story which must be nearly as old as mankind, for it has been told over and over again, in different countries and ages, of a great many famous kings and heroes. This of Sharrukin is the oldest known version of it, and the inscription on his statue puts it into the king's own mouth. It makes him say that he knew not his father, and that his mother, a princess, gave him birth in a hiding-place, (or " an inaccessible place "), near the Euphrates, but that his family were the rulers of the land. " She placed me in a basket of rushes," the king is further made to say; " with bitumen the door of my ark she closed. She launched me on the river, which drowned me not. The river bore me along; to Akki, the water-carrier, it brought me. Akki, the water-carrier, in the tenderness of his heart lifted me up. Akki, the water-carrier, as his own child brought me up. Akki, the water-carrier, made me his gardener. And in my gardenership the goddess Ishtar loved me. . . . ."

19. Whatever his origin and however he came by the royal power, Sargon was a great monarch. It is said that he undertook successful expeditions into Syria, and a campaign into Elam ; that with captives of the conquered races he partly peopled his new capital, Agadê, where he built a palace and a magnificent temple; that on one occasion he was absent three years, during which time he advanced to the very shores of the Mediterranean, which he calls " the sea of the setting sun," and where he left memorial records of his deeds, and returned home in triumph, bringing with him immense spoils. The

inscription contains only the following very moderate mention of his military career: "For forty-five years the kingdom I have ruled. And the black-head race (Accadian) I have governed. In multi-

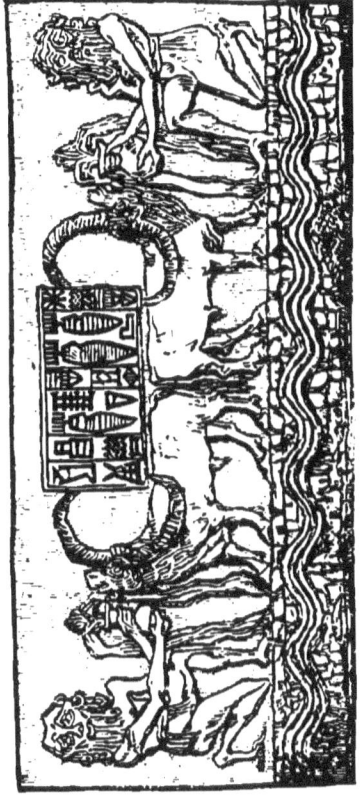

58.—CYLINDER OF SARGON, FROM AGADE.
(Hommel, "Gesch. Babyloniens u. Assyriens.")

tudes of bronze chariots I rode over rugged lands. I governed the upper countries. Three times to the coast of the (Persian) sea I advanced. . . ."*

20. This Sharrukin must not be confounded with

---

* Translation of Professor A. H. Sayce.

another king of the same name, who reigned also in Agadè, some 1800 years later (about 2000 B.C.), and in whose time was completed and brought into definite shape a vast religious reform which had been slowly working itself out ever since the Semitic and Accadian elements began to mix in matters of spiritual speculation and worship. What was the result of the amalgamation will form the subject of the next chapter. Suffice it here to say that the religion of Chaldea in the form which it assumed under the second Sharrukin remained fixed forever, and when Babylonian religion is spoken of, it is that which is understood by that name. The great theological work demanded a literary undertaking no less great. The incantations and magic forms of the first, purely Turanian, period had to be collected and put in order, as well as the hymns and prayers of the second period, composed under the influence of a higher and more spiritual religious feeling. But all this literature was in the language of the older population, while the ruling class—the royal houses and the priesthood—were becoming almost exclusively Semitic. It was necessary, therefore, that they should study the old language and learn it so thoroughly as not only to understand and read it, but to be able to use it, in speaking and writing. For that purpose Sargon not only ordered the ancient texts, when collected and sorted, to be copied on clay tablets with the translation—either between the lines, or on opposite columns—into the now generally used modern Semitic language, which we may as well begin to call by its usual name, Assyrian, but gave directions for the compilation of grammars and vocabularies,—the very works which have enabled the scholars of the present day to arrive at the understanding of that prodigiously ancient tongue which, without such assistance, must have remained a sealed book forever.

21. Such is the origin of the great collection in three books and two hundred tablets, the contents of which made the subject of the preceding chapter. To this must be added another great work, in seventy tablets, in Assyrian, on astrology, i.e., the supposed influence of the heavenly bodies, according to their positions and conjunctions, on the fate of nations and individuals and on the course of things on earth generally—an influence which was firmly believed in; and probably yet a third work, on omens, prodigies and divination. To carry out these extensive literary labors, to treasure the results worthily and safely, Sargon II. either founded or greatly enlarged the library of the priestly college at Urukh (Erech), so that this city came to be called "the City of Books." This repository became the most important one in all Chaldea, and when, fourteen centuries later, the Assyrian Asshurbanipal sent his scribes all over the country, to collect copies of the ancient, sacred and scientific texts for his own royal library at Nineveh, it was at Erech that they gathered their most abundant harvest, being specially favored there by the priests, who were on excellent terms with the king after he had

brought back from Shushan and restored to them the statue of their goddess Nana. Agadè thus became the headquarters, as it were, of the Semitic influence and reform, which spread thence towards the South, forming a countercurrent to the culture of Shumir, which had steadily progressed from the Gulf northward.

22. It is just possible that Sargon's collection may have also comprised literature of a lighter nature than those ponderous works on magic and astrology. At least, a work on agriculture has been found, which is thought to have been compiled for the same king's library,* and which contains bits of popular poetry (maxims, riddles, short peasant songs) of the kind that is now called "folk-lore." Of the correctness of the supposition there is, as yet, no absolute proof, but as some of these fragments, of which unfortunately but few could be recovered, are very interesting and pretty in their way, this is perhaps the best place to insert them. The following four may be called "Maxims," and the first is singularly pithy and powerfully expressed.

> 1. Like an oven that is old
>   Against thy foes be hard and strong.
>
> 2. May he suffer vengeance,
>   May it be returned to him,
>   Who gives the provocation.
>
> 3. If evil thou doest,
>   To the everlasting sea
>   Thou shalt surely go.

---

* A. H. Sayce.

4. Thou wentest, thou spoiledst
The land of the foe,
For the foe came and spoiled
Thy land, even thine.

23. It will be noticed that No. 3 alone expresses moral feeling of a high standard, and is distinctively Semitic in spirit, the same spirit which is expressed in a loftier and purely religious vein, and a more poetical form in one of the "Penitential Psalms," where it says:

Whoso fears not his god—will be cut off even like a reed.
Whoso honors not the goddess—his bodily strength shall waste away;
Like a star of heaven, his light shall wane; like waters of the night he shall disappear.

Some fragments can be well imagined as being sung by the peasant at work to his ploughing team, in whose person he sometimes speaks:

5. A heifer am I,—to the cow I am yoked;
The plough handle is strong—lift it up! lift it up!

6. My knees are marching—my feet are not resting;
With no wealth of thy own—grain thou makest for me.*

24. A great deal of additional interest in the elder Sargon of Agadê has lately been excited by an extraordinary discovery connected with him, which produced a startling revolution in the hitherto accepted Chaldean chronology. This question of dates is always a most intricate and puzzling one in dealing with ancient Oriental nations, because they did not date their years from some particular event,

---

* Translated by A. H. Sayce, in his paper "Babylonian Folklore" in the "Folk-lore Journal," Vol. I., Jan., 1883.

as we do, and as did the Mohammedans, the Greeks and the Romans. In the inscriptions things are said to have happened in the year so-and-so of such a king's reign. Where to place that king is the next question—unanswerable, unless, as fortunately is mostly the case, some clue is supplied, to borrow a legal term, by circumstantial evidence. Thus, if an eclipse is mentioned, the time can easily be determined by the help of astronomy, which can calculate backward as well as forward. Or else, an event or a person belonging to another country is alluded to, and if they are known to us from other sources, that is a great help. Such a coincidence (which is called a SYNCHRONISM) is most valuable, and dates established by synchronisms are generally reliable. Then, luckily for us, Assyrian and Babylonian kings of a late period, whose dates are fixed and proved beyond a doubt, were much in the habit, in their historical inscriptions, of mentioning events that had taken place before their time and specifying the number of years elapsed, often also the king under whose reign the event, whatever it was, had taken place. This is the most precious clue of all, as it is infallible, and besides ascertaining one point, gives a firm foothold, whereby to arrive at many others. The famous memorandum of Asshurbanipal, already so often referred to, about the carrying away of the goddess Nana, (i.e., her statue) from her temple at Erech is evidence of this kind. Any dates suggested without any of these clues as basis are of necessity untrustworthy, and no true scholar dreams of offering any such date, except as a temporary suggestion, awaiting confirmation or abolition from subsequent researches. So it was with Sargon I. of Agadê. There was no positive indication of the time at which he lived, except that he could not possibly have lived later than 2000 B.C. Scholars therefore agreed to assign that date to him, approximatively — a little more or less — thinking they could not go very far wrong in so doing. Great therefore was the commotion produced by the discovery of a cylinder of Nabonidus, the last king of Babylon (whose date is 550 B.C.), wherein he speaks of repairs he made in the great Sun-temple at Sippar, and declares having dug deep in its foundations for the cylinders of the founder, thus describing his success: "Shamash (the Sun-god), the great lord . . . suffered me to behold the foundation-cylinder of NARAM-SIN, the son of Sharrukin, which for thrice thousand and twice hundred years none of the kings that lived before me had seen." The simple addition 3200 + 550 gives 3750 B.C. as the date of Naram-Sin, and 3800 as that of his father Sargon, allowing for the latter's long reign! A scene-shifting of 1800 years at one slide seemed something so startling that there was much hesitation in accepting the evidence, unanswerable as it seemed, and the possibility of an error of the engraver was seriously considered. Some other documents, however, were found independently of each other and in different places, corroborating the statement on Nabonidus' cylinder, and the tremendously ancient date of 3800 B.C. is now generally accepted the elder Sargon of Agadè—perhaps the remotest *authentic* date yet arrived at in history.

25. When we survey and attempt to grasp and classify the materials we have for an early "History of Chaldea," it appears almost presumptuous to grace so necessarily lame an attempt with so ambitious a name. The landmarks are so few and far between, so unconnected as yet, and there is so much uncertainty about them, especially about placing them. The experience with Sargon of Agadè has not been encouraging to conjectural chronology; yet with such we must in many cases be content until more lucky finds turn up to set us right. What, for instance, is the proper place of GUDÊA, the *patesi* of SIRBURLA (also read SIRGULLA or SIRTILLA, and, lately, ZIRLABA), whose magnificent statues Mr. de Sarzec found in the principal hall of the temple of which the bricks bear his stamp? (See p. 217.) The title of *patesi*, (not "king"), points to great antiquity, and he is pretty generally understood to have lived somewhere between 4000 and 3000 B.C. That he was not a Semite, but an Accadian prince, is to be concluded not only from the language of his inscriptions and the writing, which is of the most archaic—i.e., ancient and old-fashioned—character, but from the fact that the head, which was found with the statues, is strikingly Turanian in form and features, shaved, too, and turbaned after a fashion still used in Central Asia. Altogether it might easily be taken for that of a modern Mongolian or Tatar.[*] The discovery of this builder and patron of art has

---

[*] See Figs. 44 and 45, p. 101.

greatly eclipsed the glory of a somewhat later ruler, UR-ÊA, King of Ur,* who had long enjoyed the reputation of being the earliest known temple-builder. He remains at all events the first powerful monarch we read of in Southern Chaldea, of which Ur appears to have been in some measure the capital, at least in so far as to have a certain supremacy over the other great cities of Shumir.

26. Of these Shumir had many, even more venerable for their age and holiness than those of Accad. For the South was the home of the old race and most ancient culture, and thence both had advanced northward. Hence it was that the old stock was hardier there and endured longer in its language, religion and nationality, and was slower in yielding to the Semitic counter-current of race and culture, which, as a natural consequence, obtained an earlier and stronger hold in the North, and from there radiated over the whole of Mesopotamia. There was ERIDHU, by the sea "at the mouth of the Rivers," the immemorial sanctuary of Êa; there was SIRGULLA, so lately unknown, now the most promising mine for research; there was LARSAM, famous with the glories of its "House of the Sun" (Ê-Babbara in the old language), the rival of Ur, the city of the Moon-god, whose kings UR-ÊA and his son DUNGI were, it appears, the first to take

---

* This name was at first read Urukh, then Likbabi, then Likbagash, then Urbagash, then Urba'u, and now Professor Friedr. Delitzsch announces that the final and correct reading is in all probability either Ur-ea or Arad-ea.

the ambitious title of "Kings of Shumir and Accad" and "Kings of the Four Regions." As for Babylon, proud Babylon, which we have so long been accustomed to think of as the very beginning of state life and political rule in Chaldea, it was perhaps not yet built at all, or only modestly beginning its existence under its Accadian name of TIN-TIR-KI ("the Place of Life"), or, somewhat later, KA-DIMIRRA ("Gate of God"), when already the above named cities, and several more, had each its famous temple with ministering college of priests, and, probably, library, and each its king. But political power was for a long time centred at Ur. The first kings of Ur authentically known to us are Ur-êa and his son Dungi, who have left abundant traces of their existence in the numerous temples they built, not in Ur alone, but in most other cities too. Their bricks have been identified at Larsam (Senkereh), and, it appears, at Sirburla (Tel-Loh), at Nipur (Niffer) and at Urukh (Erech, Warka), and as the two latter cities belonged to Accad, they seem to have ruled at least part of that country and thus to have been justified in assuming their high-sounding title.

27. It has been noticed that the bricks bearing the name of Ur-êa "are found in a lower position than any others, at the very foundation of buildings;" that "they are of a rude and coarse make, of many sizes and ill-fitted together;" that baked bricks are rare among them; that they are held together by the oldest substitutes for mortar—mud and bitumen—and that the writing upon them is

curiously rude and imperfect.* But whatever King Ur-êa's architectural efforts may lack in perfection, they certainly make up in size and number. Those

59.—STATUE OF GUDÊA, WITH INSCRIPTION; FROM TELL-LOH, (SIRBURLA OR SIRGULLA). SARZEC COLLECTION.
(Hommel).

that he did not complete, his son Dungi continued after him. It is remarkable that these great build-

---

* Geo. Rawlinson, " Five Great Monarchies of the Ancient Eastern World" (1862), Vol. I., pp. 198 and ff.

ers seem to have devoted their energies exclusively to religious purposes; also that, while their names are Shumiro-Accadian, and their inscriptions are often in that language, the temples they constructed were dedicated to various deities of the new, or rather reformed religion. When we see the princes of the South, according to an ingenious remark of Mr. Lenormant, thus begin a sort of practical preaching of the Semitized religion, we may take it as a sign of the times, as an unmistakable proof of the influence of the North, political as well as religious. A very curious relic of King Ur-ea was found—his own signet cylinder—which was lost by an accident, then turned up again and is now in the British Museum. It represents the Moon-god seated on a throne,—as is but meet for the king of the Moon-god's special city— with priests presenting worshippers. No definite date is of course assignable to Ur-êa and the important epoch of Chaldean history which he represents. But a very probable approximative one can be arrived at, thanks to a clue supplied by the same Nabonidus, last King of Babylon, who settled the Sargon question for us so unexpectedly. That monarch was as zealous a repairer of temples as his predecessors had been zealous builders. He had reasons of his own to court popularity, and could think of nothing better than to restore the time-honored sanctuaries of the land. Among others he repaired the Sun-temple (Ê-Babbara) at Larsam, whereof we are duly informed by a special cylinder. In it he tells posterity that he found a cylinder of

King Hammurabi intact in its chamber under the corner-stone, which cylinder states that the temple was founded 700 years before Hammurabi's time; as Ur-êa was the founder, it only remains to determine the latter king's date in order to know that of the earlier one.* Here unfortunately scholars differ, not having as yet any decisive authority to build upon. Some place Hammurabi *before* 2000 B.C., others a little later. It is perhaps safest, therefore, to assume that Ur-êa can scarcely have lived much earlier than 2800 or much later than 2500 B.C. At all events, he must necessarily have lived somewhat before 2300 B.C., for about this latter year took place the Elamite invasion recorded by Asshurbanipal, an invasion which, as this King expressly mentions, laid waste the land of Accad and desecrated its temples—evidently the same ones which Ur-êa and Dungi so piously constructed. Nor was this a passing inroad or raid of booty-seeking mountaineers. It was a real conquest. Khudur-Nankhundi and his successors remained in Southern Chaldea, called themselves kings of the country, and reigned, several of them in succession, so that this series of foreign rulers has become known in history as "the Elamite dynasty." There was no room then for a powerful and temple-building national dynasty like that of the kings of Ur.

28. This is the first time we meet authentic monumental records of a country which was destined

---

* Geo. Smith, in "Records of the Past," Vol. V., p. 75. Fritz Hommel, "Die Semiten," p. 210 and note 101.

through the next sixteen centuries to be in continual contact, mostly hostile, with both Babylonia and her northern rival Assyria, until its final annihilation by the latter. Its capital was SHUSHAN, (afterwards pronounced by foreigners "Susa"), and its own original name SHUSHINAK. Its people were of Turanian stock, its language was nearly akin to that of Shumir and Accad. But at some time or other Semites came and settled in Shushinak. Though too few in number to change the country's language or customs, the superiority of their race asserted itself. They became the nobility of the land, the ruling aristocracy from which the kings were taken, the generals and the high functionaries. That the Turanian mass of the population was kept in subjection and looked down upon, and that the Semitic nobility avoided intermarrying with them is highly probable; and it would be difficult otherwise to explain the difference of type between the two classes, as shown in the representations of captives and warriors belonging to both on the Assyrian sculptures. The common herd of prisoners employed on public labor and driven by overseers brandishing sticks have an unmistakably Turanian type of features—high cheek-bones, broad, flattened face, etc., while the generals, ministers and nobles have all the dignity and beauty of the handsomest Jewish type. "Elam," the name under which the country is best known both from the Bible and later monuments, is a Turanian word, which means, like "Accad," "Highlands." It is the only name under which the historian of Chap. X. of

Genesis admits it into his list of nations, and, consistently following out his system of ignoring all members of the great yellow race, he takes into consideration only the Semitic aristocracy, and makes of Elam a son of Shem, a brother of Asshur and Arphakhshad. (Gen. x. 22.)

29. One of Khudur-Nankhundi's next successors, KHUDUR-LAGAMAR, was not content with the addition of Chaldea to his kingdom of Elam. He had the ambition of a born conqueror and the generalship of one. The Chap. XIV. of Genesis—which calls him Chedorlaomer—is the only document we have descriptive of this king's warlike career, and a very striking picture it gives of it, sufficient to show us that we have to do with a very remarkable character. Supported by three allied and probably tributary kings, that of Shumir (Shinear), of Larsam, (Ellassar) and of the GOÏM, (in the unrevised translation of the Bible "king of nations") i.e., the nomadic tribes which roamed on the outskirts and in the yet unsettled, more distant portions of Chaldea, Khudur-Lagamar marched an army 1200 miles across the desert into the fertile, wealthy and populous valleys of the Jordan and the lake or sea of Siddim, afterwards called the Dead Sea, where five great cities—Sodom, Gomorrah, and three others— were governed by as many kings. Not only did he subdue these kings and impose his rule on them, but contrived, even after he returned to the Persian Gulf, to keep on them so firm a hand, that for twelve years they "served" him, i.e., paid him tribute regularly, and only in the thirteenth year, en-

couraged by his prolonged absence, ventured to rebel. But they had underrated Khudur-Lagamar's vigilance and activity. The very next year he was among them again, together with his three faithful allies, encountered them in the vale of Siddim and beat them, so that they all fled. This was the battle of the "four kings with five." As to the treatment to which the victor subjected the conquered country it is very briefly but clearly described: "And they took all the goods of Sodom and Gomorrah, and all their victuals, and went their way."

30. Now there dwelt in Sodom a man of foreign race and great wealth, Lot, the nephew of Abraham. For Abraham and his tribe no longer lived at Chaldean Ur. The change of masters, and very probably the harsher rule, if not positive oppression, consequent on the Elamite conquest, had driven them thence. It was then they went forth into the land of Canaan, led by Terah and his son Abraham, and when Terah died, Abraham became the patriarch and chief of the tribe, which from this time begins to be called in the Bible "Hebrews," from an eponymous ancestor, Heber or Eber, whose name alludes to the passing of the Euphrates, or, perhaps, in a wider sense, to the passage of the tribe through the land of Chaldea.* For years the tribe travelled without dividing, from pasture to

---

* It should be mentioned, however, that scholars have of late been inclined to see in this name an allusion to the passage of the Jordan at the time of the conquest of Canaan by Israel, after the Egyptian bondage.

pasture, over the vast land where dwelt the Canaanites, well seen and even favored of them, into Egypt and out of it again, until the quarrel occurred between Abraham's herdsmen and Lot's, (see Genesis, Chap. XIII.), and the separation, when Lot chose the plain of the Jordan and pitched his tent toward Sodom, while Abraham dwelt in the land of Canaan as heretofore, with his family, servants and cattle, in the plain of Mamre. It was while dwelling there, in friendship and close alliance with the princes of the land, that one who had escaped from the battle in the vale of Siddim, came to Abraham and told him how that among the captives whom Khudur-Lagamar had taken from Sodom, was Lot, his brother's son, with all his goods. Then Abraham armed his trained servants, born in his own household, three hundred and eighteen, took with him his friends, Mamre and his brothers, with their young men, and starting in hot pursuit of the victorious army, which was now carelessly marching home towards the desert with its long train of captives and booty, overtook it near Damascus in the night, when his own small numbers could not be detected, and produced such a panic by a sudden and vigorous onslaught that he put it to flight, and not only rescued his nephew Lot with his goods and women, but brought back all the captured goods and the people too. And the King of Sodom came out to meet him on his return, and thanked him, and wanted him to keep all the goods for himself, only restoring the persons. Abraham consented that a proper share of the rescued goods should be given to his friends and their young men, but refused all presents offered to himself, with the haughty words: "I have lift up mine hand unto the Lord, the most high God, the possessor of heaven and earth, that I will not take a thread, even to a shoe-latchet, and that I will not take anything that is thine, lest thou shouldest say, I have made Abraham rich."

31. Khudur-Lagamar, of whom the spirited Biblical narrative gives us so life-like a sketch, lived, according to the most probable calculations, about 2200 B.C. Among the few vague forms whose blurred outlines loom out of the twilight of those dim and doubtful ages, he is the second with any flesh-and-blood reality about him, probably the first conqueror of whom the world has any authentic record. For Egypt, the only country which rivals in antiquity the primitive states of Mesopotamia, although it had at this time already reached the height of its culture and prosperity, was as yet confined by its rulers strictly to the valley of the Nile, and had not entered on that career of foreign wars and conquests which, some thousand years later, made it a terror from the Mediterranean to the Persian Gulf.

32. The Elamitic invasion was not a passing raid. It was a real conquest, and established a heavy foreign rule in a highly prosperous and flourishing land—a rule which endured, it would appear, about three hundred years. That the people chafed under it, and were either gloomily despondent or angrily rebellious as long as it lasted, there is plenty of evidence in their later literature. It is even thought, and with great moral probability, that the

special branch of religious poetry which has been called " Penitential Psalms " has arisen out of the sufferings of this long period of national bondage and humiliation, and if, as seems to be proved by some lately discovered interesting fragments of texts, these psalms were sung centuries later in Assyrian temples on mournful or very solemn public occasions, they must have perpetuated the memory of the great national calamity that fell on the mother-country as indelibly as the Hebrew psalms, of which they were the models, have perpetuated that of King David's wanderings and Israel's tribulations.

33. But there seems to have been one Semitic royal house which preserved a certain independence and quietly gathered power against better days. To do this they must have dissembled and done as much homage to the victorious barbarians as would ensure their safety and serve as a blind while they strengthened their home rule. This dynasty, destined to the glorious task of restoring the country's independence and founding a new national monarchy, was that of Tin-tir-ki, or Kadimirra—a name now already translated into the Semitic BAB-ILU, (" the Gate of God "); they reigned over the large and important district of KARDUNY-ASH, important from its central position, and from the fact that it seems to have belonged neither to Accad, nor to Shumir, but to have been politically independent, since it is always mentioned by itself. Still, to the Hebrews, Babylon lay in the land of Shinar, and it is strongly supposed that the " Am-

raphel king of Shinar" who marched with Khudur-Lagamar, as his ally, against the five kings of the Jordan and the Dead Sea, was no other than a king of Babylon, one of whose names has been read AMARPAL, while "Ariokh of Ellassar" was an Elamite, ERI-AKU, brother or cousin of Khudur-Lagamar, and King of Larsam, where the conquerors had established a powerful dynasty, closely allied by blood to the principal one, which had made the venerable Ur its headquarters. This Amarpal, more frequently mentioned under his other name of SIN-MUBALLIT, is thought to have been the father of HAMMURABI, the deliverer of Chaldea and the founder of the new empire.

34. The inscriptions which Hammurabi left are numerous, and afford us ample means of judging of his greatness as warrior, statesman and administrator. In his long reign of fifty-five years he had, indeed, time to achieve much, but what he did achieve *was* much even for so long a reign. In what manner he drove out the foreigners we are not told, but so much is clear that the decisive victory was that which he gained over the Elamite king of Larsam. It was probably by expelling the hated race by turns from every district they occupied, that Hammurabi gathered the entire land into his own hands and was enabled to keep it together and weld it into one united empire, including both Accad and Shumir, with all their time-honored cities and sanctuaries, making his own ancestral city, Babylon, the head and capital of them all. This king was in every respect a great and wise ruler,

for, after freeing and uniting the country, he was very careful of its good and watchful of its agricultural interests. Like all the other kings, he restored many temples and built several new ones. But he also devoted much energy to public works of a more generally useful kind. During the first part of his reign inundations seem to have been frequent and disastrous, possibly in consequence of the canals and waterworks having been neglected under the oppressive foreign rule. The inscriptions speak of a city having been destroyed " by a great flood," and mention " a great wall along the Tigris"—probably an embankment, as having been built by Hammurabi for protection against the river. But probably finding the remedy inadequate, he undertook and completed one of the greatest public works that have ever been carried out in any country : the excavation of a gigantic canal, which he called by his own name, but which was afterwards famous under that of " Royal Canal of Babylon." From this canal innumerable branches carried the fertilizing waters through the country. It was and remained the greatest work of the kind, and was, fifteen centuries later, the wonder of the foreigners who visited Babylon. Its constructor did not overrate the benefit he had conferred when he wrote in an inscription which can scarcely be called boastful : " I have caused to be dug the Nahr-Hammurabi, a benediction for the people of Shumir and Accad. I have directed the waters of its branches over the desert plains ; I have caused them to run in the dry channels and thus given unfailing waters to the people.... I have changed desert plains into well-watered lands. I have given them fertility and plenty, and made them the abode of happiness."

35. There are inscriptions of Hammurabi's son. But after him a new catastrophe seems to have overtaken Chaldea. He is succeeded by a line of foreign kings, who must have obtained possession of the country by conquest. They were princes of a fierce and warlike mountain race, the KASSHI, who lived in the highlands that occupy the whole north-western portion of Elam, where they probably began to feel cramped for room. This same people has been called by the later Greek geographers COSSAEANS or CISSIANS, and is better known under either of these names. Their language, of which very few specimens have survived, is not yet understood; but so much is plain, that it is very different both from the Semitic language of Babylon and that of Shumir and Accad, so that the names of the Kasshi princes are easily distinguishable from all others. No dismemberment of the empire followed this conquest, however, if conquest there was. The kings of the new dynasty seem to have succeeded each other peacefully enough in Babylon. But the conquering days of Chaldea were over. We read no more of expeditions into the plains of Syria and to the "Sea of the Setting Sun." For a power was rising in the North-West, which quickly grew into a formidable rival: through many centuries Assyria kept the rulers of the Southern kingdom too busy guarding their frontiers and repelling inroads to allow them to think of foreign conquests.

V.

BABYLONIAN RELIGION.

1. IN relating the legend of the Divine Man-Fish, who came out of the Gulf, and was followed, at intervals, by several more similar beings, Berosus assures us, that he "taught the people all the things that make up civilization," so that "nothing new was invented after that any more." But if, as is suggested, "this monstrous Oannes" is really a personification of the strangers who came into the land, and, being possessed of a higher culture, began to teach the Turanian population, the first part of this statement is as manifestly an exaggeration as the second. A people who had invented writing, who knew how to build, to make canals, to work metals, and who had passed out of the first and grossest stage of religious conceptions, might have much to learn, but certainly not *everything*. What the newcomers—whether Cushites or Semites—did teach them, was a more orderly way of organizing society and ruling it by means of laws and an established government, and, above all, astronomy and mathematics—sciences in which the Shumiro-Accads were little proficient, while the later and mixed nation, the Chaldeans, attained in

them a very high perfection, so that many of their discoveries and the first principles laid down by them have come down to us as finally adopted facts, confirmed by later science. Thus, the division of the year into twelve months corresponding to as many constellations, known as "the twelve signs of the Zodiac," was familiar to them. They had also found out the division of the year into twelve months, only all their months had thirty days. So they were obliged to add an extra month—an intercalary month, as the scientific term is—every six years, to start even with the sun again, for they knew where the error in their reckoning lay. These things the strangers probably taught the Shumiro-Accads, but at the same time borrowed from them their way of counting. The Turanian races to this day have this peculiarity, that they do not care for the decimal system in arithmetic, but count by dozens and sixties, preferring numbers that can be divided by twelve and sixty. The Chinese even now do not measure time by centuries or periods of a hundred years, but by a cycle or period of sixty years. This was probably the origin of the division, adopted in Babylonia, of the sun's course into 360 equal parts or degrees, and of the day into twelve "*kasbus*" or double hours, since the kasbu answered to two of our hours, and was divided into sixty parts, which we might thus call "double minutes," while these again were composed of sixty "double seconds." The natural division of the year into twelve months made this so-called "docenal" and "sexagesimal" system of calculation particularly convenient, and it was applied to everything—measures of weight, distance, capacity and size as well as time.

2. Astronomy is a strangely fascinating science, with two widely different and seemingly contradictory aspects, equally apt to develop habits of hard thinking and of dreamy speculation. For, if on one hand the study of mathematics, without which astronomy cannot subsist, disciplines the mind and trains it to exact and complicated operations, on the other hand, star-gazing, in the solitude and silence of a southern night, irresistibly draws it into a higher world, where poetical aspirations, guesses and dreams take the place of figures with their demonstrations and proofs. It is probably to these habitual contemplations that the later Chaldeans owed the higher tone of religious thought which distinguished them from their Turanian predecessors. They looked for the deity in heaven, not on earth. They did not cower and tremble before a host of wicked goblins, the creation of a terrified fancy. The spirits whom they worshipped inhabited and ruled those beautiful bright worlds, whose harmonious, concerted movements they watched admiringly, reverently, and could calculate correctly, but without understanding them. The stars generally became to them the visible manifestations and agents of divine power, especially the seven most conspicuous heavenly bodies: the Moon, whom they particularly honored, as the ruler of night and the measurer of time, the Sun and the five planets then known, those which we call Saturn,

Jupiter, Mars, Venus and Mercury. It is but just to the Shumiro-Accads to say that the perception of the divine in the beauty of the stars was not foreign to them. This is amply proved by the fact that in their oldest writing the sign of a star is used to express the idea not of any particular god or goddess, but of the divine principle, the deity generally. The name of every divinity is preceded by the star, meaning "the god so-and-so." When used in this manner, the sign was read in the old language "Dingir"—"god, deity." The Semitic language of Babylonia which we call "Assyrian," while adapting the ancient writing to its own needs, retained this use of the sign "star," and read it *ilu*, "god." This word—ILU or EL—we find in all Semitic languages, either ancient or modern, in the names they give to God, in the Arabic ALLAH as well as in the Hebrew ELOHIM.

3. This religion, based and centred on the worship of the heavenly bodies, has been called *Sabeism*, and was common to most Semitic races, whose primitive nomadic life in the desert and wide, flat pasture-tracts, with the nightly watches required by the tending of vast flocks, inclined them to contemplation and star-gazing. It is to be noticed that the Semites gave the first place to the Sun, and not, like the Shumiro-Accads, to the Moon, possibly from a feeling akin to terror, experiencing as they did his destructive power, in the frequent droughts and consuming heat of the desert.*

---
* See A. H. Sayce, "The Ancient Empires of the East" (1883), p. 389.

4. A very prominent feature of the new order of things was the great power and importance of the priesthood. A successful pursuit of science requires two things: intellectual superiority and leisure to study, i.e., freedom from the daily care how to procure the necessaries of life. In very ancient times people in general were quite willing to acknowledge the superiority of those men who knew more than they did, who could teach them and help them with wise advice; they were willing also to support such men by voluntary contributions, in order to give them the necessary leisure. That a race with whom science and religion were one should honor the men thus set apart and learned in heavenly things and allow them great influence in private and public affairs, believing them, as they did, to stand in direct communion with the divine powers, was but natural; and from this to letting them take to themselves the entire government of the country as the established rulers thereof, was but one step. There was another circumstance which helped to bring about this result. The Chaldeans were devout believers in astrology, a form of superstition into which an astronomical religion like Sabeism is very apt to degenerate. For once it is taken for granted that the stars are divine beings, possessed of intelligence, and will, and power, what more natural than to imagine that they can rule and shape the destinies of men by a mysterious influence? This influence was supposed to depend on their movements, their position in the sky, their ever changing combinations and rela-

tions to each other; under this supposition every movement of a star—its rising, its setting, or crossing the path of another—every slightest change in the aspect of the heavens, every unusual phenomenon—an eclipse, for instance—must be possessed of some weighty sense, boding good or evil to men, whose destiny must constantly be as clearly written in the blue sky as in a book. If only one could learn the language, read the characters! Such knowledge was thought to be within the reach of men, but only to be acquired by the exceptionally gifted and learned few, and those whom they might think worthy of having it imparted to them. That these few must be priests was self-evident. They were themselves fervent believers in astrology, which they considered quite as much a real science as astronomy, and to which they devoted themselves as assiduously. They thus became the acknowledged interpreters of the divine will, partakers, so to speak, of the secret councils of heaven. Of course such a position added greatly to their power, and that they should never abuse it to strengthen their hold on the public mind and to favor their own ambitious views, was not in human nature. Moreover, being the clever and learned ones of the nation, they really were at the time the fittest to rule it—and rule it they did. When the Semitic culture spread over Shumir, whither it gradually extended from the North., *i.e.*, the land of Accad, there arose in each great city—Ur, Eridhu, Larsam, Erech,—a mighty temple, with its priests, its library, its *Ziggurat* or observatory. The cities and the tracts of country belonging to them were governed by their respective colleges. And when in progress of time, the power became centred in the hands of single men, they still were priest-kings, *patesis*, whose royalty must have been greatly hampered and limited by the authority of their priestly colleagues. Such a form of government is known under the name of *theocracy*, composed of two Greek words and meaning "divine government."

5. This religious reform represents a complete though probably peaceable revolution in the condition of the "Land between the Rivers." The new and higher culture had thoroughly asserted itself as predominant in both its great provinces, and in nothing as much as in the national religion, which, coming in contact with the conceptions of the Semites, was affected by a certain nobler spiritual strain, a purer moral feeling, which seems to have been more peculiarly Semitic, though destined to be carried to its highest perfection only in the Hebrew branch of the race. Moral tone is a subtle influence, and will work its way into men's hearts and thoughts far more surely and irresistibly than any amount of preaching and commanding, for men are naturally drawn to what is good and beautiful when it is placed before them. Thus the old settlers of the land, the Shumiro-Accads, to whom their gross and dismal goblin creed could not be of much comfort, were not slow in feeling this ennobling and beneficent influence, and it is assuredly to that we owe the beautiful prayers and hymns which mark the higher stage of their religion. The con-

sciousness of sin, the feeling of contrition, of dependence on an offended yet merciful divine power, so strikingly conspicuous in the so-called "Penitential Psalms" (see p. 178), the fine poetry in some of the later hymns, for instance those to the Sun (see p. 171), are features so distinctively Semitic, that they startle us by their resemblance to certain portions of the Bible. On the other hand, a nation never forgets or quite gives up its own native creed and religious practices. The wise priestly rulers of Shumir and Accad did not attempt to compel the people to do so, but even while introducing and propagating the new religion, suffered them to go on believing in their hosts of evil spirits and their few beneficent ones, in their conjuring, soothsaying, casting and breaking of spells and charms. Nay, more. As time went on and the learned priests studied more closely the older creed and ideas, they were struck with the beauty of some few of their conceptions—especially that of the ever benevolent, ever watchful Spirit of Earth, Êa, and his son Meridug, the mediator, the friend of men. These conceptions, these and some other favorite national divinities, they thought worthy of being adopted by them and worked into their own religious system, which was growing more complicated, more elaborate every day, while the large bulk of spirits and demons they also allowed a place in it, in the rank of inferior "Spirits of heaven" and "Spirits of earth," which were lightly classed together and counted by hundreds. By the time a thousand years had passed, the fusion had become so complete that there really was both a new religion and a new nation, the result of a long work of amalgamation. The Shumiro-Accads of pure yet low race were no longer, nor did the Semites preserve a separate existence; they had become merged into one nation of mixed races, which at a later period became known under the general name of Chaldeans, whose religion, regarded with awe for its prodigious antiquity, yet was comparatively recent, being the outcome of the combination of two infinitely older creeds, as we have just seen. When Hammurabi established his residence at Babel, a city which had but lately risen to importance, he made it the capital of the empire first completely united under his rule (see p. 226), hence the name of Babylonia is given by ancient writers to the old land of Shumir and Accad, even more frequently than that of Chaldea, and the state religion is called indifferently the Babylonian or Chaldean, and not unfrequently Chaldeo-Babylonian.

6. This religion, as it was definitely established and handed down unchanged through a succession of twenty centuries and more, had a twofold character, which must be well grasped in order to understand its general drift and sense. On the one hand, as it admitted the existence of many divine powers, who shared between them the government of the world, it was decidedly POLYTHEISTIC—"a religion of many gods." On the other hand, a dim perception had already been arrived at, perhaps through observation of the strictly regulated movements of the stars, of the presence of One supreme ruling

and directing Power. For a class of men given to the study of astronomy could not but perceive that all those bright Beings which they thought so divine and powerful, were not absolutely independent; that their movements and combinations were too regular, too strictly timed, too identical in their ever recurring repetition, to be entirely voluntary; that, consequently, they *obeyed*—obeyed a Law, a Power above and beyond them, beyond heaven itself, invisible, unfathomable, unattainable by human thought or eyes. Such a perception was, of course, a step in the right direction, towards MONOTHEISM, i.e., the belief in only one God. But the perception was too vague and remote to be fully realized and consistently carried out. The priests who, from long training in abstract thought and contemplation, probably could look deeper and come nearer the truth than other people, strove to express their meaning in language and images which, in the end, obscured the original idea and almost hid it out of sight, instead of making it clearer. Besides, they did not imagine the world as *created* by God, made by an act of his will, but as being a form of him, a manifestation, part of himself, of his own substance. Therefore, in the great all of the universe, and in each of its portions, in the mysterious forces at work in it—light and heat and life and growth—they admired and adored not the power of God, but his very presence; one of the innumerable and infinitely varied forms in which he makes himself known and visible to men, manifests himself to them—in short, *an emanation of God.* The word "emanation" has been adopted as the only one which to a certain extent conveys this very subtle and complicated idea. An emanation is not quite a thing itself, but it is a portion of it, which comes out of it and separates itself from it, yet cannot exist without it. So the fragrance of a flower is not the flower, nor is it a growth or development of it, yet the flower gives it forth and it cannot exist by itself without the flower—it is an emanation of the flower. The same can be said of the mist which visibly rises from the warm earth in low and moist places on a summer evening—it is an emanation of the earth.

7. The Chaldeo-Babylonian priests knew of many such divine emanations, which, by giving them names and attributing to them definite functions, they made into so many separate divine persons. Of these some ranked higher and some lower, a relation which was sometimes expressed by the human one of "father and son." They were ordered in groups, very scientifically arranged. Above the rest were placed two TRIADS or "groups of three." The first triad comprised ANU, ÊA and BEL, the supreme gods of all—all three retained from the old Shumiro-Accadian list of divinities. ANU is ANA, "Heaven," and the surnames or epithets which are given him in different texts, sufficiently show what conception had been formed of him: he is called "the Lord of the starry heavens," "the Lord of Darkness," "the first-born, the oldest, the Father of the Gods." ÊA, retaining his ancient attributions as "Lord of the Deep," the

pre-eminently wise and beneficent spirit, represents the Divine Intelligence, the founder and maintainer of order and harmony, while the actual task of separating the elements of chaos and shaping them into the forms which make up the world as we know it, as well as that of ordering the heavenly bodies, appointing them their path and directing them thereon, was devolved on the third person of the triad, BEL, the son of ÊA. Bel is a Semitic name, which means simply "the lord."

8. From its nature and attributions, it is clear that to this triad must have attached a certain vagueness and remoteness. Not so the second triad, in which the Deity manifested itself as standing in the nearest and most direct relation to man as most immediately influencing him in his daily life. The persons of this triad were the Moon, the Sun, and the Power of the Atmosphere,—SIN, SHAMASH, and RAMÂN, the Semitic names for the Shumiro-Accadian URU-KI or NANNAR, UD or BABBAR, and IM or MERMER. Very characteristically, Sin is frequently called "the god Thirty," in allusion to his functions as the measurer of time presiding over the month. Of the feelings with which the Sun was regarded and the beneficent and splendid qualities attributed to him, we know enough from the beautiful hymns quoted in Chap. III. (see p. 172). As to the god RAMÂN, frequently represented on tablets and cylinders by his characteristic sign, the double or triple-forked lightning-bolt—his importance as the dispenser of rain, the lord of the whirlwind and tempest, made him very popular, an

object as much of dread as of gratitude ; and as the crops depended on the supply of water from the canals, and these again could not be full without abundant rains, it is not astonishing that he should have been particularly entitled "protector or lord of canals," giver of abundance and "lord of fruitfulness." In his more terrible capacity, he is thus described : " His standard titles are the minister of heaven and earth," " the lord of the air," " he who makes the tempest to rage." He is regarded as the destroyer of crops, the rooter-up of trees, the scatterer of the harvest. Famine, scarcity, and even their consequence, pestilence, are assigned to him. He is said to have in his hand a " flaming sword " with which he effects his works of destruction, and this "flaming sword, which probably represents lightning, becomes his emblem upon the tablets and cylinders." *

9. The astronomical tendencies of the new religion fully assert themselves in the third group of divinities. They are simply the five planets then known and identified with various deities of the old creed, to whom they are, so to speak, assigned as their own particular provinces. Thus NINDAR (also called NINIP or NINÊB), originally another name or form of the Sun (see p. 172), becomes the ruler of the most distant planet, the one we now call Saturn ; the old favorite, Meridug, under the Semitized name of MARDUK, rules the planet Jupiter. It is he whom later Hebrew writers have called MERODACH,

---

* Rawlinson's " Five Monarchies," Vol. I., p. 164.

the name we find in the Bible. The planet Mars belongs to NERGAL, the warrior-god, and Mercury to NEBO, more properly NABU, the "messenger of the gods" and the special patron of astronomy, while the planet Venus is under the sway of a feminine deity, the goddess ISHTAR, one of the most important and popular on the list. But of her more anon. She leads us to the consideration of a very essential and characteristic feature of the Chaldeo-Babylonian religion, common, moreover, to all Oriental heathen religions, especially the Semitic ones.

10. There is a distinction—the distinction of sex—which runs through the whole of animated nature, dividing all things that have life into two separate halves—male and female—halves most different in their qualities, often opposite, almost hostile, yet eternally dependent on each other, neither being complete or perfect, or indeed able to exist without the other. Separated by contrast, yet drawn together by an irresistible sympathy which results in the closest union, that of love and affection, the two sexes still go through life together, together do the work of the world. What the one has not or has in an insufficient degree it finds in its counterpart, and it is only their union which makes of the world a whole thing, full, rounded, harmonious. The masculine nature, active, strong, and somewhat stern, even when merciful and bounteous, inclined to boisterousness and violence and often to cruelty, is well set off, or rather completed and moderated, by the feminine nature, not less active, but more quietly so, dispens-

ing gentle influences, open to milder moods, more uniformly soft in feeling and manner.

11. In no relation of life is the difference, yet harmony, of masculine and feminine action so plain as in that between husband and wife, father and

60.—A BUST INSCRIBED WITH THE NAME OF NEBO.
(British Museum.)

mother. It requires no very great effort of imagination to carry the distinction beyond the bounds of animated nature, into the world at large. To men for whom every portion or force of the universe was endowed with a particle of the divine nature and power, many were the things which seemed to be paired in a contrasting, yet joint action similar to that of the sexes. If the great and distant Heaven appeared to them as the universal ruler and lord, the source of all things—the Father of the Gods, as they put it—surely the beautiful Earth, kind nurse, nourisher and preserver of all things that have life, could be called the universal Mother. If the fierce summer and noonday sun could be looked on as the resistless conqueror, the dread King of the world, holding death and disease in his hand, was not the quiet, lovely moon, of mild and soothing light, bringing the rest of coolness and healing dews, its gentle Queen? In short, there is not a power or a phenomenon of nature which does not present to a poetical imagination a twofold aspect, answering to the standard masculine and feminine qualities and peculiarities. The ancient thinkers— priests—who framed the vague guesses of the groping, dreaming mind into schemes and systems of profound meaning, expressed this sense of the twofold nature of things by worshipping a double divine being or principle, masculine and feminine. Thus every god was supplied with a wife, through the entire series of divine emanations and manifestations. And as all the gods were in reality only different names and forms of the Supreme and Unfathomable ONE, so all the goddesses represent only BELIT, the great feminine principle of nature —productiveness, maternity, tenderness—also contained, like everything else, in that ONE, and emanating from it in endless succession. Hence it comes that the goddesses of the Chaldeo-Babylonian religion, though different in name and apparently in attributions, become wonderfully alike when looked at closer. They are all more or less repetitions of BELIT, the wife of BEL. Her name —which is only the feminine form of the god's, meaning "the Lady," as Bel means "the Lord,"— sufficiently shows that the two are really one. Of the other goddesses the most conspicuous are ANAT or NANA (Earth), the wife of Anu (Heaven), ANUNIT (the Moon), wife of Shamash (the Sun), and lastly ISHTAR, the ruler of the planet Venus in her own right, and by far the most attractive and interesting of the list. She was a great favorite, worshipped as the Queen of Love and Beauty, and also as the Warrior-Queen, who rouses men to deeds of bravery, inspirits and protects them in battle—perhaps because men have often fought and made war for the love of women, and also probably because the planet Venus, her own star, appears not only in the evening, close after sunset, but also immediately before daybreak, and so seems to summon the human race to renewed efforts and activity. Ishtar could not be an exception to the general principle and remain unmated. But her husband, DUMUZ (a name for the Sun), stands to her in an entirely subordinate position, and, indeed, would be but little known were it not for a beautiful story that was told of them in a very old poem, and which will find its place among many more in one of the next chapters.

12. It would be tedious and unnecessary to recite here more names of gods and goddesses, though

there are quite a number, and more come to light
all the time as new tablets are discovered and read.
Most of them are in reality only different names for
the same conceptions, and the Chaldeo-Babylonian
pantheon—or assembly of divine persons—is very
sufficiently represented by the so-called "twelve
great gods," who were universally acknowledged to
be at its head, and of whom we will here repeat the
names: ANU, ÊA and BEL, SIN, SHAMASH and RA-
MÂN, NINDAR, MARUDUK, NERGAL, NEBO, BELIT
and ISHTAR. Each had numerous temples all over
the country. But every great city had its favorite whose temple was the oldest, largest and most
sumptuous, to whose worship it was especially devoted from immemorial times. Êa, the most beloved god of old Shumir, had his chief sanctuary,
which he shared with his son Meridug, at ERIDHU
(now Abu-Shahrein), the most southern and almost
the most ancient city of Shumir, situated near the
mouth of the Euphrates, since the Persian Gulf
reached quite as far inland in the year 4000 B.C.,
and this was assuredly an appropriate station for
the great "lord of the deep," the Fish-god Oannes,
who emerged from the waters to instruct mankind. UR, as we have seen, was the time-honored seat of the Moon-god. At ERECH Anu and
Anat or Nana—Heaven and Earth—were specially
honored from the remotest antiquity, being jointly
worshipped in the temple called "the House of
Heaven." This may have been the reason of the
particular sacredness attributed to the ground all
around Erech, as witnessed by the exceeding per-

sistency with which people strove for ages to bury their dead in it, as though under the immediate protection of the goddess of Earth* (see Ch. III. of Introduction). Larsam paid especial homage to Shamash and was famous for its very ancient "House of the Sun." The Sun and Moon—Shamash and Anunit—had their rival sanctuaries at SIPPAR on the "Royal Canal," which ran nearly parallel to the Euphrates, and AGADÊ, the city of Sargon, situated just opposite on the other bank of the canal. The name of Agadê was lost in the lapse of time, and both cities became one, the two portions being distinguished only by the addition "Sippar of the Sun" and "Sippar of Anunit." The Hebrews called the united city "The two Sippars"—SEPHARVAIM, the name we find in the Bible.

13. The site of this important city was long doubtful; but in 1881 one of the most skilful and indefatigable searchers, Mr. Hormuzd Rassam, a gentleman who began his career as assistant to Layard, made a discovery which set the question at rest. He was digging in a mound known to the Arabs by the name of Abu-Habba, and had made his way into the apartments of a vast structure which he knew to be a temple. From room to room he passed until he came to a smaller chamber, paved with asphalt, which he at once surmised to be the archive-room of the temple. "Heretofore," says Mr. Rassam in his report, "all Assy-

---

* It was the statue of this very goddess Nana which was carried away by the Elamite conqueror, Khudur-Nankhundi in 2280 B.C. and restored to its place by Assurbanipal in 645 B.C.

rian and Babylonian structures were found to be paved generally either with stone or brick, consequently this novel discovery led me to have the asphalt broken into and examined. On doing so we found, buried in a corner of the chamber, about three feet below the surface, an inscribed earthenware coffer, inside which was deposited a stone tablet. . . ." Rassam had indeed stumbled on the archive of the famous Sun-temple, as was proved not only by the tablet, but by the numerous documents which accompanied it, and which gave the names of the builders and restorers of the temple. As to the tablet, it is the finest and best preserved work of art of the kind which has yet been found. It was deposited about the year 880 B.C. on occasion of a restoration, and represents the god himself, seated on a throne, receiving the homage of worshippers, while above him the sun-disc is held suspended from heaven on two strong cords, like a gigantic lamp, by two ministering beings, who may very probably belong to the host of Igigi or spirits of heaven. The inscription, in beautifully clear and perfectly preserved characters, informs us that this is "The image of Shamash, the great lord, who dwells in the 'House of the Sun,' (*Ê-Babbara*) which is within the city of Sippar."* (See Frontispiece.) This was a truly magnificent find, and who knows but something as unexpected and as conclusive may turn up to fix for us the exact

---

* The three circles above the god represent the Moon-god, the Sun-god, and Ishtar. So we are informed by the two lines of writing which run above the roof.

place of the temple of Anunit, and consequently of the venerable city of Agade. As to Babylon, it was originally placed under divine protection generally, as shown by its proper Semitic name, BABILU, which means, as we have already seen, "the Gate of God," and exactly answers to the Shumiro-Accadian name of the city (KA-DINGIRRA, or KA-DIMIRRA); but later on it elected a special protector in the person of MARUDUK, the old favorite, Meridug. When Babylon became the capital of the united monarchy of Shumir and Accad, its patron divinity, under the name of BEL-MARUDUK, ("the Lord Maruduk") rose to a higher rank than he had before occupied ; his temple outshone all others and became a wonder of the world for its wealth and splendor. He had another, scarcely less splendid, and founded by Hammurabi himself in Borsip. In this way religion was closely allied to politics. For in the days before the reunion of the great cities under the rule of Hammurabi, whichever of them was the most powerful at the time, its priests naturally claimed the pre-eminence for their local deity even beyond their own boundaries. So that the fact of the old Kings of Ur, Ur-ea and his descendants, not limiting themselves to the worship of their national Moon-god, but building temples in many places and to many gods, was perhaps a sign of a conciliating general policy as much as of liberal religious feeling.

14. One would think that so very perfect a system of religion, based too on so high and noble an order of ideas, should have entirely superseded the coarse

materialism and conjuring practices of the goblin-creed of the primitive Turanian settlers. Such, however, was far from being the case. We saw that the new religion made room, somewhat contemptuously perhaps, for the spirits of the old creed, carelessly massing them wholesale into a sort of regiment, composed of the three hundred IGIGI, or spirits of heaven, and the six hundred ANUNNAKI, or spirits of earth. The conjurers and sorcerers of old were even admitted into the priesthood in an inferior capacity, as a sort of lower order, probably more tolerated than encouraged—tolerated from necessity, because the people clung to their ancient beliefs and practices. But if their official position as a priestly class were subordinate, their real power was not the less great, for the public favor and credulity were on their side, and they were assuredly more generally popular than the learned and solemn priests, the counsellors and almost the equals of the kings, whose thoughts dwelt among the stars, who reverently searched the heavens for revelations of the divine will and wisdom, and who, by pursuing accurate observation and mathematical calculation together with the wildest dreams, made astronomy and astrology the inextricable tangle of scientific truth and fantastic speculation that we see it in the great work (in seventy tablets) prepared for the library of Sargon II. at Agadê. That the ancient system of conjuring and incantations remained in full force and general use, is sufficiently proved by the contents of the first two parts of the great collection in two hundred tablets compiled in the reign of the same king, and from the care with which the work was copied and recopied, commented on and translated in later ages, as we see from the copy made for the Royal Library at Nineveh, the one which has reached us.

15. There was still a third branch of so-called "science," which greatly occupied the minds of the Chaldeo-Babylonians from their earliest times down to the latest days of their existence: it was the art of Divination, i.e., of divining and foretelling future events from signs and omens, a superstition born of the old belief in every object of inanimate nature being possessed or inhabited by a spirit, and the later belief in a higher power ruling the world and human affairs to the smallest detail, and constantly manifesting itself through all things in nature as through secondary agents, so that nothing whatever could occur without some deeper significance, which might be discovered and expounded by specially trained and favored individuals. In the case of atmospheric prophecies concerning weather and crops, as connected with the appearance of clouds, sky and moon, the force and direction of winds, etc., there may have been some real observation to found them on. But it is very clear that such a conception, if carried out consistently to extreme lengths and applied indiscriminately to *everything*, must result in arrant folly. Such was assuredly the case with the Chaldeo-Babylonians, who not only carefully noted and explained dreams, drew lots in doubtful cases by means of inscribed arrows, interpreted the rustle of trees, the plashing

of fountains and murmur of streams, the direction and form of lightnings, not only fancied that they could see things in bowls of water and in the shifting forms assumed by the flame which consumed sacrifices, and the smoke which rose therefrom, and that they could raise and question the spirits of the dead, but drew presages and omens, for good or evil, from the flight of birds, the appearance of the liver, lungs, heart and bowels of the animals offered in sacrifice and opened for inspection, from the natural defects or monstrosities of babies or the young of animals—in short, from any and everything that they could possibly subject to observation.

16. This idlest of all kinds of speculation was reduced to a most minute and apparently scientific system quite as early as astrology and incantation, and forms the subject of a third collection, in about one hundred tablets, and probably compiled by those same indefatigable priests of Agadé for Sargon, who was evidently of a most methodical turn of mind, and determined to have all the traditions and the results of centuries of observation and practical experiences connected with any branch of religious science fixed forever in the shape of thoroughly classified rules, for the guidance of priests for all coming ages. This collection has come to us in an even more incomplete and mutilated condition than the others; but enough has been preserved to show us that a right-thinking and religiously-given Chaldeo-Babylonian must have spent his life taking notes of the absurdest trifles, and

questioning the diviners and priests about them, in order not to get into scrapes by misinterpreting the signs and taking that to be a favorable omen which boded dire calamity—or the other way, and thus doing things or leaving them undone at the wrong moment and in the wrong way. What excites, perhaps, even greater wonder, is the utter absurdity of some of the incidents gravely set down as affecting the welfare, not only of individuals, but of the whole country. What shall we say, for instance, of the importance attached to the proceedings of stray dogs? Here are some of the items as given by Mr. Fr. Lenormant in his most valuable and entertaining book on Chaldean Divination:—

"If a gray dog enter the palace, the latter will be consumed by flames.—If a yellow dog enter the palace, the latter will perish in a violent catastrophe.—If a tawny dog enter the palace, peace will be concluded with the enemies.—If a dog enter the palace and be not killed, the peace of the palace will be disturbed.—If a dog enter the temple, the gods will have no mercy on the land.—If a white dog enter the temple, its foundations will subsist.—If a black dog enter the temple, its foundations will be shaken.—If a gray dog enter the temple, the latter will lose its possessions. . . . If dogs assemble in troops and enter the temple, no one will remain in authority. . . . If a dog vomits in a house, the master of that house will die."

17. The chapter on monstrous births is extensive. Not only is every possible anomaly registered, from an extra finger or toe to an ear smaller than the

other, with its corresponding presage of good or evil to the country, the king, the army, but the most impossible monstrosities are seriously enumerated, with the political conditions of which they are supposed to be the signs. For instance:—If a woman give birth to a child with lion's ears, a mighty king will rule the land . . . with a bird's beak, there will be peace in the land. . . . If a queen give birth to a child with a lion's face, the king will have no rival . . . if to a snake, the king will be mighty. . . . If a mare give birth to a foal with a lion's mane, the lord of the land will annihilate his enemies . . . with a dog's paws, the land will be diminished . . . with a lion's paws, the land will be increased. . . . If a sheep give birth to a lion, there will be war, the king will have no rival. . . . If a mare give birth to a dog, there will be disaster and famine."

18. The three great branches of religious science —astrology, incantation and divination—were represented by three corresponding classes of "wise men," all belonging, in different degrees, to the priesthood: the star-gazers or astrologers, the magicians or sorcerers, and the soothsayers or fortune-tellers. The latter, again, were divided into many smaller classes according to the particular kind of divination which they practised. Some specially devoted themselves to the interpretation of dreams, others to that of the flight of birds, or of the signs of the atmosphere, or of casual signs and omens generally. All were in continual demand, consulted alike by kings and private persons, and all proceeded in strict accordance with the rules and principles

laid down in the three great works of King Sargon's time. When the Babylonian empire ceased to exist and the Chaldeans were no longer a nation, these secret arts continued to be practised by them, and the name "Chaldean" became a by-word, a synonym for "a wise man of the East,"—astrologer, magician or soothsayer. They dispersed all over the world, carrying their delusive science with them, practising and teaching it, welcomed everywhere by the credulous and superstitious, often highly honored and always richly paid. Thus it is from the Chaldeans and their predecessors the Shumiro-Accads that the belief in astrology, witchcraft and every kind of fortune-telling has been handed down to the nations of Europe, together with the practices belonging thereto, many of which we find lingering even to our day among the less educated classes. The very words "magic" and "magician" are probably an inheritance of that remotest of antiquities. One of the words for "priest" in the old Turanian tongue of Shumir was *imga*, which, in the later Semitic language, became *mag*. The *Rab-mag*—"great priest," or perhaps "chief conjurer," was a high functionary at the court of the Assyrian kings. Hence "magus," "magic," "magician," in all the European languages, from Latin downward.

19. There can be no doubt that we have little reason to be grateful for such an heirloom as this mass of superstitions, which have produced so much evil in the world and still occasionally do mischief enough. But we must not forget to set off against it the many excellent things, most important dis-

coveries in the province of astronomy and mathematics which have come to us from the same distant source. To the ancient Chaldeo-Babylonians we owe not only our division of time, but the invention of the sun-dial, and the week of seven days, dedicated in succession to the Sun, the Moon, and the five planets—an arrangement which is still maintained, the names of our days being merely translations of the Chaldean ones. And more than that; there were days set apart and kept holy, as days of rest, as far back as the time of Sargon of Agadê; it was from the Semites of Babylonia—perhaps the Chaldeans of Ur—that both the name and the observance passed to the Hebrew branch of the race, the tribe of Abraham. George Smith found an Assyrian calendar where the day called *Sabattu* or *Sabattuv* is explained to mean "completion of work, a day of rest for the soul." On this day, it appears it was not lawful to cook food, to change one's dress, to offer a sacrifice; the king was forbidden to speak in public, to ride in a chariot, to perform any kind of military or civil duty, even to take medicine.[*] This, surely, is a keeping of the Sabbath as strict as the most orthodox Jew could well desire. There are, however, essential differences between the two. In the first place, the Babylonians kept *five* Sabbath days every month, which made more than one a week; in the second place,

---

[*] Friedrich Delitzsch, "Beigaben" to the German translat. of Smith's "Chaldean Genesis" (1876), p. 300. A. H. Sayce, "The Ancient Empires of the East" (1883), p. 402. W. Lotz, "Quæstiones de Historia Sabbati."

they came round on certain dates of each month, independently of the day of the week: on the 7th, 14th, 19th, 21st and 28th. The custom appears to have passed to the Assyrians, and there are indications which encourage the supposition that it was shared by other nations connected with the Jews, the Babylonians and Assyrians, for instance, by the Phœnicians.

VI.

LEGENDS AND STORIES.

1. In every child's life there comes a moment when it ceases to take the world and all it holds as a matter of course, when it begins to wonder and to question. The first, the great question naturally is—"Who made it all? The sun, the stars, the sea, the rivers, the flowers, and the trees—whence come they? who made them?" And to this question we are very ready with our answer:—"God made it all. The One, the Almighty God created the world, and all that is in it, by His own sovereign will." When the child further asks: "*How* did He do it?" we read to it the story of the Creation which is the beginning of the Bible, our Sacred Book, either without any remarks upon it, or with the warning, that, for a full and proper understanding of it, years are needed and knowledge of many kinds. Now, these same questions have been asked, by children and men, in all ages. Ever since man has existed upon the earth, ever since he began, in the intervals of rest, in the hard labor and struggle for life and limb, for food and warmth, to raise his head and look abroad, and take in the wonders that surround him, he has thus pondered

and questioned. And to this questioning, each nation, after its own lights, has framed very much the same answer; the same in substance and spirit (because the only possible one), acknowledging the agency of a Divine Power, in filling the world with life, and ordaining the laws of nature,—but often very different in form, since, almost every creed having stopped short of the higher religious conception, that of One Deity, indivisible and all-powerful, the great act was attributed to many gods—"the gods,"—not to God. This of course opened the way to innumerable, more or less ingenious, fancies and vagaries as to the part played in it by this or that particular divinity. Thus all races, nations, even tribes have worked out for themselves their own COSMOGONY, i.e., their own ideas on the Origin of the World. The greatest number, not having reached a very high stage of culture or attained literary skill, preserved the teachings of their priests in their memory, and transmitted them orally from father to son; such is the case even now with many more peoples than we think of— with all the native tribes of Africa, the islanders of Australia and the Pacific, and several others. But the nations who advanced intellectually to the front of mankind and influenced the long series of coming races by their thoughts and teachings, recorded in books the conclusions they had arrived at on the great questions which have always stirred the heart and mind of man; these were carefully preserved and recopied from time to time, for the instruction of each rising generation. Thus many great nations of olden times have possessed Sacred Books, which, having been written in remote antiquity by their best and wisest men, were reverenced as something not only holy, but beyond the unassisted powers of the human intellect, something imparted, revealed directly by the deity itself, and therefore to be accepted, undisputed, as absolute truth. It is clear that it was in the interest of the priests, the keepers and teachers of all religious knowledge, to encourage and maintain in the people at large this unquestioning belief.

2. Of all such books that have become known to us, there are none of greater interest and importance than the sacred books of Ancient Babylonia. Not merely because they are the oldest known, having been treasured in the priestly libraries of Agadè, Sippar, Cutha, etc., at an incredibly early date, but principally because the ancestors of the Hebrews, during their long station in the land of Shinar, learned the legends and stories they contained, and working them over after their own superior religious lights, remodelled them into the narrative which was written down many centuries later as part of the Book of Genesis.

3. The original sacred books were attributed to the god Êa himself, the impersonation of the Divine Intelligence, and the teacher of mankind in the shape of the first Man-Fish, Oannes—(the name being only a Greek corruption of the Accadian ÊA-HAN, "Êa the Fish").* So Berosus informs us.

---

* See Fr. Lenormant, "Die Magie und Wahrsagekunst der Chaldäer," p. 377.

After describing Oannes and his proceedings (see p. 185), he adds that " he wrote a Book on the Origin of things and the beginnings of civilization, and gave it to men." The "origin of things" is the history of the Creation of the world, Cosmogony. Accordingly, this is what Berosus proceeds to expound, quoting directly from the Book, for he begins:— "There was a time, *says he*, (meaning Oannes) when all was darkness and water." Then follows a very valuable fragment, but unfortunately only a fragment, one of the few preserved by later Greek writers who quoted the old priest of Babylon for their own purposes, while the work itself was, in some way, destroyed and lost. True, these fragments contain short sketches of several of the most important legends; still, precious as they are, they convey only second-hand information, compiled, indeed, from original sources by a learned and conscientious writer, but for the use of a foreign race, extremely compressed, and, besides, with the names all altered to suit that race's language. So long as the "original sources" were missing, there was a gap in the study both of the Bible and the religion of Babylon, which no ingenuity could fill. Great, therefore, were the delight and excitement, both of Assyriologists and Bible scholars, when George Smith, while sorting the thousands of tablet-fragments which for years had littered the floor of certain remote chambers of the British Museum, accidentally stumbled on some which were evidently portions of the original sacred legends partly rendered by Berosus. To search for all available fragments of the precious documents and piece them together became the task of Smith's life. And as nearly all that he found belonged to copies from the Royal Library at Nineveh, it was chiefly in

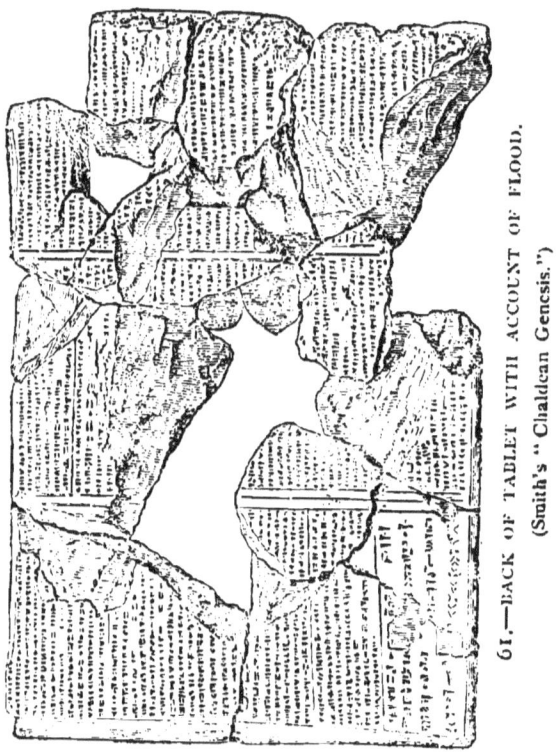

61.—BACK OF TABLET WITH ACCOUNT OF FLOOD. (Smith's "Chaldean Genesis.")

order to enlarge the collection that he undertook his first expedition to the Assyrian mounds, from which he had the good fortune to bring back many missing fragments, belonging also to different copies, so that one frequently completes the other.

Thus the oldest Chaldean legends were in a great measure restored to us, though unfortunately very few tablets are in a sufficiently well preserved condition to allow of making out an entirely intelligible and uninterrupted narrative. Not only are many parts still missing altogether, but of those which have been found, pieced and collected, there is not one of which one or more columns have not been injured in such a way that either the beginning or the end of all the lines are gone, or whole lines broken out or erased, with only a few words left here and there. How hopeless the task must sometimes have seemed to the patient workers may be judged from the foregoing specimen pieced together of sixteen bits, which Geo. Smith gives in his book. This is one of the so-called "Deluge-tablets," i.e., of those which contain the Chaldean version of the story of the Deluge. Luckily more copies have been found of this story than of any of the others, or we should have had to be content still with the short sketch of it given by Berosus.

4. If, therefore, the ancient Babylonian legends of the beginnings of the world will be given here in a connected form, for the sake of convenience and plainness, it must be clearly understood that they were not preserved for us in such a form, but are the result of a long and patient work of research and restoration, a work which still continues; and every year, almost every month, brings to light some new materials, some addition, some correction to the old ones. Yet even as the work now stands, it justifies us in asserting that our knowledge of this

marvellous antiquity is fuller and more authentic than that we have of many a period and people not half so remote from us in point of place and distance.

5. The cosmogonic narrative which forms the first part of what Geo. Smith has very aptly called "the Chaldean Genesis" is contained in a number of tablets. As it begins by the words "*When above*," they are all numbered as No. 1, or 3, or 5 "of the series WHEN ABOVE. *The property of Asshurbanipal, king of nations, king of Assyria.*" The first lines are intact :—" When the heaven above and the earth below were as yet unnamed,"—(i.e., according to Semitic ideas, *did not exist*)—APSU (the "Abyss") and MUMMU-TIAMAT (the "billowy Sea") were the beginning of all things; their waters mingled and flowed together; that was the Primeval Chaos; it contained the germs of life but "the darkness was not lifted" from the waters, and therefore nothing sprouted or grew—(for no growth or life is possible without light). The gods also were not; "they were as yet unnamed and did not rule the destinies." Then the great gods came into being, and the divine hosts of heaven and earth (the Spirits of Heaven and Earth). "And the days stretched themselves out, and the god Anu (Heaven.) . . . ." Here the text breaks off abruptly; it is probable, however, that it told how, after a long lapse of time, the gods Anu, Êa and Bel, the first and supreme triad, came into being. The next fragment, which is sufficiently well preserved to allow of a connected translation, tells of the

establishment of the heavenly bodies : " He " (Anu, whose particular dominion the highest heavens were, hence frequently called " the heaven of Anu ") " he appointed the mansions of the great gods " (signs of the Zodiac), established the stars, ordered the months and the year, and limited the beginning and end thereof ; established the planets, so that none should swerve from its allotted track; "he appointed the mansions of Bel and Êa with his own ; he also opened the great gates of heaven, fastening their bolts firmly to the right and to the left " (east and west) ; he made Nannar (the Moon) to shine and allotted the night to him, determining the time of his quarters which measure the days, and saying to him " rise and set, and be subject to this law." Another tablet, of which only the beginning is intelligible, tells how the gods (in the plural this time) created the living beings which people the earth, the cattle of the field and the city, and the wild beasts of the field, and the things that creep in the field and in the city, in short all the living creatures.

6. There are some tablets which have been supposed to treat of the creation of man and perhaps to give a story of his disobedience and fall, answering to that in Genesis ; but unfortunately they are in too mutilated a condition to admit of certainty, and no other copies have as yet come to light. However, the probability that such was really the case is very great, and is much enhanced by a cylinder of very ancient Babylonian workmanship, now in the British Museum, and too important not to

be reproduced here. The tree in the middle, the human couple stretching out their hands for the fruit, the serpent standing *behind the woman* in— one might almost say—a whispering attitude, all this tells its own tale. And the authority of this artistic presentation, which so strangely fits in to fill the blank in the written narrative, is doubled by the fact that the engravings on the cylinders are invariably taken from subjects connected with relig-

62.—BABYLONIAN CYLINDER, SUPPOSED TO REPRESENT THE TEMPTATION AND FALL.

ion, or at least religious beliefs and traditions. As to the creation of man, we may partly eke out the missing details from the fragment of Berosus already quoted. He there tells us—and so well-informed a writer must have spoken on good authority—that Bel gave his own blood to be kneaded with the clay out of which men were formed, and that is why they are endowed with reason and have a share of the divine nature in them—certainly a most ingenious way of expressing the blending of the earthly and the divine elements which has made human nature so deep and puzzling a problem to the profounder thinkers of all ages.

7. For the rest of the creation, Berosus' account (quoted from the book said to have been given men by the fabulous Oannes), agrees with what we find in the original texts, even imperfect as we have them. He says that in the midst of Chaos—at the time when all was darkness and water—the principle of life which it contained, restlessly working, but without order, took shape in numberless monstrous formations: there were beings like men, some winged, with two heads, some with the legs and horns of goats, others with the hind part of horses; also bulls with human heads, dogs with four bodies and a fish's tail, horses with the heads of dogs, in short, every hideous and fantastical combination of animal forms, before the Divine Will had separated them, and sorted them into harmony and order. All these monstrous beings perished the moment Bel separated the heavens from the earth creating light,—for they were births of darkness and lawlessness and could not stand the new reign of light and law and divine reason. In memory of this destruction of the old chaotic world and production of the new, harmonious and beautiful one, the walls of the famous temple of Bel-Mardouk at Babylon were covered with paintings representing the infinite variety of monstrous and mixed shapes with which an exuberant fancy had peopled the primeval chaos; Berosus was a priest of this temple and he speaks of those paintings as still existing. Though nothing has remained of

them in the ruins of the temple, we have representations of the same kind on many of the cylinders which, used as seals, did duty both as personal badges—(one is almost tempted to say "coats of arms")—and as talismans, as proved by the fact of such cylinders being so frequently found on the wrists of the dead in the sepulchres.

8. The remarkable cylinder with the human couple and the serpent leads us to the consideration of a most important object in the ancient Babylonian or Chaldean religion—the Sacred Tree, the Tree of Life. That it was a very holy symbol is clear from its being so continually reproduced on cylinders and on sculptures. In this particular cylinder, rude as the design is, it bears an unmistakable likeness to a real tree—of some coniferous species, cypress or fir. But art soon took hold of it and began to load it with symmetrical embellishments, until it produced a tree of entirely conventional design, as shown by the following specimens, of which the first leans more to the palm, while the second seems rather of the coniferous type. (Figs. No. 63 and 65.) It is probable that such artificial trees, made up of boughs—perhaps of the palm and cypress—tied together and intertwined with ribbons (something like our Maypoles of old), were set up in the temples as reminders of the sacred symbol, and thus gave rise to the fixed type which remains invariable both in such Babylonian works of art as we possess and on the Assyrian sculptures, where the tree, or a portion of it, appears not only in the running ornaments on the walls but on seal

63.—FEMALE WINGED FIGURES BEFORE THE SACRED TREE.
(From a photograph in the British Museum.)

cylinders and even in the embroidery on the robes of kings. In the latter case indeed, it is almost certain, from the belief in talismans which the Assyrians had inherited, along with the whole of their religion from the Chaldean mother country, that this ornament was selected not only as appropriate to the sacredness of the royal person, but as a consecration and protection. The holiness of the symbol is further evidenced by the kneeling posture of the animals which sometimes accompany it (see Fig. 22, page 67), and the attitude of adoration of the human figures, or winged spirits attending it, by the prevalence of the sacred number seven in its component parts, and by the fact that it is reproduced on a great many of those glazed earthenware coffins which are so plentiful at Warka (ancient Erech). This latter fact clearly shows that the tree-symbol not only meant life in general, life on earth, but a hope of life eternal, beyond the grave, or why should it have been given to the dead? These coffins at Warka belong, it is true, to a late period, some as late as a couple of hundred years after Christ, but the ancient traditions and their meaning had, beyond a doubt, been preserved. Another significant detail is that the cone is frequently seen in the hands of men or spirits, and al-

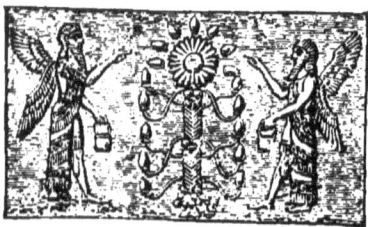

64.—WINGED SPIRITS BEFORE THE SACRED TREE.
(Smith's "Chaldea.")

65.—SARGON OF ASSYRIA BEFORE THE SACRED TREE
(Perrot and Chipiez.)

ways in a way connected with worship or auspicious protection; sometimes it is held to the king's nostrils by his attendant protecting spirits, (known by their wings); a gesture of unmistakable significancy, since in ancient languages "the breath of the nostrils" is synonymous with "the breath of life."

9. There can be no association of ideas more natural than that of vegetation, as represented by a tree, with life. By its perpetual growth and development, its wealth of branches and foliage, its blossoming and fruit-bearing, it is a noble and striking illustration of the world in the widest sense—the Universe, the Cosmos, while the sap which courses equally through the trunk and through the veins of the smallest leaflet, drawn by an incomprehensible process through invisible roots from the nourishing earth, still more forcibly suggests that mysterious principle, Life, which we *think* we understand because we see its effects and feel it in ourselves, but the sources of which will never be reached, as the problem of it will never be solved, either by the prying of experimental science or the musings of contemplative speculation; life eternal, also,—for the workings of nature *are* eternal, —and the tree that is black and lifeless to-day, we know from long experience is not dead, but will revive in the fulness of time, and bud, and grow and bear again. All these things *we* know are the effects of laws; but the ancients attributed them to living Powers,—the CHTHONIC POWERS (from the Greek word CHTHON, "earth, soil"), which have by some later and dreamy thinkers been

66.—EAGLE-HEADED FIGURE BEFORE THE SACRED TREE.
(Smith's "Chaldea.")

called weirdly but not unaptly, "the Mothers," mysteriously at work in the depths of silence and darkness, unseen, unreachable, and inexhaustibly productive. Of these powers again, what more perfect symbol or representative than the Tree, as standing for vegetation, one for all, the part for the whole? It lies so near that, in later times, it was enlarged, so as to embrace the whole universe, in the majestic conception of the Cosmic Tree which has its roots on earth and heaven for its crown, while its fruit are the golden apples—the stars, and Fire,—the red lightning.

10. All these suggestive and poetical fancies would in themselves suffice to make the tree-symbol a favorite one among so thoughtful and profound a people as the old Chaldeans. But there is something more. It is intimately connected with another tradition, common, in some form or other, to all nations who have attained a sufficiently high grade of culture to make their mark in the world —that of an original ancestral abode, beautiful, happy, and remote, a Paradise. It is usually imagined as a great mountain, watered by springs which become great rivers, bearing one or more trees of wonderful properties and sacred character, and is considered as the principal residence of the gods. Each nation locates it according to its own knowledge of geography and vague, half-obliterated memories. Many texts, both in the old Accadian and the Assyrian languages, abundantly prove that the Chaldean religion preserved a distinct and reverent conception of such a mountain, and placed it

FOUR-WINGED HUMAN FIGURE BEFORE THE SACRED TREE.
(Perrot and Chipiez.)

in the far north or north-east, calling it the "Father of Countries," plainly an allusion to the original abode of man—the "Mountain of Countries," (i.e., "Chief Mountain of the World") and also ARALLU, because there, where the gods dwelt, they also imagined the entrance to the Arali to be the Land of the Dead. There, too, the heroes and great men were to dwell forever after their death. There is the land with a sky of silver, a soil which produces crops without being cultivated, where blessings are for food and rejoicing, which it is hoped the king will obtain as a reward for his piety after having enjoyed all earthly goods during his life.* In an old Accadian hymn, the sacred mount, which is identical with that imagined as the pillar joining heaven and earth, the pillar around which the heavenly spheres revolve, (see page 153)—is called "the mountain of Bel, in the east, whose double head reaches unto the skies; which is like to a mighty buffalo at rest, whose double horn sparkles as a sunbeam, as a star." So vivid was the conception in the popular mind, and so great the reverence entertained for it, that it was attempted to reproduce the type of the holy mountain in the palaces of their kings and the temples of their gods. That is one of the reasons why they built both on artificial hills. There is in the British Museum a sculpture from Koyunjik, representing such a temple, or perhaps palace, on the summit of a mound, converted into a garden and watered by a stream

---

* François Lenormant, "Origines de l'Histoire," Vol. II., p. 130.

which issues from the "hanging garden" on the right, the latter being laid out on a platform of masonry raised on arches ; the water was brought up by machinery. It is a perfect specimen of a

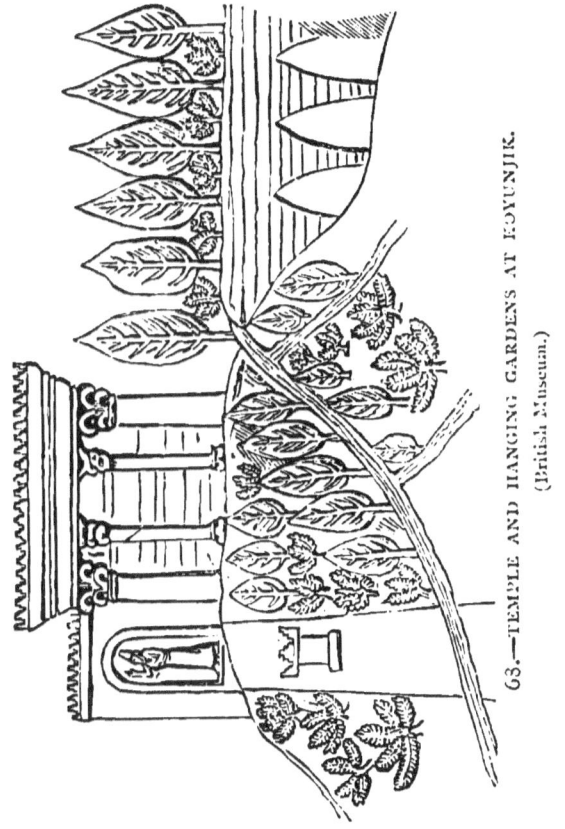

63.—TEMPLE AND HANGING GARDENS AT KOYUNJIK.
(British Museum.)

"Paradise," as these artificial parks were called by the Greeks, who took the word (meaning "park" or "garden") from the Persians, who, in their turn, had borrowed the thing from the Assyrians and Babylonians, when they conquered the latter's empire. The *Ziggurat*, or pyramidal construction in stages, with the temple or shrine on the top, also owed its peculiar shape to the same original conception: as the gods dwelt on the summit of the Mountain of the World, so their shrines should

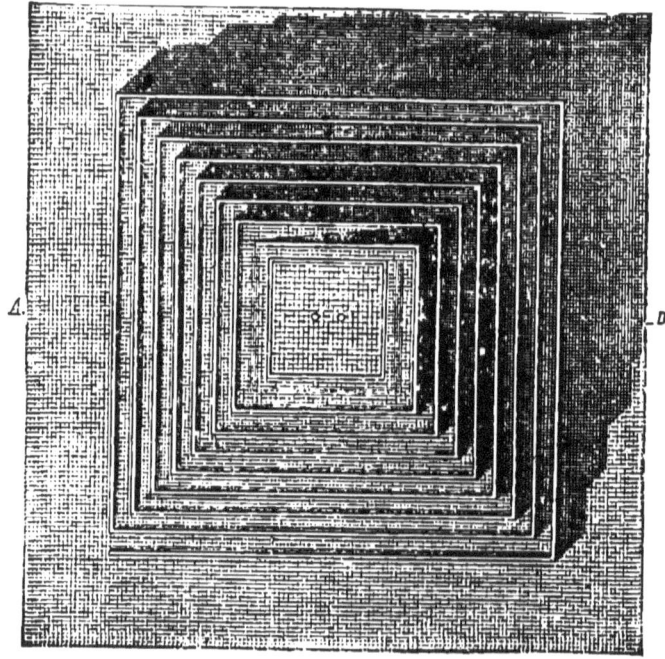

69.—PLAN OF A ZIGGURAT.
(Perrot and Chipiez.)

occupy a position as much like their residence as the feeble means of man would permit. That this is no idle fancy is proved by the very name of "Ziggurat," which means "*mountain peak*," and also by the names of some of these temples: one of the old-

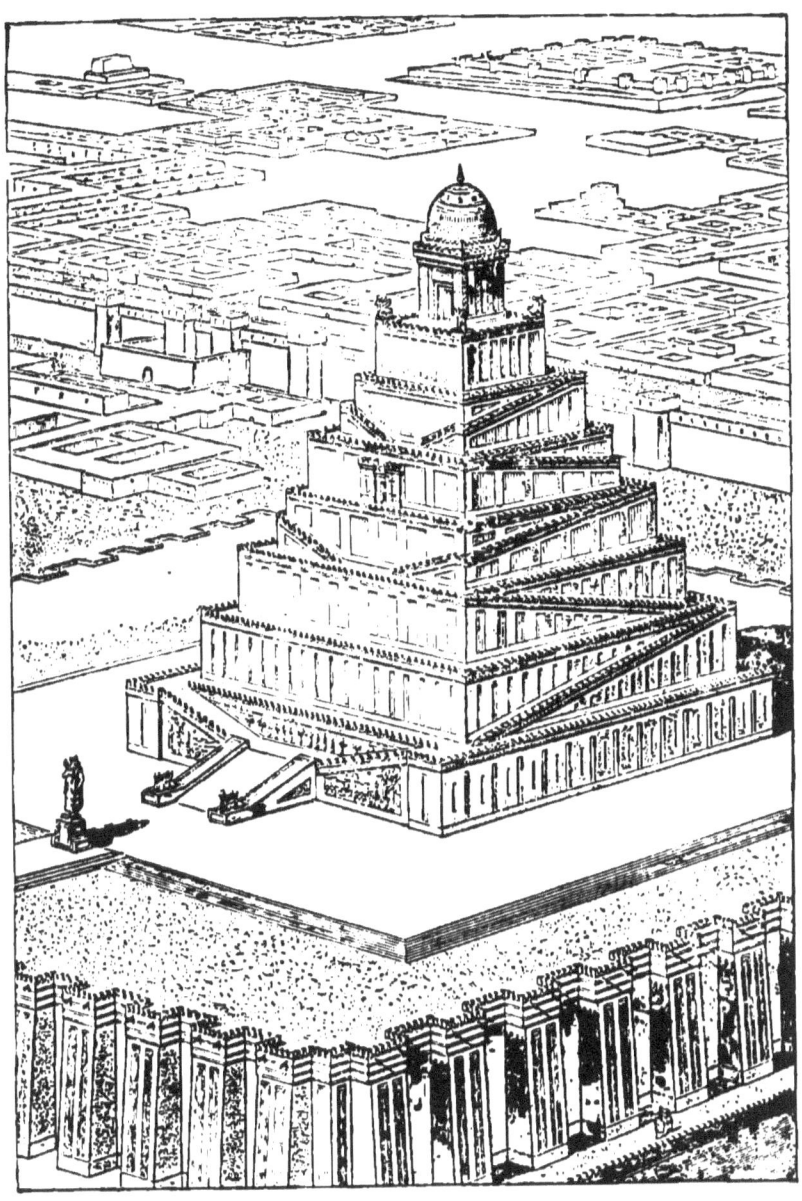

"ZIGGURAT" RESTORED, ACCORDING TO PROBABILITIES.
(Perrot and Chipiez.)

est and most famous indeed, in the city of Asshur, was named "the House of the Mountain of Countries." An excellent representation of a Ziggurat, as it must have looked with its surrounding palm grove by a river, is given us on a sculptured slab, also from Koyunjik. The original is evidently a small one, of probably five stages besides the platform on which it is built, with its two symmetrical paths up the ascent. Some, like the great temple at Ur, had only three stages, others again seven—always one of the three sacred numbers: three, corresponding to the divine Triad; five, to the five planets; seven, to the planets, sun and moon. The famous Temple of the Seven Spheres at Borsip (the Birs-Nimrud), often mentioned already, and rebuilt by Nebuchadnezzar about 600 B.C. from a far older structure, as he explains in his inscription (see p. 72), was probably the most gorgeous, as it was the largest; besides, it is the only one of which we have detailed and reliable descriptions and measurements, which may best be given in this place, almost entirely in the words of George Rawlinson: *

11. The temple is raised on a platform exceptionally low—only a few feet above the level of the plain; the entire height, including the platform, was 156 feet in a perpendicular line. The stages—of which the four upper were lower than the first three—receded equally on three sides, but doubly as much on the fourth, probably in order to present a more imposing front from the plain, and an easier ascent.

---

* "Five Monarchies," Vol. III., pp. 380-387.

71.—BIRS-NIMRUD. (ANCIENT BORSIP.)
(Perrot and Chipiez.)

"The ornamentation of the edifice was chiefly by means of color. The seven Stages represented the Seven Spheres, in which moved, according to ancient Chaldean astronomy, the seven planets. To each planet fancy, partly grounding itself upon fact, had from of old assigned a peculiar tint or hue. The Sun (Shamash) was golden ; the Moon (Sin or Nannar), silver ; the distant Saturn (Adar), almost beyond the region of light, was black ; Jupiter (Marduk) was orange ; the fiery Mars (Nergal) was red ; Venus (Ishtar) was a pale yellow ; Mercury (Nebo or Nabu, whose shrine stood on the top stage), a deep blue. The seven stages of the tower gave a visible embodiment to these fancies. The basement stage, assigned to Saturn, was blackened by means of a coating of bitumen spread over the face of the masonry ; the second stage, assigned to Jupiter, obtained the appropriate orange color by means of a facing of burnt bricks of that hue ; the third stage, that of Mars, was made blood-red by the use of half-burnt bricks formed of a bright-red clay ; the fourth stage, assigned to the Sun, appears to have been actually covered with thin plates of gold ; the fifth, the stage of Venus, received a pale yellow tint from the employment of bricks of that hue ; the sixth, the sphere of Mercury, was given an azure tint by vitrifaction, the whole stage having been subjected to an intense heat after it was erected, whereby the bricks composing it were converted into a mass of blue slag ; the seventh stage, that of the moon, was probably, like the fourth, coated with actual plates of metal. Thus the building rose up in stripes of varied color, arranged almost as nature's cunning hand arranges hues in the rainbow, tones of red coming first, succeeded by a broad stripe of yellow, the yellow being followed by blue. Above this the glowing silvery summit melted into the bright sheen of the sky. . . . The Tower is to be regarded as fronting the north-east, the coolest side, and that least exposed to the sun's rays from the time that they become oppressive in Babylonia. On this side was the ascent, which consisted probably of a broad staircase extending along the whole front of the building. The side platforms, at any rate of the first and second stages, probably of all, were occupied by a series of chambers. . . . In these were doubtless lodged the priests and other attendants upon the temple service. . . ."

12. The interest attaching to this temple, wonderful as it is in itself, is greatly enhanced by the circumstance that its ruins have through many centuries been considered as those of the identical Tower of Babel of the Bible. Jewish literary men who travelled over the country in the Middle Ages started this idea, which quickly spread to the West. It is conjectured that it was suggested by the vitrified fragments of the outer coating of the sixth, blue, stage, (that of Mercury or Nebo), the condition of which was attributed to lightning having struck the building.

13. That the Ziggurats of Chaldea should have been used not only as pedestals to uphold shrines, but as observatories by the priestly astronomers

and astrologers, was quite in accordance with the strong mixture of star-worship grafted on the older religion, and with the power ascribed to the heavenly bodies over the acts and destinies of men. These constructions, therefore, were fitted for astronomical uses by being very carefully placed with their corners pointing exactly to the four cardinal points—North, South, East and West. Only two exceptions have been found to this rule, one in Babylon, and the Assyrian Ziggurat at Kalah, (Nimrud) explored by Layard, of which the sides, not the corners, face the cardinal points. For the Assyrians, who carried their entire culture and religion northward from their ancient home, also retained this consecrated form of architecture, with the difference that with them the Ziggurats were not temple and observatory in one, but only observatories attached to the temples, which were built on more independent principles and a larger scale, often covering as much ground as a palace.

14. The singular orientation of the Chaldean Ziggurats (subsequently retained by the Assyrians),—i.e., the manner in which they are placed, turned to the cardinal points with their angles, and not with their faces, as are the Egyptian pyramids, with only one exception,—has long been a puzzle which no astronomical considerations were sufficient to solve. But quite lately, in 1883, Mr. Pinches, Geo. Smith's successor in the British Museum, found a small tablet, giving lists of signs, eclipses, etc., affecting the various countries, and containing

the following short geographical notice, in illustration of the position assigned to the cardinal points: "The South is Elam, the North is Accad, the East is Suedin and Gutium, the West is Phœnicia. On the right is Accad, on the left is Elam, in front is Phœnicia, behind are Suedin and Gutium." In order to appreciate the bearing of this bit of topography on the question in hand, we must examine an ancient map, when we shall at once perceive that the direction given by the tablet to the *South* (Elam) answers to our *South-East;* that given to the *North* (Accad) answers to our *North-West;* while *West* (Phœnicia, i.e., the coast-land of the Mediterranean, down almost to Egypt) stands for our *South-West*, and *East* (Gutium, the highlands where the Armenian mountains join the Zagros, now Kurdish Mountains,) for our *North-East*. If we turn the map so that the Persian Gulf shall come in a perpendicular line under Babylon, we shall produce the desired effect, and then it will strike us that the Ziggurats *did* face the cardinal points, according to Chaldean geography, *with their sides*, and that the discovery of the small tablet, as was remarked on the production of it, "settles the difficult question of the difference in orientation between the Assyrian and Egyptian monuments." It was further suggested that "the two systems of cardinal points originated no doubt from two different races, and their determination was due probably *to the geographical position of the primitive home of each race.*" Now the South-West is called "the front," "and the migrations of the people *therefore*

must have been from North-East to South-West."*
This beautifully tallies with the hypothesis, or conjecture, concerning the direction from which the Shumiro-Accads descended into the lowlands by the Gulf (see pp. 146-8), and, moreover, leads us to the question whether the fact of the great Ziggurat of the Seven Spheres at Borsip facing the North-East with its front may not have some connection with the holiness ascribed to that region as the original home of the race and the seat of that sacred mountain so often mentioned as "the Great Mountain of Countries" (see p. 280), doubly sacred, as the meeting-place of the gods and the place of entrance to the "Arallu" or Lower World.†

15. It is to be noted that the conception of the divine grove or garden with its sacred tree of life was sometimes separated from that of the holy primeval mountain and transferred by tradition to a more immediate and accessible neighborhood. That the city and district of Babylon may have been the centre of such a tradition is possibly shown by the most ancient Accadian name of the former —TIN-TIR-KI meaning "the Place of Life," while the latter was called GAN-DUNYASH or KAR-DUNYASH—"the garden of the god Dunyash,"

---

* See "Proceedings of the Society of Biblical Archæology," Feb., 1883, pp. 74-76, and "Journal of the Royal Asiatic Society," Vol. XVI., 1884, p. 302.

† The one exception to the above rule of orientation among the Ziggurats of Chaldea is that of the temple of Bel, in Babylon, (E-SAGGILA in the old language,) which is oriented in the usual way —its sides facing the *real* North, South, East and West.

(probably one of the names of the god Êa)—an appellation which this district, although situated in the land of Accad or Upper Chaldea, preserved to the latest times as distinctively its own. Another sacred grove is spoken of as situated in Eridhu. This city, altogether the most ancient we have any mention of, was situated at the then mouth of the Euphrates, in the deepest and flattest of lowlands, a sort of borderland between earth and sea, and therefore very appropriately consecrated to the great spirit of both, the god Êa, the amphibious Oannes. It was so much identified with him, that in the Shumirian hymns and conjurings his son Meridug is often simply invoked as "Son of Eridhu." It must have been the oldest seat of that spirit-worship and sorcerer-priesthood which we find crystallized in the earliest Shumiro-Accadian sacred books. This prodigious antiquity carries us to something like 5000 years B.C., which explains the fact that the ruins of the place, near the modern Arab village of Abu-Shahrein, are now so far removed from the sea, being a considerable distance even from the junction of the two rivers where they form the Shat-el-arab. The sacred grove of Eridhu is frequently referred to, and that it was connected with the tradition of the tree of life we see from a fragment of a most ancient hymn, which tells of "a black pine, growing at Eridhu, sprung up in a pure place, with roots of lustrous crystal extending downwards, even into the deep, marking the centre of the earth, in the dark forest into the heart whereof man hath not penetrated." Might not this be the reason why the wood of the pine was so much used in charms and conjuring, as the surest safeguard against evil influences, and its very shadow was held wholesome and sacred? But we return to the legends of the Creation and primeval world.

16. Mummu-Tiamat, the impersonation of chaos, the power of darkness and lawlessness, does not vanish from the scene when Bel puts an end to her reign, destroys, by the sheer force of light and order, her hideous progeny of monsters and frees from her confusion the germs and rudimental forms of life, which, under the new and divine dispensation, are to expand and combine into the beautifully varied, yet harmonious world we live in. Tiamat becomes the sworn enemy of the gods and their creation, the great principle of opposition and destruction. When the missing texts come to light,—if ever they do—it will probably be found that the serpent who tempts the woman in the famous cylinder, is none other than a form of the rebellious and vindictive Tiamat, who is called now a "Dragon," now "the Great Serpent." At last the hostility cannot be ignored, and things come to a deadly issue. It is determined in the council of the gods that one of them must fight the wicked dragon; a complete suit of armor is made and exhibited by Anu himself, of which the sickle-shaped sword and the beautifully bent bow are the principal features. It is Bel who dares the venture and goes forth on a matchless war chariot, armed with the sword, and the bow, and his great weapon, the

thunderbolt, sending the lightning before him and scattering arrows around. Tiamat, the Dragon of the Sea, came out to meet him, stretching her immense body along, bearing death and destruction, and attended by her followers. The god rushed on

72.—BEL FIGHTS THE DRAGON—TIAMAT (ASSYRIAN CYLINDER.)
(Perrot and Chipiez.)

73. - BEL FIGHTS THE DRAGON—TIAMAT (BABYLONIAN CYLINDER).

the monster with such violence that he threw her down and was already fastening fetters on her limbs, when she uttered a great shout and started up and attacked the righteous leader of the gods, while banners were raised on both sides as at a pitched battle. Meridug drew his sword and wounded her; at the same time a violent wind struck against her face. She opened her jaws to swallow up Meridug, but before she could close them he bade the wind to enter into her body. It entered and filled her with its violence, shook her heart and tore her entrails and subdued her courage. Then the god bound her, and put an end to her works, while her followers stood amazed, then broke their lines and fled, full of fear, seeing that Tiamat, their leader, was conquered. There she lay, her weapons broken, herself like a sword thrown down on the ground, in the dark and bound, conscious of her bondage and in great grief, her might suddenly broken by fear.

17. The battle of Bel-Marduk and the Dragon was a favorite incident in the cycle of Chaldean tradition, if we judge from the number of representations we have of it on Babylonian cylinders, and even on Assyrian wall-sculptures. The texts which relate to it are, however, in a frightful state of mutilation, and only the last fragment, describing the final combat, can be read and translated with anything like completeness. With it ends the series treating of the Cosmogony or Beginnings of the World. But it may be completed by a few more legends of the same primitive character and preserved on detached tablets, in double text, as usual—Accadian and Assyrian. To these belongs a poem narrating the rebellion, already alluded to, (see p. 182,) of the seven evil spirits, originally the messengers and throne-bearers of the gods, and their war against the moon, the whole being evidently a fanciful ren-

74.—BATTLE BETWEEN BEL AND THE DRAGON (TIAMAT).
(Smith's "Chaldea.")

dering of an eclipse. "Those wicked gods, the rebel spirits," of whom one is likened to a leopard, and one to a serpent, and the rest to other animals —suggesting the fanciful shapes of storm-clouds— while one is said to be the raging south wind, began the attack " with evil tempest, baleful wind," and " from the foundations of the heavens like the lightning they darted." The lower region of the sky was reduced to its primeval chaos, and the gods sat in anxious council. The moon-god (Sin), the sungod (Shamash), and the goddess Ishtar had been appointed to sway in close harmony the lower sky and to command the hosts of heaven; but when the moon-god was attacked by the seven spirits of evil, his companions basely forsook him, the sun-god retreating to his place and Ishtar taking refuge in the highest heaven (the heaven of Anu). Nebo is despatched to Êa, who sends his son Meridug with this instruction :—" Go, my son Meridug ! The light of the sky, my son, even the moon-god, is grievously darkened in heaven, and in eclipse from heaven is vanishing. Those seven wicked gods, the serpents of death who fear not, are waging unequal war with the laboring moon." Meridug obeys his father's bidding, and overthrows the seven powers of darkness.*

18. There is one more detached legend known from the surviving fragments of Berosus, also supposed to be derived from ancient Accadian texts: it is that of the great tower and the confusion of

---

* See A. H. Sayce, " Babylonian Literature," p. 35.

tongues. One such text has indeed been found by the indefatigable George Smith, but there is just enough left of it to be very tantalizing and very unsatisfactory. The narrative in Berosus amounts to this: that men having grown beyond measure proud and arrogant, so as to deem themselves superior even to the gods, undertook to build an immense tower, to scale the sky; that the gods, offended with this presumption, sent violent winds to overthrow the construction when it had already reached a great height, and at the same time caused men to speak different languages,—probably to sow dissension among them, and prevent their ever again uniting in a common enterprise so daring and impious. The site was identified with that of Babylon itself, and so strong was the belief attaching to the legend that the Jews later on adopted it unchanged, and centuries afterwards, as we saw above, fixed on the ruins of the hugest of all Ziggurats, that of Borsip, as those of the great Tower of the Confusion of Tongues. Certain it is, that the tradition, under all its fanciful apparel, contains a very evident vein of historical fact, since it was indeed from the plains of Chaldea that many of the principal nations of the ancient East, various in race and speech, dispersed to the north, the west, and the south, after having dwelt there for centuries as in a common cradle, side by side, and indeed to a great extent as one people.

VII.

MYTHS.—HEROES AND THE MYTHICAL EPOS.

1. THE stories by which a nation attempts to account for the mysteries of creation, to explain the Origin of the World, are called, in scientific language, COSMOGONIC MYTHS. The word Myth is constantly used in conversation, but so loosely and incorrectly, that it is most important once for all to define its proper meaning. It means simply *a phenomenon of nature presented not as the result of a law but as the act of divine or at least superhuman persons, good or evil powers*—(for instance, the eclipse of the Moon described as the war against the gods of the seven rebellious spirits). Further reading and practice will show that there are many kinds of myths, of various origins; but there is none, which, if properly taken to pieces, thoroughly traced and cornered, will not be covered by this definition. A Myth has also been defined as a legend connected more or less closely with some religious belief, and, in its main outlines, handed down from prehistoric times. There are only two things which can prevent the contemplation of nature and speculation on its mysteries from running into mythology: a knowledge

of the physical laws of nature, as supplied by modern experimental science, and a strict, unswerving belief in the unity of God, absolute and undivided, as affirmed and defined by the Hebrews in so many places of their sacred books: "The Lord he is God, there is none else beside him." "The Lord he is God, in Heaven above and upon the earth beneath there is none else." "I am the Lord, and there is none else, there is no God beside me." "I am God and there is none else." But experimental science is a very modern thing indeed, scarcely a few hundred years old, and Monotheism, until the propagation of Christianity, was professed by only one small nation, the Jews, though the chosen thinkers of other nations have risen to the same conception in many lands and many ages. The great mass of mankind has always believed in the personal individuality of all the forces of nature, i.e., in many gods; everything that went on in the world was to them the manifestation of the feelings, the will, the acts of these gods—hence the myths. The earlier the times, the more unquestioning the belief and, as a necessary consequence, the more exuberant the creation of myths.

2. But gods and spirits are not the only actors in myths. Side by side with its sacred traditions on the Origin of things, every nation treasures fond but vague memories of its own beginnings—vague, both from their remoteness and from their not being fixed in writing, and being therefore liable to the alterations and enlargements which a story invariably undergoes when told many times to and

by different people, i.e., when it is transmitted from generation to generation by oral tradition. These memories generally centre around a few great names, the names of the oldest national heroes, of the first rulers, lawgivers and conquerors of the nation, the men who by their genius *made* it a nation out of a loose collection of tribes or large families, who gave it social order and useful arts, and safety from its neighbors, or, perhaps, freed it from foreign oppressors. In their grateful admiration for these heroes, whose doings naturally became more and more marvellous with each generation that told of them, men could not believe that they should have been mere imperfect mortals like themselves, but insisted on considering them as directly inspired by the deity in some one of the thousand shapes they invested it with, or as half-divine of their own nature. The consciousness of the imperfection inherent to ordinary humanity, and the limited powers awarded to it, has always prompted this explanation of the achievements of extraordinarily gifted individuals, in whatever line of action their exceptional gifts displayed themselves. Besides, if there is something repugnant to human vanity in having to submit to the dictates of superior reason and the rule of superior power as embodied in mere men of flesh and blood, there is on the contrary something very flattering and soothing to that same vanity in the idea of having been specially singled out as the object of the protection and solicitude of the divine powers; this idea at all events takes the galling sting from the constraint of obedience. Hence every nation has very jealously insisted on and devoutly believed in the divine origin of its rulers and the divine institution of its laws and customs. Once it was implicitly admitted that the world teemed with spirits and gods, who, not content with attending to their particular spheres and departments, came and went at their pleasure, had walked the earth and directly interfered with human affairs, there was no reason to disbelieve *any* occurrence, however marvellous—provided it had happened very, very long ago. (See p. 197.)

3. Thus, in the traditions of every ancient nation, there is a vast and misty tract of time, expressed, if at all, in figures of appalling magnitude—hundreds of thousands, nay, millions of years—between the unpierceable gloom of an eternal past and the broad daylight of remembered, recorded history. There, all is shadowy, gigantic, superhuman. There, gods move, dim yet visible, shrouded in a golden cloud of mystery and awe; there, by their side, loom other shapes, as dim but more familiar, human yet more than human—the Heroes, Fathers of races, founders of nations, the companions, the beloved of gods and goddesses, nay, their own children, mortal themselves, yet doing deeds of daring and might such as only the immortals could inspire and favor, the connecting link between these and ordinary humanity—as that gloaming, uncertain, shifting, but not altogether unreal streak of time is the border-land between Heaven and Earth, the very hot-bed of myth, fiction and romance. For of their favorite

heroes, people began to tell the same stories as of their gods, in modified forms, transferred to their own surroundings and familiar scenes. To take one of the most common transformations: if the Sun-god waged war against the demons of darkness and destroyed them in heaven (see p. 171), the hero hunted wild beasts and monsters on earth, of course always victoriously. This one theme could be varied by the national poets in a thousand ways and woven into a thousand different stories, which come with full right under the head of "myths." Thus arose a number of so-called HEROIC MYTHS, which, by dint of being repeated, settled into a certain defined traditional shape, like the well-known fairy-tales of our nurseries, which are the same everywhere and told in every country with scarcely any changes. As soon as the art of writing came into general use, these favorite and time-honored stories, which the mass of the people probably still received as literal truth, were taken down, and, as the work naturally devolved on priests and clerks, i.e., men of education and more or less literary skill, often themselves poets, they were worked over in the process, connected, and re-modelled into a continuous whole. The separate myths, or adventures of one or more particular heroes, formerly recited severally, somewhat after the manner of the old songs and ballads, frequently became so many chapters or books in a long, well-ordered poem, in which they were introduced and distributed, often with consummate art, and told with great poetical beauty. Such poems, of which several have come down to us, are called EPIC POEMS, or simply EPICS. The entire mass of fragmentary materials out of which they are composed in the course of time, blending almost inextricably historical reality with mythical fiction, is the NATIONAL EPOS of a race, its greatest intellectual treasure, from which all its late poetry and much of its political and religious feeling draws its food ever after. A race that has no national epos is one devoid of great memories, incapable of high culture and political development, and no such has taken a place among the leading races of the world. All those that have occupied such a place at any period of the world's history, have had their Mythic and Heroic Ages, brimful of wonders and fanciful creations.

4. From these remarks it will be clear that the preceding two or three chapters have been treating of what may properly be called the Religious and Cosmogonic Myths of the Shumiro-Accads and the Babylonians. The present chapter will be devoted to their Heroic Myths or Mythic Epos, as embodied in an Epic which has been in great part preserved, and which is the oldest known in the world, dating certainly from 2000 years B.C., and probably more.

5. Of this poem the few fragments we have of Berosus contain no indication. They only tell of a great deluge which took place under the last of that fabulous line of ten kings which is said to have begun 259,000 years after the apparition of the

divine Man-Fish, Oannes, and to have reigned in the aggregate a period of 432,000 years. The description has always excited great interest from its extraordinary resemblance to that given by the Bible. Berosus tells how XISUTHROS, the last of the ten fabulous kings, had a dream in which the deity announced to him that on a certain day all men should perish in a deluge of waters, and ordered him to take all the sacred writings and bury them at Sippar, the City of the Sun, then to build a ship, provide it with ample stores of food and drink and enter it with his family and his dearest friends, also animals, both birds and quadrupeds of every kind. Xisuthros did as he had been bidden. When the flood began to abate, on the third day after the rain had ceased to fall, he sent out some birds, to see whether they would find any land, but the birds, having found neither food nor place to rest upon, returned to the ship. A few days later, Xisuthros once more sent the birds out; but they again came back to him, this time with muddy feet. On being sent out a third time, they did not return at all. Xisuthros then knew that the land was uncovered; made an opening in the roof of the ship and saw that it was stranded on the top of a mountain. He came out of the ship with his wife, daughter and pilot, built an altar and sacrificed to the gods, after which he disappeared together with these. When his companions came out to seek him they did not see him, but a voice from heaven informed them that he had been translated among the gods to live forever, as a reward for his piety and righteousness. The voice went on to command the survivors to return to Babylonia, unearth the sacred writings and make them known to men. They obeyed and, moreover, built many cities and restored Babylon.

6. However interesting this account, it was received at second-hand and therefore felt to need confirmation and ampler development. Besides which, as it stood, it lacked all indication that could throw light on the important question which of the two traditions—that reproduced by Berosus or the Biblical one—was to be considered as the oldest. Here again it was George Smith who had the good fortune to discover the original narrative (in 1872), while engaged in sifting and sorting the tablet-fragments at the British Museum. This is how it happened : *—" Smith found one-half of a whitish-yellow clay tablet, which, to all appearance, had been divided on each face into three columns. In the third column of the obverse or front side he read the words: 'On the mount Nizir the ship stood still. Then I took a dove and let her fly. The dove flew hither and thither, but finding no resting-place, returned to the ship.' Smith at once knew that he had discovered a fragment of the cuneiform narrative of the Deluge. With indefatigable perseverance he set to work to search the thousands of Assyrian tablet-fragments heaped up in the British Museum, for more pieces. His efforts were crowned with success. He did not

---

* Paul Haupt, " Der Keilinschriftliche Sündfluthbericht," 1881.

indeed find a piece completing the half of the tablet first discovered, but he found instead fragments of two more copies of the narrative, which completed the text in the most felicitous manner and supplied several very important variations of it. One of these duplicates, which has been pieced out of sixteen little bits (see illustration on p. 262), bore the usual inscription at the bottom: 'The property of Asshurbanipal, King of hosts, King of the land of Asshur,' and contained the information that the Deluge-narrative was the eleventh tablet of a series, several fragments of which, Smith had already come across. With infinite pains he put all these fragments together and found that the story of the Deluge was only an incident in a great Heroic Epic, a poem written in twelve books, making in all about three thousand lines, which celebrated the deeds of an ancient king of Erech.

7. Each book or chapter naturally occupied a separate tablet. All are by no means equally well preserved. Some parts, indeed, are missing, while several are so mutilated as to cause serious gaps and breaks in the narrative, and the first tablet has not yet been found at all. Yet, with all these drawbacks it is quite possible to build up a very intelligible outline of the whole story, while the eleventh tablet, owing to various fortunate additions that came to light from time to time, has been restored almost completely.

8. The epic carries us back to the time when Erech was the capital of Shumir, and when the

land was under the dominion of the Elamite conquerors, not passive or content, but striving manfully for deliverance. We may imagine the struggle to have been shared and headed by the native kings, whose memory would be gratefully treasured by later generations, and whose exploits would naturally become the theme of household tradition and poets' recitations. So much for the bare historical groundwork of the poem. It is easily to be distinguished from the rich by-play of fiction and wonderful adventure gradually woven into it from the ample fund of national myths and legends, which have gathered around the name of one hero-king, GISDHUBAR or IZDUBAR,* said to be a native of the ancient city of MARAD and a direct descendant of the last antediluvian king HÂSISADRA, the same whom Berosus calls Xisuthros.

9. It is unfortunate that the first tablet and the top part of the second are missing, for thus we lose the opening of the poem, which would probably give us valuable historical indications. What there is of the second tablet shows the city of Erech groaning under the tyranny of the Elamite conquerors. Erech had been governed by the divine Dumuzi, the husband of the goddess Ishtar. He had met an untimely and tragic death, and been succeeded by Ishtar, who had not been able, however, to make a stand against the foreign invaders, or, as the text picturesquely expresses it,

---

*There are difficulties in the way of reading this name, and scholars are not sure that this is the right pronunciation of it; but they retain it, until some new discovery helps to settle the question.

"to hold up her head against the foe." Izdubar, as yet known to fame only as a powerful and indefatigable huntsman, then dwelt at Erech, where he had a singular dream. It seemed to him that the stars of heaven fell down and struck him on the back in their fall, while over him stood a terrible being, with fierce, threatening countenance and claws like a lion's, the sight of whom paralyzed him with fear.

10. Deeply impressed with this dream, which appeared to him to portend strange things, Izdubar sent forth to all the most famous seers and wise men, promising the most princely rewards to whoever would interpret it for him: he should be ennobled with his family; he should take the high seat of honor at the royal feasts; he should be clothed in jewels and gold; he should have seven beautiful wives and enjoy every kind of distinction. But there was none found of wisdom equal to the task of reading the vision. At length he heard of a wonderful sage, named ÊABÂNI, far-famed for "his wisdom in all things and his knowledge of all that is either visible or concealed," but who dwelt apart from mankind, in a distant wilderness, in a cave, amidst the beasts of the forest.

"With the gazelles he ate his food at night, with the beasts of the field he associated in the daytime, with the living things of the waters his heart rejoiced."

This strange being is always represented on the Babylonian cylinders as a Man-Bull, with horns on his head and a bull's feet and tail. He was not easily accessible, nor to be persuaded to come to Erech, even though the Sun-god, Shamash, himself "opened his lips and spoke to him from heaven," making great promises on Izdubar's behalf :—

"They shall clothe thee in royal robes, they shall make thee great; and Izdubar shall become thy friend, and he shall place thee in a luxurious seat at his left hand; the kings of the earth shall kiss thy feet; he shall enrich thee and make the men of Erech keep silence before thee."

The hermit was proof against ambition and refused to leave his wilderness. Then a follower of Izdubar, ZAIDU, the huntsman, was sent to bring him; but he returned alone and reported that, when he had approached the seer's cave, he had been seized with fear and had not entered it, but had crawled back, climbing the steep bank on his hands and feet.

11. At last Izdubar bethought him to send out Ishtar's handmaidens, SHAMHATU ("Grace") and HARIMTU ("Persuasion"), and they started for the wilderness under the escort of Zaidu. Shamhatu was the first to approach the hermit, but he heeded her little; he turned to her companion, and sat down at her feet; and when Harimtu ("Persuasion") spoke, bending her face towards him, he listened and was attentive. And she said to him :

"Famous art thou, Eabâni, even like a god; why then associate with the wild things of the desert? Thy place is in the midst of Erech, the great city, in the temple, the seat of Anu and Ishtar, in the palace of Izdubar, the man of might, who towers amidst the leaders as a bull." "She spoke to him, and before her words the wisdom of his heart fled and vanished."

75.—IZDUBAR AND THE LION (BAS-RELIEF FROM KHORSABAD).
(Smith's "Chaldea.")

He answered:

"I will go to Erech, to the temple, the seat of Anu and Ishtar, to the palace of Izdubar, the man of might, who towers amidst the leaders as a bull. I will meet him and see his might. But I shall bring to Erech a lion—let Izdubar destroy him if he can. He is bred in the wilderness and of great strength."

76.—IZDUBAR AND THE LION.
(British Museum.)

So Zaidu and the two women went back to Erech, and Éabâni went with them, leading his lion. The chiefs of the city received him with great honors and gave a splendid entertainment in sign of rejoicing.

12. It is evidently on this occasion that Izdubar conquers the seer's esteem by fighting and kill-

ing the lion, after which the hero and the sage enter into a solemn covenant of friendship. But the third tablet, which contains this part of the story, is so much mutilated as to leave much of the substance to conjecture, while all the details, and the interpretation of the dream which is probably given, are lost. The same is unfortunately the case with the fourth and fifth tablets, from which we can only gather that Izdubar and Êabâni, who have become inseparable, start on an expedition against the Elamite tyrant, KHUMBABA, who holds his court in a gloomy forest of cedars and cypresses, enter his palace, fall upon him unawares and kill him, leaving his body to be torn and devoured by the birds of prey, after which exploit Izdubar, as his friend had predicted to him, is proclaimed king in Erech. The sixth tablet is far better preserved, and gives us one of the most interesting incidents almost complete.

13. After Izdubar's victory, his glory and power were great, and the goddess Ishtar looked on him with favor and wished for his love.

"Izdubar," she said, "be my husband and I will be thy wife: pledge thy troth to me. Thou shalt drive a chariot of gold and precious stones, thy days shall be marked with conquests; kings, princes and lords shall be subject to thee and kiss thy feet; they shall bring thee tribute from mountain and valley, thy herds and flocks shall multiply doubly, thy mules shall be fleet, and thy oxen strong under the yoke. Thou shalt have no rival."

But Izdubar, in his pride, rejected the love of the goddess; he insulted her and taunted her with having loved Dumuzi and others before him. Great was the wrath of Ishtar; she ascended to heaven and stood before her father Anu:

"My father, Izdubar has insulted me. Izdubar scorns my beauty and spurns my love."

She demanded satisfaction, and Anu, at her request, created a monstrous bull, which he sent against the city of Erech. But Izdubar and his friend went out to fight the bull, and killed him.

77.—IZDUBAR AND ÊABÂNI FIGHT THE BULL OF ISHTAR.—IZDUBAR FIGHTS EABANI'S LION (BABYLONIAN CYLINDER).
(Smith's "Chaldea.")

Êabâni took hold of his tail and horns, and Izdubar gave him his deathblow. They drew the heart out of his body and offered it to Shamash. Then Ishtar ascended the wall of the city, and standing there cursed Izdubar. She gathered her handmaidens around her and they raised loud lamentations over the death of the divine bull. But Izdubar called together his people and bade them lift up the body and carry it to the altar of Shamash and lay it before the god. Then they washed their hands in the Euphrates and returned to the city, where they made a feast of rejoicing and revelled deep into the night, while in the streets a proclamation to the people of Erech was called out, which began with the triumphant words:

"Who is skilled among leaders? Who is great among men? Izdubar is skilled among leaders; Izdubar is great among men."

14. But the vengeance of the offended goddess was not to be so easily defeated. It now fell on the hero in a more direct and personal way. Ishtar's

78.—IZDUBAR AND ÊABÂNI (BABYLONIAN CYLINDER).
(Perrot and Chipiez.)

mother, the goddess Anatu, smote Êabâni with sudden death and Izdubar with a dire disease, a sort of leprosy, it would appear. Mourning for his friend, deprived of strength and tortured with intolerable pains, he saw visions and dreams which oppressed and terrified him, and there was now no wise, familiar voice to soothe and counsel him. At length he decided to consult his ancestor, Hâsisadra, who dwelt far away, "at the mouth of the rivers," and was immortal, and to ask of him how he might find healing and strength. He started on his way alone and came to a strange country, where he met gigantic, monstrous beings, half men, half scorpions: their feet were below the earth, while their heads touched the gates of heaven; they were the warders of the sun and kept their watch over its rising and setting. They said one to another: "Who is this that comes to us with the mark of the divine wrath on his body?" Izdubar made his person and errand known to them; then they gave him directions how to reach the land of the blessed at the mouth of the rivers, but warned him that the way was long and full of hardships. He set out again and crossed a vast tract of country, where there was nothing but sand, not one cultivated field; and he walked on and on, never looking behind him, until he came to a beautiful grove by the seaside, where the trees bore fruits of emerald and other precious stones; this grove was guarded by two beautiful maidens, SIDURI and SABITU, but they looked with mistrust on the stranger with the mark of the gods on his body, and closed their dwelling against him.

79.—SCORPION-MEN.
(Smith's "Chaldea.")

15. And now Izdubar stood by the shore of the Waters of Death, which are wide and deep, and separate the land of the living from that of the blessed and immortal dead. Here he encountered the ferryman URUBÊL; to him he opened his heart and spoke of the friend whom he had loved and

86.—STONE OBJECT FOUND AT ABU-HABBA (SIPPAR) BY MR. H. RASSAM, SHOWING, AMONG OTHER MYTHICAL DESIGNS, SHAMASH AND HIS WARDER, THE SCORPION-MAN.

lost, and Urubêl took him into his ship. For one month and fifteen days they sailed on the Waters of Death, until they reached that distant land by the mouth of the rivers, where Izdubar at length met his renowned ancestor face to face, and, even while he prayed for his advice and assistance, a very natural feeling of curiosity prompted him to ask "how he came to be translated alive into the assembly of the gods." Hâsisadra, with great complaisance, answered his descendant's question and gave him a full account of the Deluge and his own share in that event, after which he informed him in what way he could be freed from the curse laid on him by the gods. Then turning to the ferryman:

"Urubêl, the man whom thou hast brought hither, behold, disease has covered his body, sickness has destroyed the strength of his limbs. Take him with thee, Urubêl, and purify him in the waters, that his disease may be changed into beauty, that he may throw off his sickness and the waters carry it away, that health may cover his skin, and the hair of his head be restored and descend in flowing locks down to his garment, that he may go his way and return to his own country."

16. When all had been done according to Hâsisadra's instruction, Izdubar, restored to health and vigor, took leave of his ancestor, and entering the ship once more was carried back to the shore of the living by the friendly Urubêl, who accompanied him all the way to Erech. But as they approached the city tears flowed down the hero's face and his heart was heavy within him for his lost friend, and he once more raised his voice in lamentation for him:

"Thou takest no part in the noble feast; to the assembly they call thee not; thou liftest not the bow from the ground; what is hit by the bow is not for thee; thy hand grasps not the club and strikes not the prey, nor stretches thy foeman dead on the earth. The wife thou lovest thou kissest not; the wife thou hatest thou strikest not. The child thou lovest thou kissest not; the child thou hatest thou strikest not. The might of the earth has swallowed thee. O Darkness, Darkness, Mother Darkness! thou enfoldest him like a mantle; like a deep well thou enclosest him!"

Thus Izdubar mourned for his friend, and went into the temple of Bel, and ceased not from lamenting and crying to the gods, till Êa mercifully inclined to his prayer and sent his son Meridug to bring Êabâni's spirit out of the dark world of shades into the land of the blessed, there to live forever among the heroes of old, reclining on luxurious couches and drinking the pure water of eternal springs. The poem ends with a vivid description of a warrior's funeral:

"I see him who has been slain in battle. His father and mother hold his head; his wife weeps over him; his friends stand around; his prey lies on the ground uncovered and unheeded. The vanquished captives follow; the food provided in the tents is consumed."

17. The incident of the Deluge, which has been merely mentioned above, not to interrupt the narrative by its disproportionate length, (the eleventh tablet being the best preserved of all), is too important not to be given in full.*

"I will tell thee, Izdubar, how I was saved from the flood," begins Hâsisadra, in answer to his descendant's question, "also will I impart to thee the decree of the great gods. Thou knowest Surippak, the city that is by the Euphrates. This city was already very ancient when the gods were moved in their hearts to ordain a great deluge,

---

* Translated from the German version of Paul Haupt, "Der Keilinschriftliche Sündfluthbericht."

all of them, their father Anu, their councillor the warlike Bel, their throne-bearer Ninib, their leader Ennugi. The lord of inscrutable wisdom, the god Êa, was with them and imparted to me their decision. 'Listen,' he said, 'and attend! Man of Surippak, son of Ubaratutu,* go out of thy house and build thee a ship. They are willed to destroy the seed of life; but thou preserve it and bring into the ship seed of every kind of life. The ship which thou shalt build let it be . . . . in length, and . . . . in width and height,† and cover it also with a deck.' When I heard this I spoke to Êa, my lord: 'If I construct the ship as thou biddest me, O lord, the people and their elders will laugh at me.' But Êa opened his lips once more and spoke to me his servant: 'Men have rebelled against me, and I will do judgment on them, high and low. But do thou close the door of the ship when the time comes and I tell thee of it. Then enter the ship and bring into it thy store of grain, all thy property, thy family, thy men-servants and thy women-servants, and also thy next of kin. The cattle of the fields, the wild beasts of the fields, I shall send to thee myself, that they may be safe behind thy door.'—Then I built the ship and provided it with stores of food and drink; I divided the interior into . . . . compartments.† I saw to the chinks and filled them; I poured bitumen over its outer side and over its inner side. All that I possessed I brought together and stowed it in the ship; all that I had of gold, of silver, of the seed of life of every kind; all my men-servants and my women-servants, the cattle of the field, the wild beasts of the field, and also my nearest friends. Then, when Shamash brought round the appointed time, a voice spoke to me:— 'This evening the heavens will rain destruction, wherefore go thou into the ship and close thy door. The appointed time has come,' spoke the voice, 'this evening the heavens will rain destruction.' And greatly I feared the sunset of that day, the day on which I was to begin my voyage. I was sore afraid. Yet I entered into the ship and closed the door behind me, to shut off the ship. And I confided the great ship to the pilot, with all its freight.—Then a great black cloud rises from the depths of the heavens, and Ramân thunders in the midst of it, while Nebo and Nergal encounter each other, and the Throne-bearers walk over mountains and vales. The mighty god of Pestilence lets loose the whirlwinds; Ninib unceasingly makes the

---

* The ninth king in the fabulous list of ten.
† The figures unfortunately obliterated.

canals to overflow; the Anunnaki bring up floods from the depths of the earth, which quakes at their violence. Ramân's mass of waters rises even to heaven; light is changed into darkness. Confusion and devastation fills the earth. Brother looks not after brother, men have no thought for one another. In the heavens the very gods are afraid; they seek a refuge in the highest heaven of Anu; as a dog in its lair, the gods crouch by the railing of heaven. Ishtar cries aloud with sorrow: 'Behold, all is turned into mud, as I foretold to the gods! I prophesied this disaster and the extermination of my creatures—men. But I do not give them birth that they may fill the sea like the brood of fishes.' Then the gods wept with her and sat lamenting on one spot. For six days and seven nights wind, flood and storm reigned supreme; but at dawn of the seventh day the tempest decreased, the waters, which had battled like a mighty host, abated their violence; the sea retired, and storm and flood both ceased. I steered about the sea, lamenting that the homesteads of men were changed into mud. The corpses drifted about like logs. I opened a port-hole, and when the light of day fell on my face I shivered and sat down and wept. I steered over the countries which now were a terrible sea. Then a piece of land rose out of the waters. The ship steered towards the land Nizir. The mountain of the land Nizir held fast the ship and did not let it go. Thus it was on the first and on the second day, on the third and the fourth, also on the fifth and sixth days. At dawn of the seventh day I took out a dove and sent it forth. The dove went forth to and fro, but found no resting-place and returned. Then I took out a swallow and sent it forth. The swallow went forth, to and fro, but found no resting-place and returned. Then I took out a raven and sent it forth. The raven went forth, and when it saw that the waters had abated, it came near again, cautiously wading through the water, but did not return. Then I let out all the animals, to the four winds of heaven, and offered a sacrifice. I raised an altar on the highest summit of the mountain, placed the sacred vessels on it seven by seven, and spread reeds, cedar-wood and sweet herbs under them. The gods smelled a savor; the gods smelled a sweet savor; like flies they swarmed around the sacrifice. And when the goddess Ishtar came, she spread out on high the great bows of her father Anu:—' By the necklace of my neck,' she said, ' I shall be mindful of these days, never shall I lose the memory of them! May all the gods come to the altar; Bel alone shall not come, for that he controlled not his wrath, and brought on the deluge, and gave up my men to destruction.' When after that Bel came nigh and saw the ship, he was perplexed, and his heart was filled with anger against the gods and against the spirits of Heaven:—'Not a soul shall escape,' he cried; 'not one man shall come alive out of destruction!' Then the god Ninîb opened his lips and spoke, addressing the warlike Bel:— 'Who but Êa can have done this? Êa knew, and informed him of everything.' Then Êa opened his lips and spoke, addressing the warlike Bel:—'Thou art the mighty leader of the gods: but why hast thou acted thus recklessly and brought on this deluge? Let the sinner suffer for his sin and the evil-doer for his misdeeds; but to this man be gracious that he may not be destroyed, and incline towards him favorably, that he may be preserved. And instead of bringing on another deluge, let lions and hyenas come and take from the number of men; send a famine to unpeople the earth; let the god of Pestilence lay men low. I have not imparted to Hâsisadra the decision of the great gods: I only sent him a dream, and he understood the warning.'—Then Bel came to his senses. He entered the ship, took hold of my hand and lifted me up; he also lifted up my wife and laid her hand in mine. Then he turned towards us, stood between us and spoke this blessing on us:—'Until now Hâsisadra was only human: but now he shall be raised to be equal with the gods, together with his wife. He shall dwell in the distant land, by the mouth of the rivers.' Then they took me and translated me to the distant land by the mouth of the rivers."

18. Such is the great Chaldean Epic, the discovery of which produced so profound a sensation, not to say excitement, not only among special scholars, but in the reading world generally, while the full importance of it in the history of human culture cannot yet be realized at this early stage of our historical studies, but will appear more and more clearly as their course takes us to later nations and other lands. We will here linger over the poem only long enough to justify and explain the name given to it in the title of this chapter, of "Mythical Epos."

19. Were the hero Izdubar a purely human person, it would be a matter of much wonder how the small nucleus of historical fact which the story of his adventures contains should have become entwined and overgrown with such a disproportionate quantity of the most extravagant fiction, oftentimes downright monstrous in its fancifulness. But the story is one far older than that of any mere human hero and relates to one far mightier: it is the story of the Sun in his progress through the year, retracing his career of increasing splendor as the spring advances to midsummer, the height of his power when he reaches the month represented in the Zodiac by the sign of the Lion, then the decay of his strength as he pales and sickens in the autumn, and at last his restoration to youth and vigor after he has passed the Waters of Death—Winter, the death of the year, the season of nature's deathlike torpor, out of which the sun has not strength sufficient to rouse her, until spring comes back and the circle begins again. An examination of the Accadian calendar, adopted by the more scientifically inclined Semites, shows that the names of most of the months and the signs by which they were represented on the maps of the corresponding constellations of the Zodiac, directly answer to various incidents of the poem, following, too, in the same order, which is that of the respective seasons of the year,—which, be it noted, began with the spring, in the middle of our month of March. If we compare the calendar months with the tablets of the poem we will find that they, in almost every case, corre-

spond. As the first tablet is unfortunately still missing, we cannot judge how far it may have answered to the name of the first month—"the Altar of Bel." But the second month, called that of "the Propitious Bull," or the "Friendly Bull," very well corresponds to the second tablet which ends with Izdubar's sending for the seer Êabâni, half bull half man, while the name and sign of the third, ": the Twins," clearly alludes to the bond of friendship concluded between the two heroes, who became inseparable. Their victory over the tyrant Khumbaba in the fifth tablet is symbolized by the sign representing the victory of the Lion over the Bull, often abbreviated into that of the Lion alone, a sign plainly enough interpreted by the name "Month of Fire," so appropriate to the hottest and driest of seasons even in moderate climes—July-August. What makes this interpretation absolutely conclusive is the fact that in the symbolical imagery of all the poetry of the East, the Lion represents the principle of heat, of fire. The seventh tablet, containing the wooing of the hero by the goddess Ishtar, is too plainly reproduced in the name of the corresponding month, "the Month of the Message of Ishtar," to need explanation. The sign, too, is that of a woman with a bow, the usual mode of representing the goddess. The sign of the eighth month, "the Scorpion," commemorates the gigantic Warders of the Sun, half men half scorpions, whom Izdubar encounters when he starts on his journey to the land of the dead. The ninth month is called "the Cloudy," surely a meet name for November-December, and in no way inconsistent with the contents of the ninth tablet, which shows Izdubar navigating the "Waters of Death." In the tenth month (December–January), the sun reaches his very lowest point, that of the winter solstice with its shortest days, whence the name "Month of the Cavern of the Setting Sun," and the tenth tablet tells how Izdubar reached the goal of his journey, the land of the illustrious dead, to which his great ancestor has been translated. To the eleventh month, "the Month of the Curse of Rain," with the sign of the Waterman,—(January–February being in the low lands of the two rivers the time of the most violent and continuous rains)—answers the eleventh tablet with the account of the Deluge. The "Fishes of Êa" accompany the sun in the twelfth month, the last of the dark season, as he emerges, purified and invigorated, to resume his triumphant career with the beginning of the new year. From the context and sequence of the myth, it would appear that the name of the first month, "the Altar of Bel," must have had something to do with the reconciliation of the god after the Deluge, from which humanity may be said to take a new beginning, which would make the name a most auspicious one for the new year, while the sign—a Ram —might allude to the animal sacrificed on the altar. Each month being placed under the protection of some particular deity it is worthy of notice that Anu and Bel are the patrons of the first month, Êa of the second, (in connection with the wisdom of Êabâni, who is called "the creature of Êa,") while

Ishtar presides over the sixth, ("Message of Ishtar,") and Ramân, the god of the atmosphere, of rain and storm and thunder, over the eleventh, ("the Curse of Rain ").

20. The solar nature of the adventurous career attributed to the favorite national hero of Chaldea, now universally admitted, was first pointed out by Sir Henry Rawlinson: but it was François Lenormant who followed it out and established it in its details. His conclusions on the subject are given in such clear and forcible language, that it is a pleasure to reproduce them:*—" 1st. The Chaldeans and Babylonians had, concerning the twelve months of the year, myths for the most part belonging to the series of traditions anterior to the separation of the great races of mankind which descended from the highlands of Pamir, since we find analogous myths among the pure Semites and other nations. As early as the time when they dwelt on the plains of the Tigris and Euphrates, they connected these myths with the different epochs of the year, not with a view to agricultural occupations, but in connection with the great periodical phenomena of the atmosphere and the different stations in the sun's yearly course, as they occurred in that particular region; hence the signs characterizing the twelve solar mansions in the Zodiac and the symbolical names given to the months by the Accads. —2d. It was those myths, strung together in their successive order, which served as foundation to the

---

* " Les Premières Civilisations," Vol. II., pp. 78 ff.

epic story of Izdubar, the fiery and solar hero, and in the poem which was copied at Erech by Asshurbanipal's order each of them formed the subject of one of the twelve tablets, making up the number of twelve separate books or chapters answering the twelve months of the year."—Even though the evidence is apparently so complete as not to need further confirmation, it is curious to note that the signs which compose the name of Izdubar convey the meaning " mass of fire," while Hâsisadra's Accadian name means " the sun of life," " the morning sun," and his father's name, Ubaratutu, is translated "the glow of sunset."

21. George Smith indignantly repudiated this mythic interpretation of the hero's exploits, and claimed for them a strictly historical character. But we have seen that the two are by no means incompatible, since history, when handed down through centuries by mere oral tradition, is liable to many vicissitudes in the telling and retelling, and people are sure to arrange their favorite and most familiar stories, the mythical signification of which has long been forgotten, around the central figure of the heroes they love best, around the most important but vaguely recollected events in their national life. Hence it came to pass that identically the same stories, with but slight local variations, were told of heroes in different nations and countries ; for the stock of original, or, as one may say, primary myths is comparatively small and the same for all, dating back to a time when mankind was not yet divided. In the course of ages and mi-

grations it has been altered, like a rich hereditary robe, to fit and adorn many and very different persons.

22. One of the prettiest, oldest, and most universally favorite solar myths is the one which represents the Sun as a divine being, youthful and of surpassing beauty, beloved by or wedded to an equally powerful goddess, but meeting a premature death by accident and descending into the dark land of shades, from which, however, after a time he returns as glorious and beautiful as before. In this poetical fancy, the land of shades symbolizes the numb and lifeless period of winter as aptly as the Waters of Death in the Izdubar Epic, while the seeming death of the young god answers to the sickening of the hero at that declining season of the year when the sun's rays lose their vigor and are overcome by the powers of darkness and cold. The goddess who loves the fair young god, and mourns him with passionate grief, until her wailings and prayers recall him from his death-like trance, is Nature herself, loving, bountiful, ever productive, but pale, and bare, and powerless in her widowhood, while the sun-god, the spring of life whence she draws her very being, lies captive in the bonds of their common foe, grim Winter, which is but a form of Death itself. Their reunion at the god's resurrection in spring is the great wedding-feast, the revel and holiday-time of the world.

23. This simple and perfectly transparent myth has been worked out more or less elaborately in all the countries of the East, and has found its way in

some form or other into all the nations of the three great white races—of Japhet, Shem, and Ham—yet here again the precedence in point of time seems due to the older and more primitive—the Yellow or Turanian race; for the most ancient, and probably original form of it is the one which was inherited by the Semitic settlers of Chaldea from their Shumiro-Accadian predecessors, as shown by the Accadian name of the young solar god, DUMUZI, "the unfortunate husband of the goddess Ishtar," as he is called in the sixth tablet of the Izdubar epic. The name has been translated " Divine Offspring," but in later times lost all signification, being corrupted into TAMMUZ. In some Accadian hymns he is invoked as "the Shepherd, the lord Dumuzi, the lover of Ishtar." Well could a nomadic and pastoral people poetically liken the sun to a shepherd, whose flocks were the fleecy clouds as they speed across the vast plains of heaven or the bright, innumerable stars. This comparison, as pretty as it is natural, kept its hold in all ages and nations on the popular fancy, which played on it an infinite variety of ingenious changes, but it is only cuneiform science which has proved that it could be traced back to the very earliest race whose culture has left its mark on the world.

24. Of Dumuzi's tragic death no text deciphered until now unfortunately gives the details. Only the remarkable fragment about the black pine of Eridhu, " marking the centre of the earth, in the dark forest, into the heart whereof man hath not penetrated," (see p. 287) tantalizingly ends with

these suggestive words: "Within it Dumuzi . . ." Scholars have found reason for conjecturing that this fragment was the beginning of a mythical narrative recounting Dumuzi's death, which must have been represented as taking place in that dark and sacred forest of Eridhu,—probably through the agency of a wild beast sent against him by a jealous and hostile power, just as the bull created by Anu was sent against Izdubar.[*] One thing, however, is sure, that both in the earlier (Turanian) and in the later (Semitic) calendary of Chaldea, there was a month set apart in honor and for the festival of Dumuzi. It was the month of June-July, beginning at the summer solstice, when the days begin to shorten, and the sun to decline towards its lower winter point—a retrograde movement, ingeniously indicated by the Zodiacal sign of that month, the Cancer or Crab. The festival of Dumuzi lasted during the six first days of the month, with processions and ceremonies bearing two distinct characters. The worshippers at first assembled in the guise of mourners, with lamentations and loud wailings, tearing of clothes and of hair, as though celebrating the young god's funeral, while on the sixth day his resurrection and reunion to Ishtar was commemorated with the noisiest, most extravagant demonstrations of rejoicing. This custom is alluded to in Izdubar's scornful answer to Ishtar's love-message, when he says to her: " Thou lovedst Du-

---

[*] A. H. Sayce, "Babylonian Literature." p. 39; Fr. Lenormant, "Il Mito di Adone-Tammuz," pp. 12-13.

muzi, *for whom they mourn year after year*," and was witnessed by the Jews when they were carried prisoners to Babylon as late as 600 B.C., as expressly mentioned by Ezekiel, the prophet of the Captivity :—" Then he brought me to the door of the Lord's house which was towards the north; *and behold, there sat the women weeping for Tammuz.*" (Ezekiel, iii. 14.)

25. A favorite version of Dumuzi's resurrection was that which told how Ishtar herself followed him into the Lower World, to claim him from their common foe, and thus yielded herself for a time into the power of her rival, the dread Queen of the Dead, who held her captive, and would not have released her but for the direct interference of the great gods. This was a rich mine of epic material, from which songs and stories must have flowed plentifully. We are lucky enough to possess a short epic on the subject, in one tablet, one of the chief gems of the indefatigable George Smith's discoveries,—a poem of great literary beauty, and nearly complete to within a few lines of the end, which are badly injured and scarcely legible. It is known under the name of " THE DESCENT OF ISHTAR," as it relates only this one incident of the myth. The opening lines are unsurpassed for splendid poetry and sombre grandeur in any, even the most advanced literature.

26. "Towards the land whence there is no return, towards the house of corruption, Ishtar, the daughter of Sin, has turned her mind . . . . towards the dwelling that has an entrance but no exit, towards the road that may be travelled but not retraced, tow-

ards the hall from which the light of day is shut out, where hunger feeds on dust and mud, where light is never seen, where the shades of the dead dwell in the dark, clothed with wings like birds. On the lintel of the gate and in the lock dust lies accumulated.—Ishtar, when she reached the land whence there is no return, to the keeper of the gate signified her command: 'Keeper, open thy gate that I may pass. If thou openest not and I may not enter, I will smite the gate, and break the lock, I will demolish the threshold and enter by force; then will I let loose the dead to return to the earth, that they may live and eat again; I will make the risen dead more numerous than the living.' The gate-keeper opened his lips and spoke:—'Be appeased, O Lady, and let me go and report thy name to Allat the Queen.'"

Here follow a few much injured lines, the sense of which could not be restored in its entirety. The substance is that the gate-keeper announces to Allat that her sister Ishtar has come for the Water of Life, which is kept concealed in a distant nook of her dominions, and Allat is greatly disturbed at the news. But Ishtar announces that she comes in sorrow, not enmity:—

"I wish to weep over the heroes who have left their wives. I wish to weep over the wives who have been taken from their husbands' arms. I wish to weep over the Only Son—(a name of Dumuzi)—who has been taken away before his time."

Then Allat commands the keeper to open the gates and take Ishtar through the sevenfold enclosure, dealing by her as by all who come to those gates, that is, stripping her of her garments according to ancient custom.

"The keeper went and opened the gate: 'Enter, O Lady, and may the halls of the Land whence there is no return be gladdened by thy presence.' At the first gate he bade her enter and laid his hand on her; he took the high headdress from her head: 'Why, O keeper, takest thou the high headdress from my head?'—'Enter, O Lady; such is Allat's command.'"

The same scene is repeated at each of the seven gates; the keeper at each strips Ishtar of some article of her attire—her earrings, her necklace, her jewelled girdle, the bracelets on her arms and the bangles at her ankles, and lastly her long flowing garment. On each occasion the same words are repeated by both. When Ishtar entered the presence of Allat, the queen looked at her and taunted her to her face: then Ishtar could not control her anger and cursed her. Allat turned to her chief minister Namtar, the god of Pestilence—meet servant of the queen of the dead!—who is also the god of Fate, and ordered him to lead Ishtar away and afflict her with sixty dire diseases,—to strike her head and her heart, and her eyes, her hands and her feet, and all her limbs. So the goddess was led away and kept in durance and in misery. Meanwhile her absence was attended with most disastrous consequences to the upper world. With her, life and love had gone out of it; there were no marriages any more, no births, either among men or animals; nature was at a standstill. Great was the commotion among the gods. They sent a messenger to Êa to expose the state of affairs to him, and, as usual, to invoke his advice and assistance. Êa, in his fathomless wisdom, revolved a scheme. He created a phantom, Uddusunamir.

"'Go,' he said to him; 'towards the Land whence there is no return direct thy face; the seven gates of the Arallu will open before thee. Allat shall see thee and rejoice at thy coming, her heart shall grow calm and her wrath shall vanish. Conjure her with the name of the great gods, stiffen thy neck and keep thy mind on the Spring of Life. Let the Lady (Ishtar) gain access to the Spring of Life and drink of its waters.'—Allat, when she heard these things, beat her breast and bit her fingers with rage. Consenting, sore against her will, she spoke:—'Go, Uddusunamir! May the great jailer place thee in durance! May the foulness of the city ditches be thy food, the waters of the city sewers thy drink! A dark dungeon be thy dwelling, a sharp pole thy seat!'"

Then she ordered Namtar to let Ishtar drink of the Spring of Life and to bear her from her sight. Namtar fulfilled her command and took the goddess through the seven enclosures, at each gate restoring to her the article of her attire that had been taken at her entrance. At the last gate he said to her:

"Thou hast paid no ransom to Allat for y deliverance; so now return to Dumuzi, the lover of thy youth; sprinkle over him the sacred waters, clothe him in splendid garments, adorn him with gems."

26. The last lines are so badly mutilated that no efforts have as yet availed to make their sense anything but obscure, and so it must remain, unless new copies come to light. Yet so much is, at all events, evident, that they bore on the reunion of Ishtar and her young lover. The poem is thus complete in itself; but some think that it was introduced into the Izdubar epic as an independent episode, after the fashion of the Deluge narrative, and, if so, it is supposed to have been part of the seventh tablet. Whether such were really the case or no, matters little in comparison with the great importance these two poems possess as being the most ancient presentations, in a finished literary form, of the two most significant and universal nature-myths—the

Solar and the Chthonic (see p. 272), the poetical fancies in which primitive mankind clothed the wonders of the heavens and the mystery of the earth, being content to admire and imagine where it could not comprehend and explain. We shall be led back continually to these, in very truth, *primary* myths, for they not only served as groundwork to much of the most beautiful poetry of the world but suggested some of its loftiest and most cherished religious conceptions.

---

*For a metrical version by Prof. Dyer of the story of "Ishtar's Descent," see Appendix, p. 367.

VIII.

RELIGION AND MYTHOLOGY.—IDOLATRY AND ANTHROPOMORPHISM.—THE CHALDEAN LEGENDS AND THE BOOK OF GENESIS.—RETROSPECT.

1. IN speaking of ancient nations, the words "Religion" and "Mythology" are generally used indiscriminately and convertibly. Yet the conceptions they express are essentially and radically different. The broadest difference, and the one from which all others flow, is that the one—Religion—is a thing of the feelings, while the other—Mythology—is a thing of the imagination. In other words, Religion comes from WITHIN—from that consciousness of limited power, that inborn need of superior help and guidance, forbearance and forgiveness, from that longing for absolute goodness and perfection, which make up the distinctively human attribute of "religiosity," that attribute which, together with the faculty of articulate speech, sets Man apart from and above all the rest of animated creation. (See p. 149.) Mythology, on the other hand, comes wholly from WITHOUT. It embodies impressions received by the senses from the outer world and transformed by the poetical faculty into images and stories.

(See definition of "Myth" on p. 294.) Professor Max Müller of Oxford has been the first, in his standard work "The Science of Language," clearly to define this radical difference between the two conceptions, which he has never since ceased to sound as a keynote through the long series of his works devoted to the study of the religions and mythologies of various nations. A few illustrations from the one nation with which we have as yet become familiar will help once for all to establish a thorough understanding on this point, most essential as it is to the comprehension of the workings of the human mind and soul throughout the long roll of struggles, errors and triumphs, achievements and failures which we call the history of mankind.

2. There is no need to repeat here instances of the Shumiro-Accadian and Chaldean myths; the last three or four chapters have been filled with them. But the instances of religious feeling, though scattered in the same field, have to be carefully gleaned out and exhibited, for they belong to that undercurrent of the soul which pursues its way unobtrusively and is often apparently lost beneath the brilliant play of poetical fancies. But it is there nevertheless, and every now and then forces its way to the surface shining forth with a startling purity and beauty. When the Accadian poet invokes the Lord " who knows lie from truth," "who knows the truth that is in the soul of man," who "maketh lies to vanish," who "turneth wicked plots to a happy issue "— this is religion, not mythology, for this is not *a story*, it is the expression of *a feeling*. That "the Lord"

whose divine omniscience and goodness is thus glorified is really the Sun, makes no difference; *that* is an error of judgment, a want of knowledge, but the religious feeling is splendidly manifest in the invocation. But when, in the same hymn, the Sun is described as " stepping forth from the background of the skies, pushing back the bolts and opening the gate of the brilliant heaven, and raising his head above the land," etc., (see p. 172) that is only a very beautiful, imaginative description of a glorious natural phenomenon—sunrise; it is magnificent poetry, religious in so far as the sun is considered as a Being, a Divine Person, the object of an intensely devout and grateful feeling ; still this is not religion, it is mythology, for it presents a material image to the mind, and one that can be easily turned into narrative, into *a story*,—which, in fact, *suggests* a hero, a king, and a story. Take, again, the so-called " Penitential Psalms." To the specimen given on p. 178, let us add, for greater completeness, the following three remarkable fragments :

I. "God, my creator, take hold of my arms ! Direct the breath of my mouth, my hands direct, O lord of light."
II. "Lord, let not thy servant sink ! Amidst the tumultuous waters take hold of his hand ! "
III. "He who fears not his God, will be cut off even like a reed. He who honors not his goddess, his bodily strength will waste away : like to a star of heaven, his splendor will pale ; he will vanish like to the waters of the night."

3. All this is religion, of the purest, loftiest kind ; fruitful, too, of good, the only real test of true religion. The deep humility, the trustful ap-

peal, the feeling of dependence, the consciousness of weakness, of sin, and the longing for deliverance from them—these are all very different from the pompous phrases of empty praise and sterile admiration; they are things which flow from the heart, not the fancy, which lighten its weight of sorrow and self-reproach, brighten it with hope and good resolutions, in short, make it happier and better—what no mere imaginative poetry, however fine, can do.

4. The radical distinction, then, between religious feeling and the poetical faculty of mythical creation, is easy to establish and follow out. On the other hand, the two are so constantly blended, so almost inextricably interwoven in the sacred poetry of the ancients, in their views of life and the world, and in their worship, that it is no wonder they should be so generally confused. The most correct way of putting the case would be, perhaps, to say that the ancient Religions—meaning by the word the whole body of sacred poetry and legends as well as the national forms of worship—were made up originally in about equal parts of religious feeling and of mythology. In many cases the exuberance of the imagination gained the upper hand, and there was such a riotous growth of mythical imagery and stories that the religious feeling was almost stifled under them. In others, again, the myths themselves suggested religious ideas of the deepest import and loftiest sublimity. Such was particularly the case with the solar and Chthonic Myths—the poetical presentation of the career of the Sun and

the Earth—as connected with the doctrine of the soul's immortality.

5. A curious and significant observation has been made in excavating the most ancient graves in the world, those of the so-called Mound-builders. This name is not that of any particular race or nation, but is given indiscriminately to all those peoples who lived, on any part of the globe, long before the earliest beginnings of even the remotest times which have been made historical by preserved monuments or inscriptions of any kind. All we know of those peoples is that they used to bury their dead—at least those of special renown or high rank—in deep and spacious stone-lined chambers dug in the ground, with a similar gallery leading to them, and covered by a mound of earth, sometimes of gigantic dimensions—a very hill. Hence the name. Of their life, their degree of civilization, what they thought and believed, we have no idea except in so far as the contents of the graves give us some indications. For, like the later, historical races, of which we find the graves in Chaldea and every other country of the ancient world, they used to bury along with the dead a multitude of things: vessels, containing food and drink; weapons, ornaments, household implements. The greater the power or renown of the dead man, the fuller and more luxurious his funeral outfit. It is indeed by no means rare to find the skeleton of a great chief surrounded by those of several women, and, at a respectful distance, more skeletons—evidently those of slaves—whose fractured skulls more than suggest the ghastly custom

of killing wives and servants to do honor to an illustrious dead and to keep him company in his narrow underground mansion. Nothing but a belief in the continuation of existence after death could have prompted these practices. For what was the sense of giving him wives and slaves, and domestic articles of all kinds, food and weapons, unless it were for his service and use on his journey to the unknown land where he was to enter on a new stage of existence, which the survivors could not but imagine to be a reproduction, in its simple conditions and needs, of the one he was leaving? There is no race of men, however primitive, however untutored, in which this belief in immortality is not found deeply rooted, positive, unquestioning. The *belief* is implanted in man by the *wish;* it answers one of the most imperative, unsilenceable longings of human nature. For, in proportion as life is pleasant and precious, death is hideous and repellent. The idea of utter destruction, of ceasing to be, is intolerable to the mind; indeed, the senses revolt against it, the mind refuses to grasp and admit it. Yet death is very real, and it is inevitable; and all human beings that come into the world have to learn to face the thought of it, and the reality too, in others, before they lie down and accept it for themselves. But what if death be *not* destruction? If it be but a passage from this into another world,—distant, unknown and perforce mysterious, but certain nevertheless, a world on the threshold of which the earthly body is dropped as an unnecessary garment? Then were death shorn of half its terrors. Indeed, the only unpleasantness about it would be, for him who goes, the momentary pang and the uncertainty as to what he is going to; and, for those who remain, the separation and the loathsome details—the disfigurement, the corruption. But these are soon gotten over, while the separation is only for a time; for all must go the same way, and the late-comers will find, will join their lost ones gone before. Surely it must be so! It were too horrible if it were not; it *must be*—it *is!* The process of feeling which arrived at this conclusion and hardened it into absolute faith, is very plain, and we can easily, each of us, reproduce it in our own souls, independently of the teachings we receive from childhood. But the mind is naturally inquiring, and involuntarily the question presents itself: this solution, so beautiful, so acceptable, so universal,—but so abstract—what suggested it? What analogy first led up to it from the material world of the senses? To this question we find no reply in so many words, for it is one of those that go to the very roots of our being, and such generally remain unanswered. But the graves dug by those old Mound-Builders present a singular feature, which almost seems to point to the answer. The tenant of the funereal chamber is most frequently found deposited in a crouching attitude, his back leaning against the stone-lined wall, and *with his face turned towards the West, in the direction of the setting sun.* .... Here, then, is the suggestion, the analogy! The career of the sun is very like that of man. His rising in the east is like the birth of man.

During the hours of his power, which we call the Day, he does his allotted work, of giving light and warmth to the world, now riding radiant and triumphant across an azure sky, now obscured by clouds, struggling through mists, or overwhelmed by tempests. How like the vicissitudes that checker the somewhat greater number of hours—or days—of which the sum makes up a human life! Then when his appointed time expires, he sinks down,—lower, lower—and disappears into darkness,—dies. So does man. What is this night, death? Is it destruction, or only a rest, or an absence? It is at all events *not* destruction. For as surely as we see the sun vanish in the west this evening, feeble and beamless, so surely shall we behold him to-morrow morning rise again in the east, glorious, vigorous and young. What happens to him in the interval? Who knows? Perhaps he sleeps, perhaps he travels through countries we know not of and does other work there; but one thing is sure: that he is not dead, for he will be up again to-morrow. Why should not man, whose career so much resembles the sun's in other respects, resemble him in this? Let the dead, then, be placed with their faces to the west, in token that theirs is but a setting like the sun's, to be followed by another rising, a renewed existence, though in another and unknown world.

6. All this is sheer poetry and mythology. But how great its beauty, how obvious its hopeful suggestiveness, if it could appeal to the groping minds of those primitive men, the old Mound-Builders,

and there lay the seed of a faith which has been more and more clung to, as mankind progressed in spiritual culture! For all the noblest races have cherished and worked out the myth of the setting sun in the most manifold ways, as the symbol of the soul's immortality. The poets of ancient India, some three thousand years ago, made the Sun the leader and king of the dead, who, as they said, followed where he had gone first, "showing the way to many." The Egyptians, perhaps the wisest and most spiritual of all ancient nations, came to make this myth the keystone of their entire religion, and placed all their burying-places in the west, amidst or beyond the Libyan ridge of hills behind which the sun vanished from the eyes of those who dwelt in the valley of the Nile. The Greeks imagined a happy residence for their bravest and wisest, which they called the Islands of the Blest, and placed in the furthest West, amidst the waters of the ocean into which the sun descends for his nightly rest.

7. But the sun's course is twofold. If it is complete—beginning and ending—within the given number of hours which makes the day, it is repeated on a larger scale through the cycle of months which makes the year. The alternations of youth and age, triumph and decline, power and feebleness, are there represented and are regularly brought around by the different seasons. But the moral, the symbol, is still the same as regards final immortality. For if summer answers to the heyday of noon, autumn to the milder glow and the extinc-

tion of evening, and winter to the joyless dreariness of night, spring, like the morning, ever brings back the god, the hero, in the perfect splendor of a glorious resurrection. It was the solar-year myth with its magnificent accompaniment of astronomical pageantry, which took the greater hold on the fancy of the scientifically inclined Chaldeans, and which we find embodied with such admirable completeness in their great epic. We shall see, later on, more exclusively imaginative and poetical races showing a marked preference for the career of the sun as the hero of a day, and making the several incidents of the solar-day myth the subject of an infinite variety of stories, brilliant or pathetic, tender or heroic. But there is in nature another order of phenomena, intimately connected with and dependent on the phases of the sun, that is, the seasons, yet very different in their individual character, though pointing the same way as regards the suggestion of resurrection and immortality— the phenomena of the Earth and the Seed. These may in a more general way be described as Nature's productive power paralyzed during the numbed trance of winter, which is as the sleep of death, when the seed lies in the ground hid from sight and cold, even as a dead thing, but awaking to new life in the good time of spring, when the seed, in which life was never extinct but only dormant, bursts its bonds and breaks into verdant loveliness and bountiful crops. This is the essence and meaning of the Chthonic or Earth-myth, as universal as the Sun-myth, but of which different features have also been unequally developed by different races according to their individual tendencies. In the Chaldean version, the " Descent of Ishtar," the particular incident of the seed is quite wanting, unless the name of Dumuzi's month, " The Boon of the Seed " ("*Le Bienfait de la Semence.*" Lenormant), may be considered as alluding to it. It is her fair young bridegroom, the beautiful Sun-god, whom the widowed goddess of Nature mourns and descends to seek among the dead. This aspect of the myth is almost exclusively developed in the religions of most Canaanitic and Semitic nations of the East, where we shall meet with it often and often. And here it may be remarked, without digressing or anticipating too far, that throughout the ancient world, the Solar and Chthonic cycles of myths have been the most universal and important, the very centre and groundwork of many of the ancient mythic religions, and used as vehicles for more or less sublime religious conceptions, according to the higher or lower spiritual level of the worshipping nations.

8. It must be confessed that, amidst the nations of Western Asia, this level was, on the whole, not a very lofty one. Both the Hamitic and Semitic races were, as a rule, of a naturally sensuous disposition; the former being, moreover, distinguished by a very decidedly material turn of mind. The Kushites, of whom a branch perhaps formed an important portion of the mixed population of Lower Mesopotamia, and especially the Canaanites, who spread themselves over all the country between the

great rivers and the Western Sea—the Mediterranean—were no exception to this rule. If their priests—their professed thinkers, the men trained through generations for intellectual pursuits—had groped their way to the perception of One Divine Power ruling the world, they kept it to themselves, or, at least, out of sight, behind a complicated array of cosmogonic myths, nature-myths, symbols and parables, resulting in Chaldea in the highly artificial system which has been sketched above—(see Chapters V. and VI.)—a system singularly beautiful and deeply significant, but of which the mass of the people did not care to unravel the subtle intricacies, being quite content to accept it entire, in the most literal spirit, elementary nature-gods, astronomical abstractions, cosmogonical fables and all—questioning nothing, at peace in their mind and righteously self-conscious if they sacrificed at the various time-honored local shrines, and conformed to the prescribed forms and ceremonies. To these they privately added those innumerable practices of conjuring and rites of witchcraft, the heirloom of the older lords of the soil, which we saw the colleges of learned priests compelled, as strangers and comparative newcomers, to tolerate and even sanction by giving them a place, though an inferior one, in their own nobler system (see p. 250). Thus it was that, if a glimmer of Truth did feebly illumine the sanctuary and its immediate ministers, the people at large dwelt in the outer darkness of hopeless polytheism and, worse still, of idolatry. For, in bowing before the altars of their temples and the images in wood, stone or metal in which art strove to express what the sacred writings taught, the unlearned worshippers did not stop to consider that these were but pieces of human workmanship, deriving their sacredness solely from the subjects they treated and the place they adorned, nor did they strive to keep their thoughts intent on the invisible Beings represented by the images. It was so much simpler, easier and more comfortable to address their adoration to what was visible and near, to the shapes that were so closely within reach of their senses, that seemed so directly to receive their offerings and prayers, that became so dearly familiar from long associations. The bulk of the Chaldean nation for a long time remained Turanian, and the materialistic grossness of the original Shumiro-Accadian religion greatly fostered its idolatrous tendencies. The old belief in the talismanic virtues of all images (see p. 162) continued to assert itself, and was easily transferred to those representing the divinities of the later and more elaborate worship. Some portion of the divine substance or spirit was supposed somehow to pass into the material representation and reside therein. This is very clear from the way in which the inscriptions speak of the statues of gods, as though they were persons. Thus the famous cylinder of the Assyrian conqueror Asshurbanipal tells how he brought back "the goddess Nana," (i.e., her statue) who at the time of the great Elamite invasion, "had gone and dwelt in Elam, a place not appointed for her," and now spoke to him the king, saying: "From the midst of Elam bring me out and cause me to enter into Bitanna"—her own old sanctuary at Erech, "which she had delighted in." Then again the Assyrian conquerors take especial pride in carrying off with them the statues of the gods of the nations they subdue, and never fail to record the fact in these words: "I carried away *their gods*," beyond a doubt with the idea that, in so doing, they put it out of their enemies' power to procure the assistance of their divine protectors.

9. In the population of Chaldea the Semitic element was strongly represented. It is probable that tribes of Semites came into the country at intervals, in successive bands, and for a long time wandered unhindered with their flocks, then gradually amalgamated with the settlers they found in possession, and whose culture they adopted, or else formed separate settlements of their own, not even then, however, quite losing their pastoral habits. Thus the Hebrew tribe, when it left Ur under Terah and Abraham (see page 121), seems to have resumed its nomadic life with the greatest willingness and ease, after dwelling a long time in or near that popular city, the principal capital of Shumir, the then dominant South. Whether this tribe were driven out of Ur, as some will have it,* or left of their own accord, it is perhaps not too bold to conjecture that the causes of their departure were partly connected with religious motives. For, alone among the Chaldeans and all the surrounding nations, this handful

---

* Maspero, "Histoire Ancienne," p. 173.

of Semites had disentangled the conception of monotheism from the obscuring wealth of Chaldean mythology, and had grasped it firmly. At least their leaders and elders, the patriarchs, had arrived at the conviction that the One living God was He whom they called "the Lord," and they strove to inspire their people with the same faith, and to detach them from the mythical beliefs, the idolatrous practices which they had adopted from those among whom they lived, and to which they clung with the tenacity of spiritual blindness and long habit. The later Hebrews themselves kept a clear remembrance of their ancestors having been heathen polytheists, and their own historians, writing more than a thousand years after Abraham's times, distinctly state the fact. In a long exhortation to the assembled tribes of Israel, which they put in the mouth of Joshua, the successor of Moses, they make him say: —" Your fathers dwelt on the other side of the flood " (i.e., the Euphrates, or perhaps the Jordan) "in old time, even Terah, the father of Abraham and the father of Nachor, *and they served other gods.*" And further on: " . . . Put away *the gods which your fathers served on the other side of the flood* and in Egypt, and serve ye the Lord. . . . . Choose you this day whom you will serve, whether the gods which your fathers served that were on the other side of the flood, or the gods of the Amorites, in whose land ye dwell; as for me and my house, we will serve the Lord." (Joshua, xxiv. 2, 14, 15.) What more probable than that the patriarchs, Terah and Abraham, should have led their people out of the midst of the Chaldeans, away from their great capital Ur, which held some of the oldest and most renowned Chaldean sanctuaries, and forth into the wilderness, partly with the object of removing them from corrupting associations. At all events that branch of the Hebrew tribe which remained in Mesopotamia with Nahor, Abraham's brother (see Gen. xxiv. xxix. and ff.), continued heathen and idolatrous, as we see from the detailed narrative in Genesis xxxi., of how Rachel "had stolen *the images that were her father's*" (xxxi. 19), when Jacob fled from Laban's house with his family, his cattle and all his goods. No doubt as to the value and meaning attached to these "images" is left when we see Laban, after having overtaken the fugitives, reprove Jacob in these words:—"And now, though thou wouldst needs be gone, because thou sore longedst for thy father's house, yet wherefore hast thou stolen *my gods?*" (xxxi. 30), to which Jacob, who knows nothing of Rachel's theft, replies:—"With whomsoever *thou findest thy gods*, let him not live" (xxxi. 32). But "Rachel had taken the images and put them in the camel's furniture, and sat upon them. And Laban searched all the tent, but found them not" (xxxi. 34). Now what could have induced Rachel to commit so dishonorable and, moreover, dangerous an action, but the idea that, in carrying away these images, her family's household "gods," she would insure a blessing and prosperity to herself and her house? That by so doing, she would, according to the heathens' notion, rob her father and old home of what she wished to secure herself (see page 344), does not seem to have disturbed her. It is clear from this that, even after she was wedded to Jacob the monotheist, she remained a heathen and idolater, though she concealed the fact from him.

10. On the other hand, wholesale emigration was not sufficient to remove the evil. Had it indeed been a wilderness, unsettled in all its extent, into which the patriarchs led forth their people, they might have succeeded in weaning them completely from the old influences. But, scattered over it and already in possession, were numerous Canaanite tribes, wealthy and powerful under their chiefs— Amorites, and Hivites, and Hittites, and many more. In the pithy and picturesque Biblical language, "the Canaanite was in the land" (Genesis, xii. 6), and the Hebrews constantly came into contact with them, indeed were dependent on their tolerance and large hospitality for the freedom with which they were suffered to enjoy the pastures of "the land wherein they were strangers," as the vast region over which they ranged is frequently and pointedly called. Being but a handful of men, they had to be cautious in their dealings and to keep on good terms with the people among whom they were brought. "I am a stranger and a sojourner with you," admits Abraham, "bowing himself down before the people of the land," (a tribe of Hittites near Hebron, west of the Dead Sea), when he offers to buy of them a field, there to institute a family burying-place for himself and his race; for he had no legal right to any of the land, not so much as

would yield a sepulchre to his dead, even though the "children of Heth" treat him with high honor, and, in speaking to him, say, "My lord," and "thou art a mighty prince among us" (Genesis, xxiii.). This transaction, conducted on both sides in a spirit of great courtesy and liberality, is not the only instance of the friendliness with which the Canaanite owners of the soil regarded the strangers, both in Abraham's lifetime and long after his death. His grandson, the patriarch Jacob, and his sons find the same tolerance among the Hivites of Shalem, who thus commune among themselves concerning them: —"These men are peaceable with us; therefore let them dwell in the land and trade therein; for the land, behold it is large enough for them; let us take their daughters for wives, and let us give them our daughters." And the Hivite prince speaks in this sense to the Hebrew chief:—"The soul of my son longeth for your daughter: I pray you, give her him to wife. And make ye marriages with us, and give your daughters unto us and take our daughters unto you. And ye shall dwell with us, and the land shall be before you; dwell and trade ye therein, and get you possessions therein."

11. But this question of intermarriage was always a most grievous one; the question of all others at which the Hebrew leaders strictly drew the line of intercourse and good-fellowship; the more stubbornly that their people were naturally much inclined to such unions, since they came and went freely among their hosts, and their daughters went out, unhindered, "to see the daughters of the land."

Now all the race of Canaan followed religions very similar to that of Chaldea, only grosser still in their details and forms of worship. Therefore, that the old idolatrous habits might not return strongly upon them under the influence of a heathen household, the patriarchs forbade marriage with the women of the countries through which they passed and repassed with their tents and flocks, and themselves abstained from it. Thus we see Abraham sending his steward all the way back to Mesopotamia to seek a wife for his son Isaac from among his own kinsfolk who had stayed there with his brother Nahor, and makes the old servant solemnly swear "by the Lord, the God of heaven and the God of earth": "Thou shalt not take a wife unto my son of the daughters of the Canaanites among whom I dwell." And when Esau, Isaac's son, took two wives from among the Hittite women, it is expressly said that they were "a grief of mind unto Isaac and Rebekah;" and Isaac's most solemn charge to his other son, Jacob, as he sends him from him with his blessing, is: "Thou shalt not take a wife of the daughters of Canaan." Whithersoever the Hebrews came in the course of their long wanderings, which lasted many centuries, the same twofold prohibition was laid on them: of marrying with native women—"for surely," they are told, "they will turn away your heart after their gods," and of following idolatrous religions, a prohibition enforced by the severest penalties, even to that of death. But nothing could keep them long from breaking the law in both respects. The very frequency and emphasis with which the command is repeated, the violence of the denunciations against offenders, the terrible punishments threatened and often actually inflicted, sufficiently show how imperfectly and unwillingly it was obeyed. Indeed the entire Old Testament is one continuous illustration of the unslackening zeal with which the wise and enlightened men of Israel—its lawgivers, leaders, priests and prophets—pursued their arduous and often almost hopeless task, of keeping their people pure from worships and practices which to them, who had realized the fallacy of a belief in many gods, were the most pernicious abominations. In this spirit and to this end they preached, they fought, they promised, threatened, punished, and in this spirit, in later ages, they wrote.

12. It is not until a nation is well established and enjoys a certain measure of prosperity, security and the leisure which accompanies them, that it begins to collect its own traditions and memories and set them down in order, into a continuous narrative. So it was with the Hebrews. The small tribe became a nation, which ceased from its wanderings and conquered for itself a permanent place on the face of the earth. But to do this took many hundred years, years of memorable adventures and vicissitudes, so that the materials which accumulated for the future historians, in stories, traditions, songs, were ample and varied. Much, too, must have been written down at a comparatively early period. *How* early must remain uncertain, since there is unfortunately nothing to show at what

time the Hebrews learned the art of writing and their characters thought, like other alphabets, to be borrowed from those of the Phœnicians. However that may be, one thing is sure: that the different books which compose the body of the Hebrew Sacred Scriptures, which we call "the Old Testament," were collected from several and different sources, and put into the shape in which they have descended to us at a very late period, some almost as late as the birth of Christ. The first book of all, that of Genesis, describing the beginnings of the Jewish people,—("*Genesis*" is a Greek word, which means "Origin")—belongs at all events to a somewhat earlier date. It is put together mainly of two narratives, distinct and often different in point of spirit and even fact. The later compiler who had both sources before him to work into a final form, looked on both with too much respect to alter either, and generally contented himself with giving them side by side, (as in the story of Hagar, which is told twice and differently, in Chap. XVI. and Chap. XXI.), or intermixing them throughout, so that it takes much attention and pains to separate them, (as in the story of the Flood, Chap. VI.-VIII.). This latter story is almost identical with the Chaldean Deluge-legend included in the great Izdubar epic, of which it forms the eleventh tablet. (See Chap. VII.) Indeed, every child can see, by comparing the Chaldean cosmogonic and mythical legends with the first chapters of the Book of Genesis, those which relate to the beginnings not so much of the Hebrew people as of the human race and the world in general, that both must originally have flowed from one and the same spring of tradition and priestly lore. The resemblances are too staring, close, continuous, not to exclude all rational surmises as to casual coincidences. The differences are such as most strikingly illustrate the transformation which the same material can undergo when treated by two races of different moral standards and spiritual tendencies. Let us briefly examine both, side by side.

13. To begin with the Creation. The description of the primeval chaos—a waste of waters, from which "the darkness was not lifted," (see p. 261)—answers very well to that in Genesis, i. 2 : "And the earth was without form and void; and darkness was upon the face of the deep." The establishment of the heavenly bodies and the creation of the animals also correspond remarkably in both accounts, and even come in the same order (see p. 264, and Genesis, i. 14-22). The famous cylinder of the British Museum (see No. 62, p. 266) is strong presumption in favor of the identity of the Chaldean version of the first couple's disobedience with the Biblical one. We have seen the important position occupied in the Chaldean religion by the symbol of the Sacred Tree, which surely corresponds to the Tree of Life in Eden (see p. 268), and probably also to that of Knowledge, and the different passages and names ingeniously collected and confronted by scholars leave no doubt as to the Chaldeans having had the legend of an Eden, a garden of God (see p. 274). A better preserved copy of the Creation tablets with the now missing passages may be recovered any

day, and there is no reason to doubt that they will be found as closely parallel to the Biblical narrative as those that have been recovered until now. But even as we have them at present it is very evident that the groundwork, the material, is the same in both. It is the manner, the spirit, which differs. In the Chaldean account, polytheism runs riot. Every element, every power of nature—Heaven, Earth, the Abyss, Atmosphere, etc.—has been personified into an individual divine being actively and severely engaged in the great work. The Hebrew narrative is severely monotheistic. In it GOD does all that "the gods" between them do in the other. Every poetical or allegorical turn of phrase is carefully avoided, lest it lead into the evil errors of the sister-nation. The symbolical myths—such as that of Bel's mixing his own blood with the clay out of which he fashions man, (see p. 266)—are sternly discarded, for the same reason. One only is retained: the temptation by the Serpent. But the Serpent being manifestly the personification of the Evil Principle which is forever busy in the soul of man, there was no danger of its being deified and worshipped; and as, moreover, the tale told in this manner very picturesquely and strikingly points a great moral lesson, the Oriental love of parable and allegory could in this instance be allowed free scope. Besides, the Hebrew writers of the sacred books were not beyond or above the superstitions of their country and age; indeed they retained all of these that did not appear to them incompatible with monotheism. Thus throughout the Books of the

Old Testament the Chaldean belief in witchcraft, divination from dreams and other signs is retained and openly professed, and astrology itself is not condemned, since among the destinations of the stars is mentioned that of serving to men " for signs " : " And God said, let there be lights in the firmament of the heaven to divide the day from the night; and let them be for signs and for seasons, and for days and years" (Genesis, i. 14). Even more explicit is the passage in the triumphal song of Deborah the prophetess, where celebrating the victory of Israel over Sisera, she says: "They fought from heaven : the stars in their courses fought against Sisera " (Judges, v. 20). But a belief in astrology by no means implies the admission of several gods. In one or two passages, indeed, we do find an expression which seems to have slipped in unawares, as an involuntary reminiscence of an original polytheism ; it is where God, communing with himself on Adam's trespass, says : " Behold, the man is become *as one of us*, to know good and evil " (Gen. iii. 22). An even clearer trace confronts us in one of the two names that are given to God. These names are " Jehovah," (more correctly " Yahveh ") and " Elohim." Now the latter name is the plural of *El*, " god," and so really means " the gods." If the sacred writers retained it, it was certainly not from carelessness or inadvertence. As they use it, it becomes in itself almost a profession of faith. It seems to proclaim the God of their religion as "the One God who is all the gods," in whom all the forces of the universe are contained and merged.

14. There is one feature in the Biblical narrative, which, at first sight, wears the appearance of mythical treatment: it is the familiar way in which God is represented as coming and going, speaking and acting, after the manner of men, especially in such passages as these: "And they heard the voice of the Lord God *walking in the garden in the cool of the day*" (Gen. iii. 8); or, "Unto Adam also and to his wife did the Lord God *make coats of skins and he clothed them*" (Gen. iii. 21). But such a judgment would be a serious error. There is nothing mythical in this; only the tendency, common to all mankind, of endowing the Deity with human attributes of form, speech and action, whenever the attempt was made to bring it very closely within the reach of their imagination. This tendency is so universal, that it has been classed, under a special name, among the distinctive features of the human mind. It has been called ANTHROPOMORPHISM, (from two Greek words *Anthropos*, "man," and *morphē*, "form,") and can never be got rid of, because it is part and parcel of our very nature. Man's spiritual longings are infinite, his perceptive faculties are limited. His spirit has wings of flame that would lift him up and bear him even beyond the endlessness of space into pure abstraction; his senses have soles of lead that ever weigh him down, back to the earth, of which he is and to which he must needs cling, to exist at all. He can *conceive*, by a great effort, an abstract idea, eluding the grasp

of senses, unclothed in matter; but he can *realize*, *imagine*, only by using such appliances as the senses supply him with. Therefore, the more fervently he grasps an idea, the more closely he assimilates it, the more it becomes materialized in his grasp, and when he attempts to reproduce it out of himself— behold! it has assumed the likeness of himself or something he has seen, heard, touched—the spirituality of it has become weighted with flesh, even as it is in himself. It is as it were a reproduction, in the intellectual world, of the eternal strife, in physical nature, between the two opposed forces of attraction and repulsion, the centrifugal and centripetal, of which the final result is to keep each body in its place, with a well-defined and limited range of motion allotted to it. Thus, however pure and spiritual the conception of the Deity may be, man, in making it real to himself, in bringing it down within his reach and ken, within the shrine of his heart, *will* and *must* perforce make of it a Being, human not only in shape, but also in thought and feeling. How otherwise could he grasp it at all? And the accessories with which he will surround it will necessarily be suggested by his own experience, copied from those among which he moves habitually himself. "Walking in the garden in the cool of the day" is an essentially Oriental and Southern recreation, and came quite naturally to the mind of a writer living in a land steeped in sunshine and sultriness. Had the writer been a Northerner, a denizen of snow-clad plains and ice-bound rivers, the Lord might probably have been represented as coming in a swift, fur-lined sleigh. Anthropomorphism, then, is in itself neither mythology nor idolatry; but it is very clear that it can with the utmost ease glide into either or both, with just a little help from poetry and, especially, from art, in its innocent endeavor to fix in tangible form the vague imaginings and gropings, of which words often are but a fleeting and feeble rendering. Hence the banishment of all material symbols, the absolute prohibition of any images whatever as an accessory of religious worship, which, next to the recognition of One only God, is the keystone of the Hebrew law:—"Thou shalt have no other gods before me. Thou shalt not make unto thee any graven image, or any likeness of anything that is in heaven above, or that is in the earth beneath, or that is in the water under the earth.—Thou shalt not bow down thyself to them, nor serve them" (Exodus, xx. 3-5).

But, to continue our parallel.

15. The ten antediluvian kings of Berosus, who succeed the apparition of the divine Man-Fish, Êa-Oannes (see p. 196), have their exact counterpart in the ten antediluvian patriarchs of Genesis, v. Like the Chaldean kings, the patriarchs live an unnatural number of years. Only the extravagant figures of the Chaldean tradition are considerably reduced in the Hebrew version. While the former allots to its kings reigns of tens of thousands of years (see p. 196), the latter cuts them down to hundreds, and the utmost that it allows to any of its

patriarchs is nine hundred and sixty-nine years of life (Methuselah).

16. The resemblances between the two Deluge narratives are so obvious and continuous, that it is not these, but the differences that need pointing out. Here again the sober, severely monotheistic character of the Hebrew narrative contrasts most strikingly with the exuberant polytheism of the Chaldean one, in which Heaven, Sun, Storm, Sea, even Rain are personified, deified, and consistently act their several appropriate and most dramatic parts in the great cataclysm, while Nature herself, as the Great Mother of beings and fosterer of life, is represented, in the person of Ishtar, lamenting the slaughter of men (see p. 327). Apart from this fundamental difference in spirit, the identity in all the essential points of fact is amazing, and variations occur only in lesser details. The most characteristic one is that, while the Chaldean version describes the building and furnishing of a *ship*, with all the accuracy of much seafaring knowledge, and does not forget even to name the pilot, the Hebrew writer, with the clumsiness and ignorance of nautical matters natural to an inland people unfamiliar with the sea or the appearance of ships, speaks only of an *ark* or *chest*. The greatest discrepancy is in the duration of the flood, which is much shorter in the Chaldean text than in the Hebrew. On the seventh day already, Hâsisadra sends out the dove (see p. 316). But then in the Biblical narrative itself, made up, as was remarked above, of two parallel texts joined together, this same point is given dif-

ferently in different places. According to Genesis, vii. 12, " the rain was upon the earth forty days and forty nights," while verse 24 of the same chapter tells us that " the waters prevailed upon the earth an hundred and fifty days." Again, the number of the saved is far larger in the Chaldean account: Hâsisadra takes with him into the ship all his men-servants, his women-servants, and even his "nearest friends," while Noah is allowed to save only his own immediate family, " his sons, and his wife, and his sons' wives " (Genesis, vi. 18). Then, the incident of the birds is differently told: Hâsisadra sends out three birds, the dove, the swallow, and the raven; Noah only two—first the raven, then three times in succession the dove. But it is startling to find both narratives more than once using the same words. Thus the Hebrew writer tells how Noah " sent forth a raven, which went to and fro," and how " the dove found no rest for the sole of her foot and returned." Hâsisadra relates: " I took out a dove and sent it forth. The dove went forth, to and fro, but found no resting-place and returned." And further, when Hâsisadra describes the sacrifice he offered on the top of Mount Nizir, after he came forth from the ship, he says: " The gods smelled a savor; the gods smelled a sweet savor." " And the Lord smelled a sweet savor," says Genesis,—viii. 21—of Noah's burnt-offering. These few hints must suffice to show how instructive and entertaining is a parallel study of the two narratives; it can be best done by attentively reading both alternately, and comparing them together, paragraph by paragraph.

17. The legend of the Tower of Languages (see above, p. 293, and Genesis, xi. 3-9), is the last in the series of parallel Chaldean and Hebrew traditions. In the Bible it is immediately followed by the detailed genealogy of the Hebrews from Shem to Abraham. Therewith evidently ends the connection between the two people, who are severed for all time from the moment that Abraham goes forth with his tribe from Ur of the Chaldees, probably in the reign of Amarpal (father of Hammurabi), whom the Bible calls Amraphel, king of Shinear. The reign of Hammurabi was, as we have already seen (see p. 219), a prosperous and brilliant one. He was originally king of Tintir (the oldest name of Babylon), and when he united all the cities and local rulers of Chaldea under his supremacy, he asserted the pre-eminence among them for his own city, which he began to call by its new name, KA-DIMIRRA (Accadian for "Gate of God," which was translated into the Semitic BAB-IL). This king in every respect opens a new chapter in the history of Chaldea. Moreover, a great movement was taking place in all the region between the Mediterranean and the Persian Gulf; nations were forming and growing, and Chaldea's most formidable rival and future conqueror, Assyria, was gradually gathering strength in the north, a fierce young lion-cub. By this newcomer among nations our attention will henceforth mainly be claimed. Let us, therefore, pause on the high

place to which we have now arrived, and, casting a glance backward, take a rapid survey of the ground we have covered.

18. Looking with strained eyes into a past dim and gray with the scarce-lifting mists of unnumbered ages, we behold our starting-point, the low land by the Gulf, Shumir, taking shape and color under the rule of Turanian settlers, the oldest known nation in the world. They drain and till the land, they make bricks and build cities, and prosper materially. But the spirit in them is dark and lives in cowering terror of self-created demons and evil things, which they yet believe they can control and compel. So their religion is one, not of worship and thanksgiving, but of dire conjuring and incantation, inconceivable superstition and witchcraft, an unutterable dreariness hardly lightened by the glimmering of a nobler faith, in the conception of the wise and beneficent Êa and his ever benevolently busy son, Meridug. But gradually there comes a change. Shumir lifts its gaze upward, and as it takes in more the beauty and the goodness of the world—in Sun and Moon and Stars, in the wholesome Waters and the purifying serviceable Fire, the good and divine Powers—the Gods multiply and the host of elementary spirits, mostly evil, becomes secondary. This change is greatly helped by the arrival of the meditative, star-gazing strangers, who take hold of the nature-worship and the nature-myths they find among the people to which they have come—a higher and more advanced race—and weave these, with their

own star-worship and astrological lore, into a new faith, a religious system most ingeniously combined, elaborately harmonized, and full of profoundest meaning. The new religion is preached not only in words, but in brick and stone: temples arise all over the land, erected by the *patesis*—the priest-kings of the different cities—and libraries in which the priestly colleges reverently treasure both their own works and the older religious lore of the country. The ancient Turanian names of the gods are gradually translated into the new Cushito-Semitic language; yet the prayers and hymns, as well as the incantations, are still preserved in the original tongue, for the people of Turanian Shumir are the more numerous, and must be ruled and conciliated, not alienated. The more northern region, Accad, is, indeed, more thinly peopled; there the tribes of Semites, who now arrive in frequent instalments, spread rapidly and unhindered. The cities of Accad with their temples soon rival those of Shumir and strive to eclipse them, and their *patesis* labor to predominate politically over those of the South. And it is with the North that the victory at first remains; its pre-eminence is asserted in the time of Sharrukin of Agadè, about 3800 B.C., but is resumed by the South some thousand years later, when a powerful dynasty (that to which belong Ur-èa and his son Dungi) establishes itself in Ur, while Tintir, the future head and centre of the united land of Chaldea, the great Babylon, if existing at all, is not yet heard of. It is these kings of Ur who first take the significant title "kings of Shumir and Accad." Meanwhile new and higher moral influences have been at work; the Semitic immigration has quickened the half mythical, half astronomical religion with a more spiritual element—of fervent adoration, of prayerful trust, of passionate contrition and self-humiliation in the bitter consciousness of sin, hitherto foreign to it, and has produced a new and beautiful religious literature, which marks its third and last stage. To this stage belong the often mentioned "Penitential Psalms," Semitic, nay, rather Hebrew in spirit, although still written in the old Turanian language (but in the northern dialect of Accad, a fact that in itself bears witness to their comparative lateness and the locality in which they sprang up), and too strikingly identical with similar songs of the golden age of Hebrew poetry in substance and form, not to have been the models from which the latter, by a sort of unconscious heredity, drew its inspirations. Then comes the great Elamitic invasion, with its plundering of cities, desecration of temples and sanctuaries, followed probably by several more through a period of at least three hundred years. The last, that of Khudur Lagamar, since it brings prominently forward the founder of the Hebrew nation, deserves to be particularly mentioned by that nation's historians, and, inasmuch as it coincides with the reign of Amarpal, king of Tintir and father of Hammurabi, serves to establish an important landmark in the history both of the Jews and of Chaldea. When we reach this comparatively recent date the mists have in great part rolled aside, and as we turn from the ages we have just surveyed to those that still lie before us, history guides us with a bolder step and shows us the landscape in a twilight which, though still dim and sometimes misleading, is yet that of breaking day, not of descending night.

19. When we attempt to realize the prodigious vastness and remoteness of the horizon thus opened before us, a feeling akin to awe overcomes us. Until within a very few years, Egypt gloried in the undisputed boast of being the oldest country in the world, i.e., of reaching back, by its annals and monuments, to an earlier date than any other. But the discoveries that are continually being made in the valley of the two great rivers have forever silenced that boast. Chaldea points to a monumentally recorded date nearly 4000 B.C. This is more than Egypt can do. Her oldest authentic monuments, —her great Pyramids, are considerably later. Mr. F. Hommel, one of the leaders of Assyriology, forcibly expresses this feeling of wonder in a recent publication:[*] "If," he says, "the Semites were already settled in Northern Babylonia (Accad) in the beginning of the fourth thousand B.C., in possession of the fully developed Shumiro-Accadian culture adopted by them,—a culture, moreover, which appears to have sprouted in Accad as a cutting from Shumir—then the latter must naturally be far, far

---

[*] Ztschr. für Keilschriftforschung, "Zur altbabylonischen Chronologie," Heft I.

older still, and have existed in its completed form IN THE FIFTH THOUSAND B.C.—an age to which I now unhesitatingly ascribe the South-Babylonian incantations." This would give our mental vision a sweep of full six thousand years, a pretty respectable figure! But when we remember that these first known settlers of Shumir came from somewhere else, and that they brought with them more than the rudiments of civilization, we are at once thrown back at least a couple of thousands of years more. For it must have taken all of that and more for men to pass from a life spent in caves and hunting the wild beasts to a stage of culture comprising the invention of a complete system of writing, the knowledge and working of metals, even to the mixing of copper and tin into bronze, and an expertness in agriculture equal not only to tilling, but to draining land. If we further pursue humanity—losing at last all count of time in years or even centuries—back to its original separation, to its first appearance on the earth,—if we go further still and try to think of the ages upon ages during which man existed not at all, yet the earth did, and was beautiful to look upon—(*had* there been any to look on it), and good for the creatures who had it all to themselves—a dizziness comes over our senses, before the infinity of time, and we draw back, faint and awed, as we do when astronomy launches us, on a slender thread of figures, into the infinity of space. The six ages of a thousand years each which are all that our mind can firmly grasp then come to seem to us a very poor and puny fraction of eternity, to which we are tempted to apply almost scornfully the words spoken by the poet of as many years: "Six ages! six little ages! six drops of time!" *

---

* Matthew Arnold, in "Mycerinus":

"Six years! six little years! six drops of time!"

APPENDIX TO CHAPTER VII.

PROFESSOR LOUIS DYER has devoted some time to preparing a free metrical translation of "Ishtar's Descent." Unfortunately, owing to his many occupations, only the first part of the poem is as yet finished. This he most kindly has placed at our disposal, authorizing us to present it to our readers.

ISHTAR IN URUGAL.

ALONG the gloomy avenue of death
To seek the dread abysm of Urugal,
In everlasting Dark whence none returns,
Ishtar, the Moon-god's daughter, made resolve,
And that way, sick with sorrow, turned her face.
    A road leads downward, but no road leads back
From Darkness' realm. There is Irkalla queen,
Named also Ninkigal, mother of pains.
Her portals close forever on her guests
And exit there is none, but all who enter,
To daylight strangers, and of joy unknown,
Within her sunless gates restrained must stay.
And there the only food vouchsafed is dust,
For slime they live on, who on earth have died.
Day's golden beam greets none and darkness reigns
Where hurtling bat-like forms of feathered men
Or human-fashioned birds imprisoned flit.
Close and with dust o'erstrewn, the dungeon doors
Are held by bolts with gathering mould o'ersealed.
    By love distracted, though the queen of love,
Pale Ishtar downward flashed toward death's domain,
And swift approached these gates of Urugal,
Then paused impatient at its portals grim;

For love, whose strength no earthly bars restrain,
Gives not the key to open Darkness' Doors.
By service from all living men made proud,
Ishtar brooked not resistance from the dead.
She called the jailer, then to anger changed
The love that sped her on her breathless way,
And from her parted lips incontinent
Swept speech that made the unyielding warder quail.
"Quick, turnkey of the pit! swing wide these doors,
And fling them swiftly open. Tarry not!
For I will pass, even I will enter in.
Dare no denial, thou, bar not my way,
Else will I burst thy bolts and rend thy gates,
This lintel shatter else and wreck these doors.
The pent-up dead I else will loose, and lead
Back the departed to the lands they left,
Else bid the famished dwellers in the pit
Rise up to live and eat their fill once more.
Dead myriads then shall burden groaning earth,
Sore tasked without them by her living throngs."
   Love's mistress, mastered by strong hate,
The warder heard, and wondered first, then feared
The angered goddess Ishtar what she spake,
Then answering said to Ishtar's wrathful might:
"O princess, stay thy hand; rend not the door.
But tarry here, while unto Ninkigal
I go, and tell thy glorious name to her."

ISHTAR'S LAMENT.

"All love from earthly life with me departed,
  With me to tarry in the gates of death;
In heaven's sun no warmth is longer hearted,
  And chilled shall cheerless men now draw slow breath.

"I left in sadness life wh'ch I had given,
  I turned from gladness and I walked with woe,
Toward living death by grief untimely driven,
  I search for Thammuz whom harsh fate laid low.

"The darkling pathway o'er the restless waters
Of seven seas that circle Death's domain
I trod, and followed after earth's sad daughters
Torn from their loved ones and ne'er seen again.

"Here must I enter in, here make my dwelling
With Thammuz in the mansion of the dead,
Driven to Famine's house by love compelling
And hunger for the sight of that dear head.

"O'er husbands will I weep, whom death has taken,
Whom fate in manhood's strength from life has swept,
Leaving on earth their living wives forsaken,—
O'er them with groans shall bitter tears be wept.

"And I will weep o'er wives, whose short day ended
Ere in glad offspring joyed their husbands' eyes ;
Snatched from loved arms they left their lords untended,—
O'er them shall tearful lamentations rise.

"And I will weep o'er babes who left no brothers,
Young lives to the ills of age by hope opposed,
The sons of saddened sires and tearful mothers,
One moment's life by death eternal closed."

NINKIGAL'S COMMAND TO THE WARDER.

"LEAVE thou this presence, slave, open the gate;
Since power is hers to force an entrance here,
Let her come in as come from life the dead,
Submissive to the laws of Death's domain.
Do unto her what unto all thou doest."

Want of space bids us limit ourselves to these few fragments—surely sufficient to make our readers wish that Professor Dyer might spare some time to the completion of his task.

INDEX.

A.

Abel, killed by Cain, 129.
Abraham, wealthy and powerful chief, 200; goes forth from Ur, 201; his victory over Khudur-Lagamar, 222-224.
Abu-Habba, see Sippar.
Abu-Shahrein, see Eridhu.
Accad, Northern or Upper Chaldea, 145; meaning of the word, ib.; headquarters of Semitism, 204-205.
Accads, see Shumiro-Accads.
Accadian language, see Shumiro-Accadian.
Agadê, capital of Accad, 205.
Agglutinative languages, meaning of the word, 136-137; characteristic of Turanian nations, ib.; spoken by the people of Shumir and Accad, 144.
Agricultural life, third stage of culture, first beginning of real civilization, 122.
Akki, the water-carrier, see Sharrukin of Agadê.
Alexander of Macedon conquers Babylon, 4; his soldiers destroy the dams of the Euphrates, 5.
Allah, Arabic for "God," see Ilu.
Allat, queen of the Dead, 327-329.
Altaï, the great Siberian mountain chain, 146; probable cradle of the Turanian race, 147.
Altaïc, another name for the Turanian or Yellow Race, 147.
Amarpal, also Sin-Muballit, king of Babylon, perhaps Amraphel, King of Shinar, 226.
Amorite, the, a tribe of Canaan, 133.
Amraphel, see Amarpal.
Ana, or Zi-ana—"Heaven," or "Spirit of Heaven," p. 154.
Anatu, goddess, mother of Ishtar, smites Êabâni with death and Izdubar with leprosy, 310.
Anthropomorphism, meaning of the word, 355; definition and causes of, 355-357.
Anu, first god of the first Babylonian Triad, same as Ana, 240; one of the "twelve great gods," 246.
Anunnaki, minor spirits of earth, 154, 250.
Anunit (the Moon), wife of Shamash, 245.
Apsu (the Abyss), 264.
Arali, or Arallu, the Land of the Dead, 157; its connection with the Sacred Mountain, 276.
Arallu, see Arali.
Aram, a son of Shem, eponymous ancestor of the Aramæans in Gen. x., 131.
Arabs, their conquest and prosperous rule in Mesopotamia, 5; Baghdad, their capital, 5; nomads in Mesopotamia, 8; their superstitious horror of the ruins and sculptures, 11; they take the gigantic head for Nimrod, 22-24; their strange ideas about the colossal winged bulls

INDEX.

and lions and their destination, 24-25; their habit of plundering ancient tombs at Warka, 86; their conquests and high culture in Asia and Africa, 118.

Arbela, city of Assyria, built in hilly region, 50.

Architecture, Chaldean, created by local conditions, 37-39; Assyrian, borrowed from Chaldea, 50.

Areph-Kasdim, see Arphaxad, meaning of the word, 200.

Arphaxad, eldest son of Shem, 200.

Arphakshad, see Arphaxad.

Asshur, a son of Shem, eponymous ancestor of the Assyrians in Genesis X., 131.

Asshurbanipal, King of Assyria, his Library, 100-112; conquers Elam, destroys Shushan, and restores the statue of the goddess Nana to Erech, 194-195.

Asshurnazirpal, King of Assyria, size of hall in his palace at Calah (Nimrud), 63.

Assyria, the same as Upper Mesopotamia, 7; rise of, 228.

Astrology, meaning of the word, 106; a corruption of astronomy, 234; the special study of priests, ib.

Astronomy, the ancient Chaldeans' proficiency in, 230; fascination of, 231; conducive to religious speculation, 232; degenerates into astrology, 234; the god Nebo, the patron of, 242.

B.

Babbar, see Ud.

Babel, same as Babylon, 237.

Bab-el-Mander, Straits of, 189.

Bab-ilu, Semitic name of Babylon; meaning of the name, 225, 249.

Babylonia, a part of Lower Mesopotamia, 7; excessive flatness of, 9; later name for "Shumir and Accad" and for "Chaldea," 237.

Baghdad, capital of the Arabs' empire in Mesopotamia, 5; its decay, 6;

Bassorah, see Busrah.

Bedouins, robber tribes of, 8; distinctively a nomadic people, 116-118.

Bel, third god of the first Babylonian Triad, 239; meaning of the name, 240; one of the "twelve great gods," 246; his battle with Tiamat, 288-290.

Belit, the wife of Bel, the feminine principle of nature, 244-245; one of the "twelve great gods," 246.

Bel-Maruduk, see Marduk.

Berosus, Babylonian priest; his History of Chaldea, 128; his version of the legend of Oannes, 184-185; his account of the Chaldean Cosmogony, 260-261, 267; his account of the great tower and the confusion of tongues, 292-293; his account of the Deluge, 299-301.

Birs-Nimrud or Birs-i-Nimrud, see Borsippa.

Books, not always of paper, 93; stones and bricks used as books, 97; walls and rocks, ib., 97-99.

Borsippa (Mound of Birs-Nimrud), its peculiar shape, 47; Nebuchadnezzar's inscription found at, 72; identified with the Tower of Babel, 293.

Botta begins excavations at Koyunjik, 14; his disappointment, 15; his great discovery at Khorsabad, 15-16.

Bricks, how men came to make, 39; sun-dried or raw, and kiln-dried or baked, 40; ancient bricks from the ruins used for modern constructions; trade with ancient bricks at Hillah, 42.

British Museum, Rich's collection presented to, 14.
Busrah, or Bassorah, bulls and lions shipped to, down the Tigris, 52.
Byblos, ancient writing material, 94.

C.

Ca-Dimirra (or Ka-Dimirra), second name of Babylon; meaning of the name, 216, 249
Cain, his crime, banishment, and posterity, 129.
Calah, or Kalah, one of the Assyrian capitals, the Larissa of Xenophon, 3.
Calendar, Chaldean, 230, 318–321, 325.
Canaan, son of Ham, eponymous ancestor of many nations, 134.
Canaanites, migrations of, 190.
Cement, various qualities of, 44.
Chaldea, the same as Lower Mesopotamia, 7; alluvial formation of, 37–38; its extraordinary abundance in cemeteries, 78; a nursery of nations, 198; more often called by the ancients " Babylonia," 237.
Chaldeans, in the sense of " wise men of the East," astrologer, magician, soothsayer,—a separate class of the priesthood, 254-255.
Charm against evil spells, 162.
Cherub, Cherubim, see Kirûbu.
China, possibly mentioned in Isaiah, 136, note.
Chinese speak a monosyllabic language, 137; their genius and its limitations, 138, 139; oldest national religion of, 180, 181; their "docenal" and "sexagesimal" system of counting, 230–231.
Chronology, vagueness of ancient, 193-194; extravagant figures of, 196-197; difficulty of establishing, 211-212.
Chthon, meaning of the word, 272.
Chthonic Powers, 272, 273.

Chthonic Myths, see Myths.
Cissians, see Kasshi.
Cities, building of, fourth stage of culture, 123, 124.
Classical Antiquity, meaning of the term; too exclusive study of, 12.
Coffins, ancient Chaldean, found at Warka: "jar-coffins," 82; "dish-cover" coffins, 84; "slipper-shaped" coffin (comparatively modern), 84–86.
Conjuring, against demons and sorcerers, 158–159; admitted into the later reformed religion, 236.
Conjurors, admitted into the Babylonian priesthood, 250.
Cossæans, see Kasshi.
Cosmogonic Myths, see Myths.
Cosmogony, meaning of the word, 259; Chaldean, imparted by Berosus, 260–261; original tablets discovered by Geo. Smith, 261–263; their contents, 264 and ff.; Berosus again, 267.
Cosmos, meaning of the word, 272.
Cuneiform writing, shape and specimen of, 10; introduced into Chaldea by the Shumiro-Accads, 145.
Cush, or Kush, eldest son of Ham, 186; probable early migrations of, 188; ancient name of Ethiopia, 189.
Cushites, colonization of Turanian Chaldea by, 192.
Cylinders: seal cylinders in hard stones, 113–114; foundation-cylinders, 114; seal-cylinders worn as talismans, 166; Babylonian cylinder, supposed to represent the Temptation and Fall, 266.

D.

Damkina, goddess, wife of Ea, mother of Meridug, 160.
Decoration: of palaces, 58–62; of walls at Warka, 87–88.

Delitzsch, Friedrich, eminent Assyriologist, favors the Semitic theory, 186.
Deluge, Berosus' account of, 299 –301; cuneiform account, in the 11th tablet of the Izdubar Epic, 314–317.
Demon of the South-West Wind, 168.
Diseases conceived as demons, 163.
Divination, a branch of Chaldean "science," in what it consists, 251–252; collection of texts on, in one hundred tablets, 252–253; specimens of, 253–254.
Draining of palace mounds, 70; of sepulchral mounds at Warka, 86–87.
Dumuzi, the husband of the goddess Ishtar, 303; the hero of a solar Myth, 323–326.
Dur-Sharrukin, (see Khorsabad), built in hilly region, 50.

E.

Ea, sometimes Zi-ki-a, the Spirit of the Earth and Waters, 154; protector against evil spirits and men, 160; his chief sanctuary at Eridhu, 215; second god of the first Babylonian Triad, 239; his attributions, 240; one of the "twelve great gods," 246.
Eabâni, the seer, 304; invited by Izdubar, 304–305; becomes Izdubar's friend, 307; vanquishes with him the Elamite tyrant Khumbaba, 308; smitten by Ishtar and Anatu, 310; restored to life by the gods, 314.
E-Babbara, "House of the Sun," 215, 248.
Eber, see Heber.
El, see Ilu.
Elam, kingdom of, conquered by Asshurbanipal, 194; meaning of the name, 220.

Elamite conquest of Chaldea, 219–221, 224–225.
Elohim, one of the Hebrew names for God, a plural of El, 354. See Ilu.
Emanations, theory of divine, 238–239; meaning of the word, 239.
Enoch, son of Cain, 129.
Enoch, the first city, built by Cain, 129.
Epic Poems, or Epics, 298–299.
Epic-Chaldæan, oldest known in the world, 299; its division into tablets, 302.
Eponym, meaning of the word, 133.
Eponymous genealogies in Genesis X., 132–134.
Epos, national, meaning of the word, 299.
Erech (now Mound of Warka), oldest name Urukh, immense burying-grounds around, 80–82; plundered by Khudur-Nankhundi, king of Elam, 195; library of, 209.
Eri-Aku (Arioch of Ellassar), Elamite king of Larsam, 226.
Eridhu (modern Abu-Shahrein), the most ancient city of Shumir, 215; specially sacred to Ea, 215, 246, 287.
Ethiopians, see Cush.
Excavations, how carried on, 30–34.

F.

Fergusson, Jas., English explorer and writer on art subjects, 56.
Finns, a nation of Turanian stock, 138.
Flood, or Deluge, possibly *not* universal, 128–129.

G.

Gan-Dunyash, or Kar-Dunyash, most ancient name of Babylonia proper, 225, 286.
Genesis, first book of the Pentateuch, 127–129; Chapter X. of,

130-142; meaning of the word, 353.
Gibil, Fire, 173; hymn to, 16; his friendliness, 174; invoked to prosper the fabrication of bronze, 16.
Gisdhubar, see Izdubar.
Gudêa, *patesi* of Sirburla, 214.

H.

Ham, second son of Noah, 130; meaning of the name, 186.
Hammurabi, king of Babylon and all Chaldea, 226; his long and glorious reign, ib.; his public works and the "Royal Canal," 227.
Harimtu ("Persuasion"), one of the handmaidens of Ishtar, 305.
Hâsisadra, same as Xisuthros, 303; gives Izdubar an account of the great Flood, 314-317.
Heber, a descendant of Shem, eponymous ancestor of the Hebrews in Genesis X., 131, 222.
Heroes, 296-298.
Heroic Ages, 299.
Heroic Myths, see Myths.
Hillah, built of bricks from the palace of Nebuchadnezzar, carries on trade with ancient bricks, 42.
Himalaya Mountains, 188.
Hindu-Cush (or Kush) Mountains, 188.
Hit, ancient Is, on the Euphrates, springs of bitumen at, 44.
Hivite, the, a tribe of Canaan, 133.
Hungarians, a nation of Turanian stock, 138.

I.

Idpa, the Demon of Fever, 156.
Igigi, three hundred, spirits of heaven, 250.
Ilu, or El, Semitic name for "god," 232.
Im, or Mermer, "Wind," 154.

India, 188.
Indus, the great river of India, 188.
Intercalary months, introduced by the Chaldeans to correct the reckoning of their year, 230.
Is, see Hit.
Ishtar, the goddess of the planet Venus, 242; the Warrior Queen and Queen of Love, 245; one of the "twelve great gods," 246; offers her love to Izdubar, 308; is rejected and sends a monstrous bull against him, 309; causes Êabâni's death and Izdubar's illness, 310; descent of, into the land of shades, 326-330.
Izdubar, the hero of the great Chaldean Epic, 303; his dream at Erech, 304; invites Êabâni, 304-305; vanquishes with his help Khumbaba, the Elamite tyrant of Erech, 308; offends Ishtar, 308; vanquishes the divine Bull, with Êabâni's help, 309; is smitten with leprosy, 310; travels to "the mouth of the great rivers" to consult his immortal ancestor Hâsisadra, 310-313; is purified and healed, 313; returns to Erech; his lament over Êabâni's death, 313-314; solar character of the Epic, 318-322.

J.

Jabal and Jubal, sons of Lamech, descendants of Cain, 129.
Japheth, third son of Noah, 130.
Javan, a son of Japhet, eponymous ancestor of the Ionian Greeks, 134.
"Jonah's Mound," see Nebbi-Yunus.
Jubal, see Jabal and Jubal.

K.

Ka-Dingirra, see Ca-Dimirra.
Kar-Dunyash, see Gan-Dunyash.

Kasbu, the Chaldean double hour, 230.
Kasr, Mound of, ruins of the palace of Nebuchadnezzar.
Kasshi (Cossæans or Cissians), conquer Chaldea, 228.
Kerbela and Nedjif, goal of pilgrim-caravans from Persia, 78.
Kerubim, see Kirûbu.
Khorsabad, Mound of, Botta's excavations and brilliant discovery at, 15-16.
Khudur-Lagamar (Chedorlaomer), king of Elam and Chaldea, his conquests, 221; plunders Sodom and Gomorrah with his allies, 222; is overtaken by Abraham and routed, 223; his probable date, 224.
Khudur-Nankhundi, king of Elam, invades Chaldea and carries the statue of the goddess Nana away from Erech, 195.
Khumbaba, the Elamite tyrant of Erech vanquished by Izdubar and Êabâni, 308.
Kirûbu, name of the Winged Bulls, 164.
Koyunjik, Mound of Xenophon's Mespila, 14; Botta's unsuccessful exploration of, 15; valuable find of small articles in a chamber at, in the palace of Sennacherib, 34.
Kurds, nomadic tribes of, 8.

L.

Lamech, fifth descendant of Cain, 129.
Larissa, ruins of ancient Calah, seen by Xenophon, 3.
Larsam (now Senkereh), city of Shumir, 215.
Layard meets Botta at Mossul in 1842, 17; undertakes the exploration of Nimrud, 17-18; his work and life in the East, 19-32; discovers the Royal Library at Nineveh (Koyunjik), 100.

Lebanon Mountains, 190.
Lenormant, François, eminent French Orientalist; his work on the religion of the Shumiro-Accads, 152-3; favors the Cushite theory, 186.
Library of Asshurbanipal in his palace at Nineveh (Koyunjik); discovered by Layard, 100; re-opened by George Smith, 103; contents and importance of, for modern scholarship, 106-109; of Erech, 209.
Loftus, English explorer; his visit to Warka in 1854-5, 80-82; procures slipper-shaped coffins for the British Museum, 36.
Louvre, Assyrian Collection at the, 17; "Sarzec collection" added, 89.
Louvre, Armenian contrivance for lighting houses, 68.

M.

Madai, a son of Japhet, eponymous ancestor of the Medes, 135.
Magician, derivation of the word, 255.
Marad, ancient city of Chaldea, 303.
Marduk, or Maruduk (Hebrew Merodach), god of the planet Jupiter, 241; one of the "twelve great gods," 246; special patron of Babylon, 249.
Maskim, the seven, evil spirits, 154; incantation against the, 155; the same, poetical version, 182.
Maspero, G., eminent French Orientalist, 197.
Medes, Xenophon's erroneous account of, 3-4; mentioned under the name of Madai in Genesis X., 135.
Media, divided from Assyria by the Zagros chain, 50.
Ménant, Joachim, French Assyriologist; his little book on

the Royal Library at Nineveh, 105.
Meridug, son of Êa, the Mediator, 160; his dialogues with Êa, 161-162.
Mermer, see Im.
Merodach, see Marduk.
Mesopotamia, meaning of the name, 5; peculiar formation of, 6; division of, into Upper and Lower, 7.
Mespila, ruins of Nineveh, seen by Xenophon, 3; now Mound of Koyunjik, 14.
Migrations of tribes, nations, races; probable first causes of prehistoric migrations, 119; caused by invasions and conquests, 125; of the Turanian races, 146-147; of the Cushites, 188; of the Canaanites, 190.
Mizraim ("the Egyptians"), a son of Ham, eponymous ancestor of the Egyptians, 133; opposed to Cush, 189.
Monosyllabic languages—Chinese, 136-137.
Monotheism, meaning of the word, 238; as conceived by the Hebrews, 344-345.
Mosul, the residence of a Turkish Pasha; origin of the name, 6; the wicked Pasha of, 20-22.
Mound-Builders, their tombs, 335-338.
Mounds, their appearance, 9-10; their contents, 11; formation of, 72; their usefulness in protecting the ruins and works of art, 74; sepulchral mounds at Warka, 79-87.
Mugheir, see Ur.
Mul-ge, "Lord of the Abyss," 154.
Mummu-Tiamat (the "Billowy Sea"), 264; her hostility to the gods, 288; her fight with Bel, 288-290.
Mythology, definition of, 331; distinction from Religion, 331-334.
Myths, meaning of the word,
294; Cosmogonic, 294; Heroic, 297-298; Solar, 322; 339-340; Chthonic, 330, 340-341.

N.

Nabonidus, last king of Babylon, discovers Naram-sin's cylinder, 213; discovers Hammurabi's cylinder at Larsam, 218-219.
Naintar, the Demon of Pestilence, 156, 157; incantation against, 167; Minister of Allat, Queen of the Dead, 328, 329.
Nana, Chaldean goddess, her statue restored by Asshurbanipal, 195, 343-344; wife of Anu, 245.
Nannar, see Uru-Ki.
Naram-Sin, son of Sargon I. of Agadê; his cylinder discovered by Nabonidus, 213.
Nations, gradual formation of, 125-126.
Nebbi-Yunus, Mound of, its sacredness, 11; its size, 49.
Nebo, or Nabu, the god of the planet Mercury, 242; one of the "twelve great gods," 246.
Nebuchadnezzar, king of Babylon; his palace, now Mound of Kasr, 42; his inscription of Borsippa, 72.
Nedjif, see Kerbela.
Nergal, the god of the planet Mars, and of War, 242; one of the "twelve great gods," 246.
Niffer, see Nippur.
Nimrod, dams on the Euphrates attributed to, by the Arabs, 5; his name preserved, and many ruins called by it, 11; gigantic head declared by the Arabs to be the head of, 22-24.
Nimrud, Mound of, Layard undertakes the exploration of, 17.
Nin-dar, the nightly sun, 175.
Nineveh, greatness and utter destruction of, 1; ruins of, seen by Xenophon, called by him

Mespila, 3; site of, opposite Mossul, 11.
Nin-ge, see Nin-ki-gal.
Ninib, or Nineb, the god of the planet Saturn, 241; one of the "twelve great gods," 246.
Nin-ki-gal, or Nin-ge, "the Lady of the Abyss," 157.
Nippur (now Niffer), city of Accad, 216.
Nizir, Mount, the mountain on which Hâsisadra's ship stood still, 301; land and Mount, 316
Noah and his three sons, 130.
Nod, land of ("Land of Exile," or "of Wanderings"), 129.
Nomads, meaning of the word, and causes of nomadic life in modern times, 118.

O.

Oannes, legend of, told by Berosus, 185.
Oasis, meaning of the word, 118.

P.

Palaces, their imposing aspect, 54; palace of Sennacherib restored by Fergusson, 56; ornamentation of palaces, 58; winged Bulls and Lions at gateways of, 58; sculptured slabs along the walls of, 58-60; painted tiles used for the friezes of, 60-62; proportions of halls, 63; roofing of, 62-66; lighting of, 66-68.
Papyrus, ancient writing material, 94.
Paradise, Chaldean legend of, see Sacred Tree and Ziggurat. Meaning of the word, 277.
Parallel between the Book of Genesis and the Chaldean legends, 350-360.
Pastoral life, second stage of culture, 120; necessarily nomadic, 121.
Patesis, meaning of the word, 203; first form of royalty in Chaldean cities, ib., 235.
Patriarchal authority, first form of government, 123; the tribe, or enlarged family, first form of the State, 123.
Penitential Psalms, Chaldean, 177-179.
Persian Gulf, flatness and marshiness of the region around, 7; reached further inland than now, 201.
Persians, rule in Asia, 2; the war between two royal brothers, 2; Persian monarchy conquered by Alexander, 4; not named in Genesis X., 134.
Platforms, artificial, 46-49.
Polytheism, meaning of the word, 237; tendency to, of the Hebrews, combated by their leaders, 345-350.
Priesthood, Chaldean, causes of its power and influence, 233-234.

R.

Races, Nations, and Tribes represented in antiquity under the name of a man, an ancestor, 130-134; black race and yellow race omitted from the list in Genesis X., 134-142; probable reasons for the omission, 135, 140.
Ramân, third god of the second Babylonian Triad, his attributions, 240-241; one of the "twelve great gods," 246.
Rassam, Hormuzd, explorer, 247, 248.
Rawlinson, Sir Henry, his work at the British Museum, 152.
Religion of the Shumiro-Accads the most primitive in the world, 148; characteristics of Turanian religions, 180, 181; definition of, as distinguished from Mythology, 331-334.
Religiosity, distinctively human

characteristic, 143; its awakening and development, 149-152.
Rich, the first explorer, 13; his disappointment at Mossul, 14.

S.

Sabattuv, the Babylonian and Assyrian "Sabbath," 256.
Sabeism, the worship of the heavenly bodies, a Semitic form of religion, 232; fostered by a pastoral and nomadic life, ib.
Sabitu, one of the maidens in the magic grove, 311.
Sacred Tree, sacredness of the Symbol, 268; its conventional appearance on sculptures and cylinders. 268-270; its signification, 272-274; its connection with the legend of Paradise, 274-276.
Sargon of Agadé, see Sharrukin.
Sarzec, E. de, French explorer; his great find at Tell-Loh, 88-90: statues found by him, 214.
Scorpion-men, the Warders of the Sun, 311.
Schrader, Eberhard, eminent Assyriologist, favors the Semitic theory, 186.
Semites (more correctly Shemites), one of the three great races given in Genesis X.; named from its eponymous ancestor, Shem. 131.
Semitic language, 199; culture, the beginning of historical times in Chaldea, 202, 203.
Sennacherib, king of Assyria, his palace at Koyunjik, 34; Fergusson's restoration of his palace, 56; his "Will" in the library of Nineveh, 109.
Senkereh, see Larsam.
Sepharvaim, see Sippar.
Seth (more correctly Sheth), third son of Adam.
Shamash, the Sun-god, second god of the Second Babylonian Triad, 240; one of the "twelve

great gods," 246; his temple at Sippar discovered by H. Rassam, 247, 248.
Shamhatu ("Grace"), one of the handmaidens of Ishtar, 305.
Sharrukin I. of Agadé (Sargon I.), 205; legend about his birth, 206; his glorious reign, 206; Sharrukin II. of Agadé (Sargon II.), 205; his religious reform and literary labors, 207, 208; probable founder of the library at Erech, 209; date of, lately discovered, 213.
Shem. eldest son of Noah, 130; meaning of the name, 193.
Shinar, or Shinear, geographical position of, 127.
Shumir, Southern or Lower Chaldea, 145.
Shumir and Accad, oldest name for Chaldea, 143, 144.
Shumiro-Accadian, oldest language of Chaldea, 108; Agglutinative, 145.
Shumiro-Accads, oldest population of Chaldea, of Turanian race, 144; their language agglutinative, 145; introduce into Chaldea cuneiform writing, metallurgy and irrigation, ib.; their probable migration, 146; their theory of the world, 153.
Shushan (Susa), capital of Elam, destroyed by Asshurbanipal, 194.
Siddim, battle in the veil of, 221, 222.
Sidon, a Phœnician city, meaning of the name, 133; the "first-born" son of Canaan, eponymous ancestor of the city in Genesis X., ib.
Siduri, one of the maidens in the magic grove, 311.
Sin, the Moon-god, first god of the Second Babylonian Triad, 240; one of the "twelve great gods," 246; attacked by the seven rebellious spirits, 291.
Sin-Muballit, see Amarpal.

Sippar, sister city of Agadê, 205; Temple of Shamash at, excavated by II. Rassam, 247, 248.
Sir-burla (also Sir-gulla, or Sirtella, or Zirbab), ancient city of Chaldea, now Mound of Tell-Loh; discoveries at, by Sarzec, 88–90.
Sir-gulla, see Sir-burla.
Smith, George, English explorer; his work at the British Museum, 102; his expeditions to Nineveh, 103; his success, and his death, 104; his discovery of the Deluge Tablets, 301.
Sorcerers believed in, 157.
Spirits, belief in good and evil, the first beginning of religion, 150; elementary, in the primitive Shumiro-Accadian religion, 153–155; evil, 155–157; allowed an inferior place in the later reformed religion, 236, 250; rebellion of the seven evil, their attack against the Moon-god, 290, 291.
Statues found at Tell-Loh, 88, 214.
Style, ancient writing instrument, 94, 109.
Synchronism, meaning of the word, 212.

T.

Tablets, in baked or unbaked clay, used as books, 109; their shapes and sizes, 109; mode of writing on, 109–110; baking of, 110; great numbers of, deposited in the British Museum, 110–112; Chaldean tablets in clay cases, 112; tablets found under the foundation stone at Khorsabad, 113, 114; "Shamash tablet," 248.
Talismans, worn on the person or placed in buildings, 164.
Tammuz, see Dumuzi.
Taurus Mountains, 190.
Tell-Loh (also Tello), see Sir-burla.

Temples of Êa and Meridug at Eridhu, 246; of the Moon-god at Ur, ib.; of Anu and Nana at Erech, ib.; of Shamash and Anunit at Sippar and Agadê, 247; of Bel Maruduk at Babylon and Borsippa, 249.
Theocracy, meaning of the word, 235.
Tiamat, see Mummu-Tiamat.
Tin-tir-ki, oldest name of Babylon, meaning of the name, 216.
Triads in Babylonian religion, and meaning of the word, 239–240.
Tubalcain, son of Lamech, descendant of Cain, the inventor of metallurgy, 129.
Turanians, collective name for the whole Yellow Race, 136; origin of the name, ib.; the limitations of their genius, 136–139; their imperfect forms of speech, monosyllabic and agglutinative, 136, 137; "the oldest of men," 137; everywhere precede the white races, 138; omitted in Genesis X., 135, 139; possibly represent the discarded Cainites or posterity of Cain, 140–142; their tradition of a Paradise in the Altaï, 147; characteristics of Turanian religions, 180–181.
Turks, their misrule in Mesopotamia, 5–6; greed and oppressiveness of their officials, 7–8; one of the principal modern representatives of the Turanian race, 136.

U.

Ubaratutu, father of Hâsisadra, 322
Ud, or Babbar, the midday Sun, 171; hymns to, 171, 172; temple of, at Sippar, 247–248.
Uddusunamir, phantom created by Êa, and sent to Allat, to rescue Ishtar, 328, 329.
Ur (Mound of Mugheir), construction of its platform, 46; earliest known capital of Shu-

nur, maritime and commercial, 200; Terah and Abraham go forth from, 201.
Ur-êa, king of Ur, 215; his buildings, 216-218; his signet cylinder, 218.
Urubêl, the ferryman on the Waters of Death, 311; purifies Izdubar and returns with him to Erech, 313.
Urukh, see Erech.
Uru-ki, or Nannar, the Shumiro-Accadian Moon-god, 240.

V.

Vaults, of drains, 70; sepulchral, at Warka, 83, 85.

W.

Warka, see Erech

X.

Xenophon leads the Retreat of the Ten Thousand, 2; passes by the ruins of Calah and Nineveh, which he calls Larissa and Mespila, 3.
Xisuthros, the king of, Berosus' Deluge-narrative, 300. See Hâsisadra.

Y.

Yahveh, the correct form of "Jehovah," one of the Hebrew names for God, 354.

Z.

Zab, river, tributary of the Tigris, 17.
Zagros, mountain range of, divides Assyria from Media, 50; stone quarried in, and transported down the Zab, 50, 51.
Zaidu, the huntsman, sent to Êabâni, 305.
Zi-ana, see Ana.
Ziggurats, their peculiar shape and uses, 48; used as observatories attached to temples, 234; meaning of the word, 278; their connection with the legend of Paradise, 278-280; their singular orientation and its causes, 284-286; Ziggurat of Birs-Nimrud (Borsippa), 280-283; identified with the Tower of Babel, 293.
Zi-ki-a, see Êa.
Zirlab, see Sir-burla.
Zodiac, twelve signs of, familiar to the Chaldeans, 230; signs of, established by Anu, 265; represented in the twelve books of the Izdubar Epic, 318-321.

www.ingramcontent.com/pod-product-compliance
Lightning Source LLC
Chambersburg PA
CBHW051243300426
44114CB00011B/870